"These nuts-and-bolts descriptions of bank robberies, dramatic prison riots, grotesque scenarios in which the offender yearns to die, and exotic hostage dramas in foreign lands make for gripping reading. A standout is . . . the 1985 siege of the Covenant, an armed survivalist cult living on a heavily defended rural Arkansas farm."

—*Publishers Weekly*

"Before retiring from the FBI in 1995, Van Zandt, one of the key figures in the formation of the agency's hostage negotiation program in the 1970s, brought the strategies of negotiation to a host of white-knuckle and high-profile hostage standoffs. In this gripping memoir, he brings readers in on the secrets behind his ability to defuse hostage situations. In casebook format, Van Zandt reviews the great standoffs of his career, including a bank robbery gone sour in Rochester, New York; a weeks-long confrontation with a white supremacist group in Arkansas; a Cuban prisoner rebellion, with staffers held hostage, in Alabama; the kidnapping of corporate executive Michael Barnes in Manila; and . . . the tragedies of Waco and Oklahoma City. The writing . . . is crisp and fast-paced, and Van Zandt's revelations about hostage negotiation tactics and actual encounters are fascinating."

—*Booklist*

"Triumphs and tragedies in the career of a former FBI agent who became one of the Bureau's first hostage-negotiation specialists. The author, who retired in 1995 after twenty-five years' service, ruminates on personal wins and losses as well as the evolution of the Federal Bureau of Investigation's policies and tactics as it moved into the era of terrorist threats under two different chiefs, J. Edgar Hoover and Louis Freeh."

—*Kirkus Reviews*

FACING DOWN EVIL

LIFE ON THE EDGE AS AN
FBI HOSTAGE NEGOTIATOR

• • •

CLINT VAN ZANDT
WITH DANIEL PAISNER

BERKLEY BOOKS, NEW YORK

THE BERKLEY PUBLISHING GROUP
Published by the Penguin Group
Penguin Group (USA) Inc.
375 Hudson Street, New York, New York 10014, USA
Penguin Group (Canada), 90 Eglinton Avenue East, Suite 700, Toronto, Ontario M4P 2Y3, Canada
(a division of Pearson Penguin Canada Inc.)
Penguin Books Ltd., 80 Strand, London WC2R 0RL, England
Penguin Group Ireland, 25 St. Stephen's Green, Dublin 2, Ireland (a division of Penguin Books Ltd.)
Penguin Group (Australia), 250 Camberwell Road, Camberwell, Victoria 3124, Australia (a division of
Pearson Australia Group Pty. Ltd.)
Penguin Books India Pvt. Ltd., 11 Community Centre, Panchsheel Park, New Delhi–110 017, India
Penguin Group (NZ), 67 Apollo Drive, Rosedale, North Shore 0745, Auckland, New Zealand
(a division of Pearson New Zealand Ltd.)
Penguin Books (South Africa) (Pty.) Ltd., 24 Sturdee Avenue, Rosebank, Johannesburg 2196, South Africa

Penguin Books Ltd., Registered Offices: 80 Strand, London WC2R 0RL, England

While the authors have made every effort to provide accurate telephone numbers and Internet addresses
at the time of publication, neither the publisher nor the authors assume any responsibility for errors, or
for changes that occur after publication. Further, the publisher does not have any control over and does
not assume any responsibility for author or third-party websites or their content.

PRINTING HISTORY
G. P. Putnam's Sons hardcover edition / September 2006
Berkley trade paperback edition / September 2007

Berkley trade paperback ISBN: 978-0-425-21163-2

The Library of Congress has catalogued the G. P. Putnam's Sons hardcover edition of this book as
follows:

Van Zandt, Clint.
Facing down evil: life on the edge as an FBI hostage negotiator /
by Clinton R. Van Zandt with Daniel Paisner.
p. cm.
ISBN 0-399-15308-X
1. Van Zandt, Clinton R.   2. Hostage negotiations—United States.
3. United States, Federal Bureau of Investigation—Officials and employees—Biography.
I. Paisner, Daniel. II. Title.
HV6598. V36   2006   2005053470
363.25'092—dc22

PRINTED IN THE UNITED STATES OF AMERICA

10 9 8 7 6 5 4 3 2 1

I'd like to dedicate this book to my family, all of whom have lived this life on the edge with me. My parents provided the solid foundation that enabled a kid from a steel town to reach his dreams, and my wife, Dianne, was a constant source of love, encouragement, and support throughout our life together. As a Christian, I know that God provided me the opportunity to live the life that led to this book. For this and so many other blessings and opportunities, I am eternally grateful.

Best wishes & travel safe!

Clint Van Zandt

ACKNOWLEDGMENTS

Writing a book is no easy task. I appreciate the hard work of my literary agent, John Silbersack of Trident Media Group, who knew the process and walked me through it as professionally and as painlessly as possible. I also want to acknowledge Dan Paisner, a real pro's pro, who listened to my adventures and helped spin them into readable chapters.

CONTENTS

FACING
DOWN
EVIL

INTRODUCTION

THE PREDATOR
DOWN THE STREET

As a child, I lived in an older one-family, two-story brown clapboard house on a quiet residential street in a blue-collar Midwestern steel mill town. Neighbors sat on front porch swings and talked to each other while their kids played ball in the street. Home plate was a metal pie tin; first and third base were marked in chalk on opposite sides of the curb; second base was a soup can crushed flat for effect. An old tennis ball or a torn, weathered softball was usually our ball of choice.

Not quite Norman Rockwell, but not bad either.

My point here is that East Twenty-fourth Street in Granite City, Illinois, was about as safe as any such urban neighborhood in the early 1950s. Safe enough that my parents would give me a nickel to walk the half block down to Poston's Pharmacy to buy a copy of the *Granite City Press-Record*. Later in life, when I had some real money of my own, I could buy a Coke for another nickel—or, if I wanted to splurge, a Cherry Coke, which Poston's sold for a nickel and two pennies. At seven, I didn't know to be afraid because there wasn't anything to be afraid of. I wasn't mature or experienced enough to understand the true purpose of fear. I was cautious, but that's a whole different thing. My parents gave me the perfunctory warnings: look both ways when you cross the street; go straight to the store and come directly home; don't talk to strangers.

"I got it," I used to say, whenever they drilled these warnings into me. "I'm seven years old. Stop treating me like a baby."

And yet I was soon to find out how little I really did know.

It was a warm summer day. The blue sky, as usual, was partially hidden by the long streams of black soot that bleached from the steel mill smokestacks nearby. On this particular afternoon, I took the nickel from my mother and pushed it deep into the pocket of my shorts and headed off to fetch her newspaper. I had the routine down cold: look both ways for cars; cross the street and head into the store; collect the newspaper; give the man my mother's coin; fold the paper under my arm; head home.

I remember seeing him coming toward me. I had crossed the street and was headed for the pharmacy when he came into my peripheral vision, just off to my left. I had never seen him before. He was an older man (although, at seven, everyone was "older"). He approached me as if he wanted to talk to me. "Hey little boy," he said, his voice all friendly and welcoming. "Do you want to see some newborn puppies?"

I wasn't frightened, but I should have been. I didn't recognize this as the textbook approach of a sexual predator. I didn't know the first thing about the fight-or-flight impulse we now try to instill in our children. It never occurred to me to kick, bite, yell, or run. So I just listened. Newborn puppies sounded good to me.

The man held out his hand, and I stood there and let him touch my hand.

"You'll really like these puppies," he said. "They were just born."

I let him do it. Fifty-five years later, I can't believe that I just let him do it, but I did. Everything my parents had told me about personal safety (a lot, by 1950s standards, hardly anything by today's) flew out the window as I let this man take me by my skinny wrist and lead me from the safety of the sidewalk just a few steps away from the storefront pharmacy. We walked between two nondescript houses, and then into an old wooden garage that faced a dirty alley running behind another row of houses. He opened a side door and pushed me into the garage. There was no car inside the garage—and, certainly, there were no puppies. The garage was dark and worn, like the man who had brought me there, but I could see the sunlight from the holes in the wall and the roof, where there were some planks and shingles missing. The dirt particles we kicked up with our shoes seemed to sparkle in the little bit of sunlight that found its way into the garage, something to momentarily take my mind off of what was going on.

We walked across the dirt floor and reached to the far side of the garage. That's when he came at me.

I didn't get it. I just didn't get it. Why had this man lied to me about the puppies? I wondered. Why had he brought me here? I couldn't understand it, but I could hear a change in his tone. His words were no longer soft or kind or beckoning. They had turned nasty, slurred, and profane. He cursed at me, and demanded that I perform a sexual act on him. At seven, I didn't even understand what he was asking me to do, but I finally knew to be afraid. I watched him loosen his belt, and then I knew what he wanted was wrong. I stepped back, but he lunged at me. He held his pants up with one hand and tried to grab at me with the other.

Everything was moving slowly. Years later, after a tour in Vietnam and a long career in the FBI, I would dream of a gun battle where I could see the bullet coming out of the gun in slow motion. I could see the smoke exit the business end of the gun barrel, and then the ever-so-slowly-spinning bullet as it left the barrel and headed straight toward me. In my dreams, I could see the round coming but I could never manage to get out of the way. Always, it was like that scene in *The Matrix*, but I couldn't maneuver my body like Keanu Reeves to avoid the hail of bullets. But that was Hollywood. This was Granite City, Illinois, circa 1952, and there were no special effects to help me out of this one. This was a 1950s predator who was determined to have his way with me, and afterwards . . . well, I didn't have time to think about what the extremes of his behavior toward me might be. What I didn't know then was that I would have been the only witness that could have identified this man, and that most predators don't like to leave behind witnesses who could talk and therefore testify against them. I did know, however, that this man was coming for me in that dark, dingy garage, and that his plans were as dirty as the garage floor on which I stood frozen.

As he lunged at me, I took a quick step to my right. The rest of his body seemed to stumble forward, and in that split-second opening that I had somehow created, I rushed to the small wooden door on the other side of the garage. *Feet, move!* I silently commanded. I shot across that garage like a bullet from the barrel, my hands out in front of me as I slammed into the door. It creaked in protest and then burst open as if spring-loaded. In seconds, I was out in the bright sunlight, running as fast as I could.

I'd never made it to the pharmacy before this monster took me, so for some reason I doubled back to Poston's to finish my mother's errand. Of course, I looked behind me for signs of my assailant, but he was nowhere to be seen, so I ducked into the store, threw the nickel on the counter, grabbed the newspaper, and raced home to the safety of the even-numbered houses on our side of the street.

My mother must have seen that I was flushed and out-of breath when I came into the house. She asked if I was all right. I thought for a second before answering. I had just violated a number of rules that she and my father had laid out for me, and it occurred to me they might be angry at me for what had almost just happened. It had been my fault, they would say, and I would be appropriately punished. Or maybe they would hold my hand and try to comfort me, and it would be awkward, and people would look at me and point at me and wonder if I was okay. And so I didn't tell her about the man and the puppies and the garage. "I'm fine," I lied. "I just ran home for fun."

My mother took me at my word, and that was the end of the discussion. In fact, it was nearly the end of the matter entirely, because I never spoke of it again, for decades. I don't know why or how I allowed this to happen, but I pushed this memory so deep into the background of my childhood experiences that when I sat down to write about my life in the FBI and the life-shaping influences that led me to a career in law enforcement—the book you now hold in your hands!—I didn't even think to include it. It was as if the incident had happened to someone else.

Of course, I knew full well that by my action (or, inaction) regarding my momentary abduction, I had allowed my potential molester to remain on the street to take another child to another dark garage to see another litter of nonexistent puppies. This haunted me, when I allowed myself to think about it. Today, I know that a person who molests young girls will average over 50 victims before being identified and arrested; a person who molests boys will average over 150 victims before one of them comes forward with charges that might stick. This haunted me as well, as did the sad fact that our criminal justice system is increasingly likely to spit out sexual predators it can't quite convict, and that these individuals are in turn increasingly likely to re-offend. Indeed, one child molester in California recently acknowledged over 25,000 incidents of molestation! And of course I know that there are probably thousands of children like me, the unspoken and unacknowledged victims who are out there but never counted.

I finally told my mother this story early in 2005, just moments before giving a speech on child predators. I had decided to share what happened to me in order to help make some compelling points in my presentation, and to shake some of these haunting personal demons at long last, when I realized that my mother was going to be in the audience. Of course, I didn't want her to hear what I had to say in front of a room full of strangers, so I took her aside before the event and asked her to relive that day with me. After I had laid it all out for her, she was stunned. "Why didn't you tell us?" she asked incredulously.

Why, indeed. Why had I allowed myself to become a double victim? It was as if I had compounded the initial incident by trying to forget that it had ever happened—or, even worse, by wondering if I was perhaps to blame. How many assault victims, rape victims, domestic violence victims, or child molestation victims have allowed themselves to walk down a similar path? Far too many, I'm afraid.

After that first revelation came another. And another. I started talking about the incident with friends and family, and found myself hoping to have an opportunity to discuss it on a more public stage. It was helpful to me to finally talk about it, at long last, and I felt certain it could be helpful for others. Then, in early 2007, some months after the initial publication of this book, I was invited by Oprah Winfrey's producers to appear on Oprah's television show to discuss the case of a Missouri boy who had been held for over four years by his kidnapper. During a pause in the taping, I happened to mention to Oprah that I had been taken by a predator when I was seven. I don't know why I mentioned this, but I guess Oprah has a way of making people feel comfortable around her, which probably explains her enormous success. Oprah, a victim of sexual abuse herself as a young girl, thought it would be powerful if her audience knew that a hardened former FBI agent such as myself had been abducted as a child, and asked me to share my story on air—which I did. Later, dozens of men and women would write to me, telling me how they had seen me on *Oprah* and how they, like me, had been a victim of a predator and how they, again like me, had kept their terrible secret to themselves.

A week or so later, my wife and I were having lunch with three other people, another married couple and a younger man in his early thirties. Someone at the table had seen me on Oprah's show and commented on my revelation. I asked those at the table if any of them had either been the attempted victim or the victim of a predator, molester, or rapist. Four of us acknowledged such an experience. (Four out of five!) The younger man looked at me with tears in his eyes and said, "Because you've been there, I'll tell you." He said he had never shared his story with anyone else, and he proceeded to tell us of a time when he was raped. He was just a boy at the time of the incident, and he'd never told anyone; as an adult, he'd never told anyone until that moment.

I was careful not to ask this young man why he had never told anyone about the incident, in part because to do so might suggest guilt or personal responsibility on his part, and also because I still couldn't explain why I had kept silent myself for all those years. The young man became very emotional as he tried to explain himself, even though none of us had pressed for an explanation. He acknowledged that, statistically, most molesters have themselves been the victim of molestation at some time in their life. He also acknowledged that most people were well aware of this fact. "I was afraid," he said, "that if I told anyone about my assault, they'd think that I could be a child molester myself. I couldn't stand the look I thought would be in their eyes."

I tried to explain to this young man that such statistics were not absolutes, that I had met many victims over the course of my career and only a few of them would become molesters or abusers themselves, but of course he knew this on an intellectual level. It was his gut that had him worried, along with the knee-jerk reaction he thought he might receive if he opened up about his experiences. And as he shared his dilemma I thought to myself how terribly sad it was that this man had allowed himself, through shame and fear, to keep such a terrible secret, to become a double victim, just as I had allowed myself to become a double victim.

And so I share my terrible secret here, in the introduction to the trade paperback edition of a book chronicling my life on the front lines of our never-ending war on child abuse, domestic violence, terror, and every other imaginable evil. I might have thought to mention it earlier, but I suppose I wasn't ready. Me, of all people. A military veteran, a veteran FBI agent, and a victim of a child predator. But I am ready now, secure in the hope that my admission might help other wrestling with the same sense of shame and fear and guilt that had kept me silent for so long.

HOW IN THE WORLD
DID I GET HERE?

It was February 1992. I was in the ornate office of the United States ambassador at the U.S. embassy in Manila, along with the local FBI legal attaché (or legat, in Bureau-speak), a U.S. military adviser, several members of the ambassador's staff, and a representative from an international crisis management company charged with the safekeeping of international executives throughout the third world—and one American executive in particular.

I had been in the Philippines for several weeks, trying to negotiate the release of a 41-year-old American oil company vice president named Michael L. Barnes, who had been kidnapped at gunpoint on the way to his office about three or four weeks earlier and subsequently blindfolded and chained to a bed in some unknown part of the city. On the one hand, I supposed things weren't going particularly well, because there we were, after all this time, and Barnes was still missing. In negotiating terms, however, I supposed we were making progress, because we were able to obtain renewed proof each week that Barnes was still alive and because we were able to keep the kidnappers talking. These were good things. I'd been in situations where the kidnappers cut off all talks for a period of weeks or months, but that hadn't happened in this case, so at least we were making progress. Barnes may have remained blindfolded and chained to a bed, but he was still alive and the lines of communication were still open.

Everything about this case was a crapshoot, not least because Manila was shot through with corruption and violence and dubious activities of every stripe. It was, to say the least, an uncertain environment. Kidnap gangs and guerrilla groups seemed to roam the streets with impunity—indeed, their ranks were as often as not composed of former or even current members of the local military or police. You never knew who you could trust, what to believe, or where to turn for reliable insight or inside information. Just a couple days before, I was headed to a command post meeting at another location downtown and walked smack into a shootout right in the middle of the street, following a jewelry store robbery that had evidently gone wrong. I had to duck into a small alley to escape the ricochet rounds, and as I peered around the wall from my position of relative safety I couldn't help but notice how the locals seemed to take an incident such as this in stride. Sure, there was a good amount of screaming and running around with hands above heads, but a great many of the locals were simply going about their business, like a shootout in the middle of the street, middle of the afternoon, was nothing much at all. I thought for a moment that I had landed in some Wild West frontier town—and wondered how the hell we'd get *ourselves* out alive, let alone Barnes.

The American embassy was like an oasis of stately calm in the middle of a frenzied storm. It's a magnificent structure, befitting the U.S. presence in the Philippines, with fine furnishings and artwork and detailed moldings, and it was sometimes incongruous to see, set against such a majestic backdrop, the long lines of down-on-their-luck Filipinos desperate to get travel documents that would allow them to flee their country for the United States. But I guess you can get used to anything. That's pretty much the scene at American embassies throughout the world, so why should Manila be any different?

In any case, I had snaked my way through all the chaos and confusion in order to arrive at our meeting at the appointed time, and all of a sudden I found myself drifting off, unable to concentrate. It wasn't like me to lose focus like this, but I wasn't feeling all that well, and it took sitting still for me to realize how *off* I truly was. I had been battling a raging case of diarrhea for the past several days, which also fell under the category of *you can get used to anything*, because there was nothing else to do but ride it out. After a tough couple days, I thought I finally had things under control. I'd been dining out on the local economy for weeks, eating all manner of godforsaken meats and custards and who can remember what else. (Monkey meat is what you usually find, in places like this, even though they might call it something else on the menu.) Like every other American in a third-world environment, I tried to eat carefully—sticking to fruits and grains and breads when I was uncertain of a particular restaurant or vendor, avoiding water and anything but canned beverages, and only attempting meats or custards or cheeses when I could be somewhat more certain of a restaurant's refrigeration situation—but I guess I'd made a bad decision on this one. I was in a reputable restaurant and sampled some type of custard, and I think that's what did me in. For two or three days, I'd been doubled over with what I'd assumed was food or salmonella poisoning, and I'd about cleaned myself out.

Somehow I was able to scrape myself off the floor of my hotel room and make it over to the embassy, thinking the worst of my stomach troubles were now behind me (so to speak), but now that I was here, listening to my colleagues figure a next move on this Barnes case, I started to fade. Yes, we had an all-important American life on the line, and yes, we had several negotiation and rescue strategies ready to be put into place, but it got to where I couldn't follow what the ambassador, or the legat, or the international consultant, was saying. Their words were all jumbled together and the room started spinning, and next thing I knew I had moved from the hard-backed chair I'd been using to a place on the floor, knees drawn close to my chest. It was the only way I could get comfortable, and as I sat there rocking myself, calming myself, the ambassador looked down and said, "Van Zandt, what the hell is the matter with you?"

"I don't know," I said, rocking still. "I'm pretty sick, I guess."

Now, it wasn't like I was some unknown quantity to these people, this deep into our negotiations. We'd been working together for some weeks, and they knew it wasn't like me to just drop to the floor and start keening, but I couldn't make out a thing anyone said from this point on. And I couldn't say with any kind of certainty what happened next. All I know is I kept hearing voices, distant voices, and I'm presuming now there was concern in those voices, but at the time I was just seeking comfort, relief. That's all I remember—that and the few loose thoughts that came rattling through my fevered brain. I rocked and rocked, slowly at first, and then I'm told I picked up the pace a bit, and after a while of this I just kind of slumped over, face-down on the plush carpet. All I could hear were these waves of sound. I couldn't really pick up what any one person was saying, just that a lot of people were talking all at once and that most of it seemed directed at me. I'd fallen into a position from which I had no desire to move, or no ability, and I lay there for a time, faced pressed full against the fine fibers of a possibly Persian rug, my loose thoughts running all over the damn place. There was Dianne back home with the kids. There were my colleagues on the Hostage Negotiations unit at the FBI Academy in Quantico, Virginia. There was this guy Barnes, and his guerrilla kidnappers, holed up somewhere here in Manila. And there were my well-meaning and now (apparently) well-concerned colleagues here in this room, wondering what to make of this mustachioed Bureau veteran who had suddenly and mysteriously gone weak at the knees and fallen limply to the ground.

These guys eventually hoisted me from the floor of the ambassador's office into the backseat of one of their cars, and raced me to the nearest hospital, where I was administered intravenous fluids through both arms and both legs. I have no firsthand recollection of anything that happened a few minutes after my face hit the ambassador's rug. Apparently, I'd lost so much fluid over the previous several days that I had become dangerously dehydrated, and it would take a few days of convalescing in Manila, and another period of time back home in Virginia, before I could return my full attention to Mike Barnes, who was still blindfolded and chained by the neck to the same bed when I returned to the case following my ordeal. And yet, there was room enough in my thinking for me to do some of that wondering myself as I lay drifting and disoriented on the floor of the ambassador's office: to look back at my life and career and to marvel at the twists and turns my life had taken. God, I thought as I faded one final time before being carted off to the hospital, what a long, strange trip it's been.

WHERE I COME FROM

I was born to be an FBI agent.

I grew up in a steel town across the river from St. Louis, Missouri, knowing only that I wanted up and out. Don't misunderstand: Granite City, Illinois—current population about 30,000-plus—was in most respects an idyllic midwestern steel town in the 1950s, if you could get past the heavy black soot that used to belch from the mills and the fact that the snow never stayed white for too long.

My father, Manuel, was an electrician for the Granite City Steel Company. We lived fairly modestly in a lower-middle-class neighborhood, a couple blocks from the grade school—although, come to think of it, everyone in Granite City lived fairly modestly in a lower-middle-class neighborhood, a couple blocks from one of the local schools. The place wasn't exactly big on distinctions.

We didn't have much, but we had enough. That is, until fifth grade or so, when my parents divorced, which was its own kind of big deal. In that environment, divorce was practically unheard-of. In fact, I'd never even come across the term before my parents separated. My mother, Fay, had to take a job to support the two of us, packaging meat in the butcher department for the Tri-City Grocery Company, and we managed to stay on in the same house, but virtually overnight my safe little world was changed forever. Everything I knew was set aside, and all of a sudden it was just my mother and me, and we went from having just enough to hardly anything, but I never thought of us as poor or deprived or disadvantaged in any way. Still, we managed, and before long my mother remarried a kind man named George, a local firefighter, who took on the financial responsibility of raising his wife's son. My father eventually remarried, too, and he continued to work the same job and live in the same town, and it was all just far enough removed from the ordinary to leave me feeling awkward and self-conscious and cut from a fabric that no one else seemed to have to wear.

Money was so tight that we were probably the last family in town to get a television. I didn't mind. I listened to radio serials like *The Lone Ranger, The Green Hornet, Gang Busters,* and *Inner Sanctum,* but my absolute favorite was *The FBI in Peace and War,* one of the most popular crime dramas on the air. I looked forward to each episode like it was the most exciting thing in the world—which, to me, it was. We had this old clunker of a radio enclosed in an old gray-metal cabinet with too many dials and tubes, but it managed to pull in signals from all over the world; and in addition to the network radio fare I used to listen to the BBC broadcasts all the time. The other kids at school were watching *Howdy Doody,* but I was glued to the radio, formulating a fairly unique world view or losing myself in chasing Nazi saboteurs or escaped bank robbers.

I got it in my head that I would someday be an FBI agent, and throughout my growing up it was the only thing I ever wanted to be. Other kids dreamed of being firemen like my stepfather, or baseball players or business tycoons, and usually they bounced from one dream to the next with each flip of the calendar. Not me. I would be a G-man, just like the guys on the radio. I would chase bad guys, preserve order, and protect my fellow man. My life would be about truth, justice, and the American way, no matter how corny or how unrealistic it may have seemed to others at the time.

It's only fitting, I suppose, that with all those changes at home I found myself seeking order out in the rest of the world. I joined the grade-school safety patrol, in a program sponsored by the American Automobile Association. In most towns, you'll find retired cops or empty-nester housewives out to make a couple extra bucks filling this same role, but in Granite City it fell to student volunteers, and I counted myself lucky to get it. I had always been a responsible kid, always following the rules. If you ask my wife, Dianne, she might say I am responsible to a fault—she might even use words like *obsessive* or *compulsive* to describe this one aspect of character—but back in grade school the folks in charge issued me a badge and a white Sam Browne belt and trained me to be a crossing guard. It was my first position of real authority. I was ten years old, and I thought I'd died and gone to heaven.

At some point, I traded my crossing guard badge for another position of responsibility: as a lifeguard. I wasn't much of a swimmer, but I managed to pass my junior lifesaving course and was well on my way to my senior lifesaving distinction when I happened across my first real opportunity to put my long-held dreams of protecting my fellow man into play. I was driving through town, idling in front of a dry-cleaning establishment just down the street from the Third Baptist Church, where my mom and I regularly attended Sunday services. I looked out the car window and noticed a crowd of people with variously panicked looks on their faces, and I followed their gazes until I noticed somebody on the ground. Half out of curiosity and half out of instinct, I spilled out of the car to see what was up. Some poor guy had suffered an apparent heart attack, and someone had called for an ambulance, and now all these well-meaning citizens were just milling about, not doing anything, waiting for help to arrive. There I was, barely 16, alongside all of these adults, people I had known my entire life, and I thought, *Somebody's got to do something.*

I knew CPR from my junior lifesaving course, so I dropped down to where this individual lay and started administering it. Didn't even think about it, really, and next thing I knew I was going through the motions, trying to save a human being's life like it was something I did every day. I kept at it for ten minutes, maybe longer. Nobody said anything. Nobody offered to help. Nobody even commented at the incongruity of this lanky kid—me!—stepping in and taking control while a dozen or so adults looked on, helpless as the man lay on the ground, dying.

I was comfortable in what I was doing, and confident, and soon enough I lost myself in the rhythm of it, and soon enough after that the ambulance arrived and some EMT type slapped an oxygen mask on this guy and loaded him onto a gurney. One of the EMTs turned to me and said, "Nice job, kid."

And that was that. Nobody took my name. Nobody shook my hand. My picture never made it into the local paper. Life simply went on—as it tends to do—and I simply crossed back to my car and drove home, a little overwhelmed for the ordeal but none the worse for it. And I might never have known what happened to this guy if I hadn't called the hospital myself a couple days later. I told them who I was and what had happened and I was finally put through to someone in the emergency room who had worked the case. "I'm sorry, kid," this someone said. "He was alive when he came in, and for a while it looked like he might make it, but then he gave out on us."

I was devastated at first that this guy had died, but then I thought, *Well, that's how it goes. You do the best you can, everything you can, and sometimes it's still not enough.* I set it out there and realized that this had been the story of my life up to this point. And then I looked around and realized it was pretty much the story of everybody's life in Granite City. You do the best you can, everything you can, and you might still never get anywhere, and I knew right then and there that if I stayed put, if I went through the same motions as everyone else, I'd keep running into the same brick walls.

Football became a place to put my frustrations and uncertainties, and offered daily life lessons on taking a hit and surviving. The great side benefits to school sports, then as now, was the way they offered a positive outlet: While other kids were out drinking and carousing, I was running laps and toeing the line. I wasn't fast. I wasn't big. Truth be told, I wasn't particularly athletic. I played offensive and defensive end, and took my licks on the extra-point squad, and I learned early on that I couldn't tackle a bigger guy head-on. I always wore rib pads, because I was just beat to pieces, throwing my body at somebody's legs and trying to take them down. If I went at them from the waist up, they would just roll me over, so I had to go right at them and cut their legs out from under them. One day one of the coaches took me aside and said, "Van Zandt, you ain't got much athletic ability, but you sure got a lot of guts." If that was a compliment, I'd take it.

It was a challenge, on the field and off—and to a growing boy this was especially so in an era before microwave ovens. Most nights, I'd trudge home from high school long after my mother and stepfather (and now sister, Peggy) had eaten, and there'd be a cold pork chop and some cold peas and cold mashed potatoes waiting for me in the oven to reheat. Not exactly a nice hot steaming meal, but again, I tried to make the best of it and counted myself lucky each season to make the team, even if I didn't play all that much or leave much of an impression when I did manage to get in for a couple downs.

At odd moments I'd catch myself thinking about what I might do next, where I'd go from there, what the rest of my life might look like. Most often my thoughts would run to the FBI and to the purposeful life I would lead, as soon as *up and out* came calling. From a Granite City perspective, St. Louis was a key first step. It was our version of the big time, our big city. St. Louis was where you went when you had money to burn, once you were old enough to drive. And that was where you'd go to build your career or your fortune, once you were old enough to leave home.

But when high school ended I found myself headed in the opposite direction, to Eastern Illinois University, in Charleston, Illinois. I had been a mediocre student, at best. Many of my fellow classmates chose to stay on in Granite City and found work in one of the local mills. Even some of the better students stayed put, I guess on the ingrained thinking that they wouldn't find anything better out in the world. Or maybe they just felt totally comfortable with what they already had. That might have been my path as well, but I couldn't see signing on and working alongside my father in the steel mill for the rest of my life, so I set off to Eastern Illinois with a suitcase and a clock radio, hoping to make something of myself—something *else,* anyway.

Unfortunately, I quickly found I was in over my head. I didn't know the first thing about studying. I didn't know the first thing about discipline. I dated a lot, and played a lot of cards and Ping-Pong—as a left-hander, I crossed up my mostly right-handed opponents and managed to control the table—but at the end of my first year I was looking at a long list of lousy grades, and a tuition bill I couldn't really afford and could no longer justify, so I let a couple university administrators convince me I wasn't really college material and came home. In the back of my head, I still thought I'd be an FBI agent, but I didn't have the first idea how to move myself from where I was to where I wanted to be.

I tried to make a go of it back home. For a while I worked for the local highway department, spreading oil on county roads. For another while, I worked for Granite City Steel, where everybody knew my father. They all called him "Van," which left me as "Van's kid." I enjoyed the association, but I was challenged by the inevitability of it. *Oh, that's Van's kid.* Meaning: It was only a matter of time before I turned up here too.

In any case, being a laborer in a steel mill was dirty, nasty, back-breaking work that I couldn't see doing for the next thirty years. No, sir. It was honorable work, don't misunderstand, but that didn't make up for the dirty, nasty, back-breaking aspects. They had me working around melted steel in brick-lined furnaces heated to hundreds of degrees. Or cleaning out those brick furnaces after some other hard-working sap had finished with the melting. They used to give us these Dutch clog–like wooden overshoes to wear over our work boots, because the heat from the furnace floor would just melt the leather to nothing at all. The heat was overwhelming, and they couldn't get any of the older guys to pull this kind of duty, so it fell to us recent high school graduates, guys like me looking at lives just like our fathers'.

It got to where I figured I had to try college again, just to get a leg up and move myself on to something better; however, a short stint at Southern Illinois University at Edwardsville, not far from where I lived, was another bust. I had to start all over again, as a freshman, and for a second time my grades were sub-par and yet another well-meaning college administrator pressed upon me the notion that I might not be college material. I might have gotten the message by this point, but instead I contented myself in thinking that at least I was consistent.

Still, I couldn't see myself signing on for the long haul at the steel mill, and marrying some local girl, and raising some local kids, and attending the same local church and going through the same local motions as everyone else in town. I don't mean to dismiss such a move, or to knock those who chose this path, because there is certainly comfort and integrity in a life so lived, but it wasn't for me. I wasn't letting go of this FBI fantasy so fast. Back of my mind, it was still front and center. Trouble was, there was no one in town to help me on this path, no guidance counselors at school, and no recruitment officers. There was, however, a local FBI agent named Walt Johnson, who encouraged me to stop by and visit and "talk a little FBI." Like a lot of kids, I thought I knew where I wanted to go, but I was just ricocheting off the walls. I was like a BB in a boxcar, rolling around trying to find the door. I had no idea. I had no education. I had no money. I had no prospects. All I had were a couple fifteen-year-old reference books in the local library, but with Walt's help I got the current address for FBI Headquarters in Washington, D.C., and sent off a letter requesting information on how to apply for a job. A couple weeks later I got back a mess of papers, including an application for a GS-2 clerical employee position—the lowest rung on the Bureau's ladder, but about the best I could hope for given my two-strikes-against-me college career.

Realize, this was 1964–65 and Vietnam was raging. For young American males looking down the barrel at a military draft, it was Topic One. Realize, too, that I'd flunked out of college twice, and the draft was looming, and I wanted desperately to be in a position to maybe call my own shots if I was called to serve. I didn't want to be some infantry grunt. If I was going to put myself on the line like that, I wanted to make a difference—to matter. I didn't mind going, like a great many young men of my generation, but I wanted my going to mean something. It occurred to me that maybe signing on at the FBI, even as a lowly GS-2 clerk, might put me in a good position to control my fate in Vietnam, if it ever came to that. Anyway, it was one reason on a long list of many to quit dreaming of a career in the Bureau and finally put in for one.

I still have the letter from J. Edgar Hoover, offering me a job as a GS-2 file clerk in the St. Louis Field Office, at what even then was an astonishingly low starting salary of $2,800. It was so *not* where I wanted to be—the whale feces on the bottom of the ocean of FBI jobs—but God knows I needed a place to start. I shelled out $400 from my meager savings to buy a relatively clean '56 Chevy, which I needed for the daily commute to St. Louis from my parents' home in Granite City, and another $50 or so for a presentable suit and a reasonable-enough-looking pair of shoes, because in those days, under J. Edgar Hoover, FBI agents didn't wear sport coats and slacks. You had to wear suits. Even clerical employees had to wear suits, and I figured I could get by with just one, to start.

It wasn't much of a job. I drove to St. Louis each morning and dutifully typed information on three-by-five cards and dutifully placed documents in files and dutifully sent teletypes and searched for pictures. There was nothing challenging in the work beyond the duty of it, nothing exciting beyond the hard-to-grasp notion that what I was doing somehow fit in with what the *real* FBI agents were doing. That's what it came down to, after all, and every now and then I caught myself reading something interesting. I wasn't supposed to read the files or the paperwork that crossed my path, but I caught enough to get that people were being arrested, suspected criminals were being interviewed, leads were being covered, and open cases were being closed. All this stuff was going on, exciting "FBI in Peace and War"–type stuff, at the hands of real-life, gun-carrying, badge-toting, wing-tip–wearing FBI agents, who when they weren't sitting in the office just next door were tooling around Greater St. Louis, driving cars with police lights on the dash, going to bank robberies, kicking in doors, making arrests. The stuff of my dreams—truth, justice, and the American way—and it was all so *right there.*

I looked forward to coffee breaks and cigarette breaks, even though I didn't drink coffee or smoke. Instead I used my break time to talk to the agents, and they were nice enough. I'd talk to them about their cases, and where they went to college, and how they'd got from there to here. I'd talk to them about their families and their futures. I even wangled an invitation to firearms training, and got to shoot with real FBI agents. (Man, it was too good to be true!) I got the message from the chief clerk that I should probably leave the agents alone, but I kept at it and they kept talking. It was a tantalizing thing, to be so close to it, to get such a front-row, once-removed glimpse, but there weren't any back doors into the FBI for would-be agents. I needed a college degree, same as everyone else, so after about a year I sent a letter to Mr. Hoover, thanking him for the experience, and informing him that I was leaving my now GS-3 position and going back to school. He sent me back a letter wishing me luck and encouraging me to finish my degree and reapply to the Bureau at that time.

I re-upped at Southern Illinois University in late 1965, as the prospect of a draft still hung over the country. All along, I'd pumped my new FBI agent friends for their insight and experience, and the advice I kept getting back was to avoid the draft entirely and enlist— specifically, to sign on for a stint in military intelligence. Better not to wait until your number is called and you get some random assignment pulling hump duty. Better to call your own shots. The consensus was that a stint in military intelligence would be like being a G-man in the military. I could learn investigative techniques, wear plain clothes, carry a badge and credentials, and realize at least some version of my lifelong dream. It wasn't the FBI—not by a long shot—but I convinced myself it was close.

I had to take a test and submit to all kinds of interviews and background checks, but my brief stint as an FBI clerk eventually got me waved into military intelligence (MI) school without my college degree, alongside other enlisted men who were all at least three or four years older than me, all of them with a bachelor's or master's, but I could not have cared less. I was in, and good to go—as far as I ever knew, the only MI agent candidate without a college degree. I thought, *Well, so be it.* It never occurred to me to quit or to feel intimidated; I wasn't going to be denied.

First stop was Fort Leonard Wood, Missouri, for eight weeks of basic training. It was March 1966, and I was so green I'd never even been on an airplane. I boarded a TWA twin-engine DC-3 (the old military C-47), and figured the next twenty years had to be a little more exciting than the twenty just past. Basic was tough but doable. I had about two months from when I enlisted to when I was called, and I filled the time by going to the gym at the local YMCA, getting myself into shape. As I've written, I wasn't the strongest athlete in the world, and now that I was two years removed from high school football I needed to build up my strength and stamina. The last thing I wanted was to show up at Fort Leonard Wood and be tagged as some bolo. I didn't need to be the best or the strongest or the fastest, and I didn't need to stand out, but I wanted to make sure I at least stood on middle ground, because even *I* knew that if I got lumped with the fat guys and the uncoordinated guys and the laggards, I was finished.

Turned out I didn't take too well to certain forms of military authority, and I wasn't the type to be easily intimidated—two aspects of character that might have served me well in most walks of life but this one, because of course the U.S. military is built on authority and intimidation, which meant that I had to learn how to accept just enough of the former and feign just enough of the latter to get by. If the folks in charge think they've got you appropriately intimidated, they tend to leave you alone; if you fall short in their estimation, they look to break you down. So I tried to find the balance. Perfect example: They used to make you get your hair cut every week, and of course they'd cut it down to a buzz. I hated how I looked with my military haircut, but more than that I hated the arbitrariness of the routine. It made no sense to me, to have to cut all my hair off each and every week, so I found myself ducking out of the line when they marched us off to the barbershop. I would just peel off and lay low behind the shrubs. At first I skipped every other haircut, but as those eight weeks wore on I started to miss a whole bunch. Three weeks in a row I ducked out of the line and laid low, until finally some young hump of an acting NCO caught me napping off by the side of some footpath and decided to give me some grief. But that's all it was, grief, and I figured I could put up with it in exchange for my little show of independence.

From Fort Leonard Wood, I was off to the U.S. Army Intelligence School at Fort Holabird in Baltimore, Maryland, all the way on the East Coast. I'd never been so far from home: I'd never even seen the Atlantic Ocean! I was surrounded by enlisted men, all a whole lot more worldly than I, all at least three or four years my senior. Here again, in a class of about thirty-five, I was the only one without a college degree, but I kept up with everyone else as best I could. There was a whole lot of classroom work and a whole lot of field exercise-type work. We learned how to conduct interviews, how to interrogate prisoners of war, how to support combat operations. If you were doing a background check on someone, for example, you had to check their LIDMC: loyalty, integrity, discretion, and moral character. That was the big MI buzzword, *LIDMC,* and I caught myself thinking that if I never came across that acronym again, it would be too soon.

The great thing about Army intelligence at the time was that the United States enjoyed a tremendous military presence in Europe, so when we got around to discussing assignments, it looked like I'd be sent to some great job in Germany or France; or there was also the possibility I could be deployed to some cushy assignment on the west coast of the United States. Either way, I wouldn't have minded. I'd serve my country and miss the front lines entirely. All around me, with about two or three weeks to go in training, guys were getting their orders. They were getting sent to San Diego, and San Francisco, and Honolulu, and Munich, and Berne, Switzerland. One great assignment after another. When my turn came, I was called to the front of the class to receive my envelope, and I tore it open and it said, "Van Zandt, Republic of Vietnam."

That night I found myself commiserating with one of the local girls at the local bar, the Holabird Inn. She wanted to know where I had been assigned. "Saigon," I said.

"Well, it could be worse," she reassured. "You could be going to Vietnam."

I thought, *So much for the Dundock Debutantes,* as we called them.

It was October 1966, and body bags were coming back from Vietnam by the dozens, but I took my assignment like I had it coming, and I flew off to Saigon not knowing what to expect. First night in-country, all incoming GIs were stacked like cordwood in a huge barracks with triple-decker beds, and guys were so tense and nervous they were yelling and screaming at each other, especially the Latinos, who were at each other's throats. Literally. One of the enlisted men was playing his music at a ridiculous volume, and another one approached him and asked him to turn it down, and the first guy pulled out a knife and looked to kill the second one for it. He had to be restrained to keep from going after the guy, and I looked on and wondered, *What am I into here?* I thought I'd be killed by one of our own before the Vietcong could ever get to me.

Like most other new, in-country MI agents, I had an enlisted rank, although we were in civilian clothes or fatigues with *U.S.* on our collars, carrying MI credentials and civilian ID cards. (If you were about to be captured, you were to bury your credentials and claim to be a civilian contractor to the military—a lame cover story, in retrospect, seeing as how the Vietcong or North Vietnamese Army would have probably assumed we were CIA and killed us anyway.) I was assigned to the 524th MI Detachment CI (for *counterintelligence*), about an hour and a half north of Saigon, not far from the large military compound at Long Bien. Every night, it seemed, there were gun battles raging on the perimeter of our compound. Our small MI unit wasn't nearly large enough to be self-contained, which meant we were typically "bunked" with a larger outfit, so we contented ourselves in knowing that our "hosts," in this case a truck transportation group that hauled ammo up-country, were covering our butts.

As MI agents, we would do anything from investigating other GIs to working with U.S. and ARVN (Army of the Republic of Vietnam) infantry units to gather intelligence from the neighboring villages, sometimes with a CIA counterpart. It was mostly routine, but it was almost always interesting. Most interesting of all was our MI team. There was Tom Erson, a great big guy who looked more than a little like Mr. Clean, a gentle giant who used to play football for Auburn University; Dave Fredericks, one of the few married men in our unit, whose wife, Jackie, had a baby during our tour; and Mickey Moore, who was somehow assigned to an undercover position in an up-country whorehouse for most his tour. The four of us had been friends since Fort Holabird. Also, there was a kindly Vietnamese woman who used to come and clean out our building, or hooch, every day. We all called her Mama San, as every GI in Vietnam addressed their local cleaning women, and she earned the equivalent of about a dollar a day. The people in Mama San's village didn't have much, so I wrote home to my mother about it, and she organized a clothing drive at the Third Baptist Church; every few months we'd get these giant boxes of clothing, which Mama San gratefully distributed, and before long all the locals were looking like they'd just stepped off the "fashionable" streets of Granite City.

It was amazing to me how we moved about in-country without any real fear. There was a lot to be afraid of, believe me, and we gave voice to those fears, but only in a lip service sort of way. See, we were all so terribly young, and at that age I guess it never occurs to you that you're in any kind of danger. Even under fire, I never once thought, *I'm going to die.* You simply couldn't function if you went around believing that the next bullet had your name on it, and so we moved about like we were invincible. Contributing to my false sense of invincibility was a .45 pistol on my hip, an old Thompson submachine gun in the seat of my jeep, and a LAW rocket launcher in the backseat. The VC could get to us, but we had the means to put up a fight. Nevertheless, once you'd made it eleven months into your twelve-month tour, there was no sense getting killed just before you were due to be sent home. This was known as being "short," or being a "short-timer," as in "I've only got a short time left in Vietnam before I get to go home."

The married guys paid particular attention to the calendar. Once, as our time was running short, my friend Dave was sent out on what could have been seen as a dangerous assignment, and I volunteered to go for him. "You've got a wife and kid," I said. "It's just me, and I don't mind going." I wasn't being heroic so much as I was being practical. He had a lot more to lose than I did, noting that I had sent my Granite City girlfriend a "Dear Jane" letter, not wanting anyone to have to worry about me other than my family.

For the most part I stayed out of harm's way, although I did get hit by a grenade fragment midpoint in my tour. A GI had short-armed the grenade, was what happened; he simply didn't throw it far enough, and the darn thing blew up right in front of us. I took a piece of it in the face, near my eye, and I was bleeding like a stuck hog, but it was just a small metal fragment and not really any kind of big deal. Like many facial wounds, it looked a whole lot worse than it actually was, although the medic who checked me out and cleaned me up said he was going to fill out the paperwork to put me in for a Purple Heart. I thought, *For this little thing?* Guys were getting their arms and legs blown off. Guys were losing their eyesight. Me, I'd gotten a superficial wound from a grenade thrown by one of our own guys, so I wouldn't let him write me up for it.

I picked up a lot through my intelligence-gathering activities while I was in Nam. I learned how to develop informants and run an information network. I learned how to chase down leads and conduct a thorough search. Most interesting of all, I learned how to psychologically soften up a subject, a suspected VC, in order to get reliable information out of him—not through torture tactics but by getting into his head a little. If MI could not get the desired information out of a VC prisoner, it was suggested that the local Republic of Korea (ROK) MI detachment be called in to do the job. The thinking here was that the ROKs understood the adversary better than we Americans did—Asian mind to Asian mind. That is, until we learned that the ROK got their information using tactics that involved "extreme prejudice" (translation: the prisoner didn't live). Subsequently, U.S. MI would turn difficult prisoners over to ARVN MPs for processing.

MI gave us some money to spread around, which was always helpful in getting the locals to talk, and I got to thinking that if I could limit the number of Americans getting killed or injured, then I was doing a good job. That was my barometer. I couldn't directly impact a war we now seemed determined to lose, but I thought if I could save a couple hides, then my time over there would be worth it.

I was promoted to sergeant during my tour, and was in line to receive the traditional handful of medals—basically for surviving and not being drunk or excessively insubordinate or exposing myself to the local social diseases—and at the end of my twelve months my commanding officer made me two offers: I could stay on for another six months and be promoted to staff sergeant, or I could stay for a full year and make second lieutenant. I didn't care about the promotions, and I wasn't looking at any kind of military career, but I did take time to admire the negotiations tactic: give the guy you're negotiating with only the choices you want him to choose from, instead of all the options available to him.

I was about halfway through my three-year term of enlistment and figured the next move was to play out my stint on home soil. I landed back in San Francisco in October 1967, just a couple months removed from the now-infamous "Summer of Love," at pretty much the height of the flower power movement. Let me tell you, the contrast between Granite City circa 1966 and San Francisco circa 1967 was enormous. It's like I'd left the planet and realighted in some strange new territory. I'd expected some of it. I'd been reading *Stars and Stripes*. I knew that American GIs were being spit on upon their return, and cussed at, and called baby killers and things of that nature. I knew that our efforts in Vietnam were being viewed as unjust and un-American by our nation's youth—so much so that I actually wrote my own orders allowing me to return home in civilian clothes. I wasn't ashamed of our efforts in Vietnam, but I wasn't about to step off that plane and get spit at for them, either.

I walked the streets of Haight-Ashbury for a couple days, just to see if I could pass as a hippie. It was like stepping into some strange performance-art exhibit with a surreally modern twist. The peace-and-love aspects of the scene were just fine, but it wasn't me. I was still a God-fearing, working-class midwestern boy, and I found myself longing for the simpler pleasures of Granite City and made hasty arrangements to return home for the balance of my leave.

Ah, the pleasures of home . . . I can still remember the quiet thrill I felt the first time I flushed a toilet, the first time I sipped real milk, the first night I slept in my own bed. After all that time on the streets of Saigon and in the jungles of Vietnam, the return to my old routines could not have been more welcome—although I needed to make a few adjustments. For example, I met up with an old high school friend who had been in the U.S. Air Force, and we walked to our local Dairy Queen one night to get an ice cream cone. I'd been looking forward to that first trip back to Dairy Queen pretty much since I left home in the first place, and there I was, lazily strolling with my cone in hand, when all of a sudden a car backfired a couple clicks up the street. Scared the you-know-what out of me and left me scrambling for safety beneath the closest parked car. (So much for my ice cream cone!) Of course, I caught myself and what I was doing, and the picture of it combined with the rapid beating of my heart and got me to thinking it might be a while before I shed some of what it meant to have fought in this war—especially since the Air Force guy, who hadn't been assigned to Vietnam, could only stand there laughing.

For the most part, though, I think I came home basically the same person I was when I left. I was hardened, somewhat, by the way everybody seemed to need to dehumanize the bad guys in a time of war: the way the Vietcong became "gooks" to most GIs, the way they were razzed for the slope of their foreheads or the slant of their eyes. I tried never to use the pejorative terminology that others tossed around so easily, but I understood the impulse behind it. I understood that in order to get to the place where you can take a human life, you need to first reduce that human life in your mind. It's the same if you're out in a rice paddy or on the front lines of some FBI standoff; otherwise, you're killing another human being, just like you. There was no time to consider any moral implications of what you had to do, because to do so would likely get yourself killed.

I had another year and a half to go on my enlistment, but I never again put on a uniform—not until the day I got out of the Army. I took about a month of leave before heading out to my next assignment—in Chicago, just in time for the 1968 Democratic National Convention. The antiwar movement in this country was reaching its peak, and the military was looking at particularly vocal opponents of the war and trying to determine if there was any kind of threat to our national security. It was, to say the very least, an interesting time to be stationed in a hotbed of unrest and protest like Chicago: there were tremendous riots during the convention; parts of the city were ablaze; and all around was bedlam and confusion. This was when then-mayor Richard Daley ordered Chicago police to shoot to wound looters and shoot to kill arsonists, which gives a good indication of the level of civil disorder.

Of course, I objected to the lawlessness and disorder, the looting and rioting, but I respected the right to protest. To speak out against the war . . . well, that was one of the basic rights we were fighting for, wasn't it? So on that one level, at least, I didn't have a problem with the protest, just the extreme methods of the protesters. And yet, the rioting and the fomenting of all that unrest was only a part of my experience there. I conducted a lot of investigations, mostly back-ground checks on draft evaders and protesters, security clearance checks and investigations on others pegged by the Army as potential trouble. Occasionally I'd fill in for the full-time MI agent at the recruiting cen-ter downtown, where we had to interview conscientious objectors. I suppose I was somewhat more empathetic than these young men had any right to expect, and as I sat across the desk from them, listening to their various reasons for opposing the war, I found myself taking up their side. I'd gotten to that place in my thinking where I didn't agree with the way the United States was fighting this war; I no longer believed we had the heart to win and felt that we should no longer be involved, that young GIs, Marines, airmen and sailors were now dying for nothing. I'd listen to some young guy about the same age as me tell me he didn't want to be sent off to die when his dying had no pur-pose, and I couldn't argue with him.

I am eternally grateful for my tour in Chicago, because that's where I met my wife, Dianne. I was rooming with one of the guys from my Vietnam MI detachment, Tom Erson; we shared an affordable two-bedroom townhouse in northern Chicago and set about having the time of our young lives. Really, to be young and single in a city like Chicago wasn't exactly difficult duty. There were a lot of interesting women running around the city at that time, and I think it's fair to say that Tom and I met most of them. Mickey Moore, having survived his assignment to that Vietnamese house of ill repute, came to visit us from time to time, and together we ran through our share of cover stories, because of course we weren't supposed to let slip that we were Army Intelligence agents. We were always something else. Sometimes I'd be a golf course designer, because I figured most people wouldn't know a whole lot about it and I could make it up as I went along. Tom might have been with the Justice Department, adjudicating financial claims. We'd get with a group of girls in a bar and just start spinning stories.

It just so happened that Dianne's mother was a dear old friend of

Mickey Moore's mother, and when he breezed into town he announced that he had arranged dates for the three of us with three single women, Dianne being one of them. I took one look at her—five foot ten, blue eyes, long blond hair—and she stood out like a supermodel. More than that, she came off as so utterly *American,* if that makes any sense. This was not all that long after I returned to the States, and the contrast between Dianne's traditional good looks and midwestern charms and the women I was used to seeing for the past year in Vietnam was startling. As a plus, she was also smart and good-natured, and we hit it off straightaway. When we first met, I was already dating a young nurse, who was decidedly less blue-eyed and blond-haired, but there was no reason to break off the one relationship for the other just yet; so I did what any other red-white-and-blue–blooded MI agent would have done at the time: I strung both women along, for as long as I could get away with it. Dianne hung out in downtown Chicago, and the nurse hung out on the north end, so I was able to keep the two relationships fairly separate. My MO was to squeeze two dates into one night, blaming my early exit each night on my job.

Things went on in this way for months, and I was dying. I was getting maybe two or three hours of sleep each night and still trying to stay reasonably sharp when I was on duty, and it all unraveled on me one night when I took the nurse to a bar and we bumped into Dianne. It was bound to happen, and she had me dead to rights. Even my practiced lines of patter couldn't help me out of this one, so I sidled sheepishly over to where Dianne was standing, and bought her a drink, and after a couple minutes I shrugged my shoulders and said something lame like "I'm sorry, but I have to go."

Her eyes drifted across the bar to the woman she'd seen me come in with, and she said, "I can see why you've got to go."

And off I went, feeling like a (caught) idiot, but feeling also like there was no other move I could make. Dianne, to her great credit, wasn't about to wait around for the likes of me that night and quickly took up with a pilot. I tried to see her a couple times the following week, and her roommates made some feeble attempts to cover for her, but my mind was really scrambling, especially when I found a matchbook in her apartment from a distant airport restaurant and realized she'd been flying with her new pilot friend. I was now 23 years old and I had meant to be single and carefree for years and years, thinking I'd get married at 35 or so. But in my scrambling, I realized that Dianne was everything I could ever want in a woman. She was intelligent. She was a person of tremendous faith. We shared a lot of the same values. She was drop-dead attractive. And above all, she was the most honest, decent, straightforward person I had ever met. I thought to myself, *Okay, Van Zandt, either you continue with your game plan and lose this glorious woman to some pilot, or you set aside your game plan and come up with a new one.* So I traded in my friend the nurse and Dianne traded in her friend the pilot, and we set about spending the rest of our lives together, right then and there.

We married and moved into a small efficiency apartment—you know, the kind where your couch turns into your bed at night—and Dianne and I began our uncertain adventure. Happily, the uncertainty had more to do with our plans and prospects than our belief in each other; we were meant to be together, no question, but I had no job lined up for when I would be discharged in March 1969. I still had no college education. And of course I still wanted to be an FBI agent. Forget any long-term uncertainties: there was still the chance that I could be reassigned at any time during the remainder of my enlistment: even back to Vietnam—although, as my enlistment wound down, this last became less and less likely.

As it happened, I stayed on in Chicago until I was discharged. My commanding officer kept hitting me up to reenlist, but I had no interest in signing on for another tour. It was nuts. Plus, I'd gotten what I wanted to get out of my military "career"—namely, some key investigatory experience and, for good measure, the GI Bill, which would enable me to go back to college. I'd be entitled to a whopping $155 per month, enough to see me back to SIU for a third try, this time with about a year and a half of accumulated credits from my various fits and starts (including a couple of courses taken through the University of Maryland's overseas extension program while I was in Vietnam), and this time with a new part-time job as a dispatcher with the campus police. Dianne was able to swing a political appointee job at the county courthouse, so we had some money coming in and every reason to look ahead. And the icing on the cake was an Illinois-backed scholarship program for Vietnam veterans, which sat on top of my GI Bill monies and paid for my books and tuition.

Life, at long last, was good, and I went from a young lifetime of wanting up and out to a young adulthood of counting myself very much in and present and anxious for more of the same. We had good friends. We had high hopes. And we had each other.

Turned out the third time was a charm, as far as SIU and I were concerned. No more all-night card games, no Ping-Pong, and no partying to all hours; studying at long last made sense, and a 3.0 grade point average was now my norm. I reapplied to the FBI in December 1970, looking ahead to college graduation the following spring. There was a Bureau regulation at the time prohibiting prospective "re-hires" from interviewing in the same office they had once worked, so I had to trek to Springfield, Illinois, to be interviewed and tested and processed, but I had made myself into an attractive candidate. Three years of military experience; an Army Intelligence agent and Vietnam veteran; one year as an FBI clerk; one semester to go for an undergraduate degree, with good grades (at last); married, with a stable home environment; and still only 25 years old, but well ahead of the game in terms of real-world experience.

The Special Agent in Charge (SAC) in Springfield determined that I was FBI material, and I joined the Bureau in July 1971, a couple weeks after graduation. Dianne was seriously pregnant with Jeff, our first child, but I had to run off to Washington, D.C., for sixteen weeks of training. This put us in a bit of a bind. The current FBI Academy had not yet been built in Quantico, Virginia, so most of my time was spent at FBI Headquarters in downtown Washington; for a portion of those weeks we were relocated to Quantico for legal and firearms training, and housed in a small barracks facility there, but it fell to us rookie agents to find our own accommodations in the D.C. area. I threw in with five other guys on a one-bedroom apartment next door to a fire station, to try to save money, and the location was a killer. Every night, it seemed, there'd be a fire, usually at two or three o'clock in the morning, and they'd sound bells and sirens and air horns that would just blow us right out of bed. But that was about all we could afford, so we got by on a little less sleep.

Dianne, meanwhile, was riding out her pregnancy with relatives in northern Wisconsin, including a cousin, a high-ranking nurse-nun in a Green Bay hospital. Dianne spent so much time with her cousin that many of the locals mistook her for a tall, blond, *pregnant* nun. When Jeff was finally born, I was stuck in the old FBI Academy building at Quantico, unable to break free. There were some interesting quirks to the FBI training program under J. Edgar Hoover, and one of them was that new agents in training had to endure a lockdown-type curfew when they were in residence. It was frustrating, to say the least, and irrational, to say a bit more. We were all adult men (there were no female agents at the time), all college graduates, many of us Vietnam veterans, made to suffer an inexplicable restriction that for the most part would have been no big deal—unless your young wife happened to be half a continent away giving birth to your first child.

But I had no business complaining. I was now a GS-10-level employee, at an annual salary of about $15,000, which from my perspective seemed like all the money in the world. It took a while getting used to some of the bizarre regulations, though. Once, during training school, I was sent back to my apartment to change into a white dress shirt and docked a couple hours of leave because I'd reported to class in a blue dress shirt, being told in no uncertain terms that FBI agents did not wear blue shirts. One of the other unusual restrictions had to do with our weight. We agents were weighed at regular intervals throughout our training—and, under Mr. Hoover, throughout our careers—and if we ever climbed above our designated thresholds for our height, weight, and physical types, we were consigned to what we all jokingly referred to as "the fat boys' club" and removed from our normal schedule until we fell into line. The up-against-authority part of me always wondered what would happen if I showed up to work one day a couple pounds overweight *and* dressed in a pink shirt and green pants, but I never pressed the point.

Add sweaty palms to the list of Bureau infractions and you'd really be up a creek, because Mr. Hoover was legendary for the way he couldn't abide sweaty palms. In fact, the man was legendary around the Bureau for a lot of things—and justifiably so, because he made the FBI the internationally respected organization that it was—but this was one of the first ways his reputation had any kind of direct impact on us rookie agents. The routine for all new agents graduating from the FBI's training program was to travel to FBI Headquarters for a small ceremony in Mr. Hoover's office. There were about thirty agents in each class, and you stood around a grand conference table in Mr. Hoover's office while he made the rounds and shook each man's hand. You were told beforehand to blot your hands with a handkerchief or against your pant legs before you went in, because Mr. Hoover was said to distrust people with sweaty palms. He thought they had something to hide, the story went. It was a strangely intimidating little dance new agents had to go through, at the heels of a director who was himself a little strangely intimidating and who may have outlasted his legacy by the time I arrived on the scene. Indeed, the FBI under J. Edgar Hoover was such an insulated culture that in many ways it remained rooted in the 1930s and 1940s, when the Bureau rose to prominence.

The world, in some ways, appeared to have passed Mr. Hoover by, and yet the rest of the FBI leadership tended to look the other way and show the man his due respect by adhering to his old-line policies.

I'd met J. Edgar Hoover one other time, not long before this brief conference-room meeting. I was returning to headquarters with a copy of my college diploma, to complete my file, and when I pressed the elevator button at the old Justice Department building in Washington the double doors of the cab opened onto the great man himself. I was fairly flummoxed to see him in just this circumstance, and I guess I hesitated for a couple beats before stepping into the elevator because he flashed me this disdainful look that seemed to say, *Well, you pressed the damn button, so either get on the elevator or let it go.* I stepped into the cab and didn't know whether to face him, or to turn away from him, or to attempt to make small talk. So I mustered up my courage and extended my undoubtedly sweaty hand in greeting and blurted out something inane like "Good morning, Mr. Hoover," and as soon as I said it I thought, *Oh, crap.* My voice came out sounding like Tinker Bell after a trip to a helium factory, and Mr. Hoover left me hanging on the handshake, silently harrumphing as if he'd like nothing better than for this sweaty-palmed, squeaky-voiced rookie to disappear and leave him to his elevator ride.

Thankfully, the rest of my FBI career went a little more smoothly than this first private meeting with Mr. Hoover might have foretold, and I was sent to the Atlanta office for my first assignment. They could have sent me anywhere, but the local SAC sent me off to a small resident agency in Rome, Georgia, a rural three-man outpost in the northern part of the state, which struck me just then as Granite City with a southern drawl.

It took us a while to get settled, with a new baby and a new dog to round out our young family. The FBI in those days offered a meager moving allowance that provided a certain amount of money for the first ten days, half that amount for the second ten days, and half that remaining amount for the third ten days. By the end of that first month in Rome we were really scraping. Finally, just when we were really up against it, another agent was reassigned and we were able to finish out the lease on his rental house.

I made one hundred arrests my first full year in Rome, which I was told was some kind of record. I know a great many agents who've logged whole careers with the FBI without ever making a single hands-on arrest, because of the type of work they were doing, so to log one hundred collars in just twelve months as a rookie agent was something of a splash. The arrests ran the gamut from bank robbers to murderers and from fugitives to military deserters. Our coverage area was mostly rural, and there was a lot of interstate activity. I wound up doing some work with local agents from the Bureau of Alcohol, Tobacco, and Firearms (ATF), shutting down local moonshiners and illegal weapons suppliers.

Mr. Hoover was big into statistics. He'd go before Congress every year and announce that the FBI had made so many arrests, responded to so many cases, recovered this much property, and returned to the American taxpayers this much on their budgeted dollar: "fines, savings, and recoveries," the FBI called it, with the Bureau consistently returning more to the public than it cost to run the FBI. It was all down to numbers and statistics with him, at that stage of his career, and the mountain of paperwork we were made to file in support of all those numbers was certainly felt by a low man on the totem pole like me. That's why that one-hundred-arrest number was such a milestone, because the folks in charge tended to inflate the importance of those kinds of numbers.

In many respects, Rome, Georgia, was a sleepy, out-of-the-way place. I remember sitting with one of the local detectives there, and our talk ran to guns. This guy had been in Rome all his life, and he was admiring my Smith & Wesson Model 19-3 .357 Magnum revolver, which I guess was a whole lot more impressive than the old five-shot Colt .38 he wore at his hip. Anyway, he said, "What you got there, Clint?" I handed it over to him, the way cops do. You open the cylinder and dump your bullets and hand the weapon to him butt first so he could give it a good once-over. It can be a real phallic-symbol, macho-male sort of thing, and I played along, and when he pulled out his .38 and handed it over I noticed it was rusted shut. It had been so long since he'd cleaned it or had any call to fire it that it was now inoperable, and aside from making a mental note to never go out on an arrest situation with this particular detective I chalked it up to the pace of the place.

Things were a little tough on Dianne on the social front. She was stuck at home with a newborn, in an unfamiliar part of the country, while I was off keeping ridiculous, unpredictable hours, having the time of my life. It made for a bit of tension between us, and so I made every effort to seek out occasions where we could get out and socialize as a couple. Unfortunately, at most Bureau or police gatherings, the agents and officers usually wound up on one side of the room, talking cases, and the spouses wound up on the other side of the room, talking babies. Most people I've known in law enforcement have been inclined to divide people into two types: cops and assholes. I'm not crazy about the term, but nothing else fits this insular worldview, and after just a couple months on the job I found I had a hard time looking at the world in just this way, so we distanced ourselves from that group, as much as possible, building our social circle around our children and their activities, and around our church.

A word or two on this last: church and organized religion had always been a central part of our lives, before we even got together. The slight hitch to our faith-based pursuits was that Dianne was a card-carrying Roman Catholic, while I was a good old Southern Baptist, but we managed to find our own middle-ground version of Bible-based Christianity without putting any kind of label on it, and more and more I found myself calling on my faith to see me through.

I'd pray as I rolled up to a bank robbery in progress. I'd pray when I found myself at some tense impasse or other. I'd pray when all else failed, and my prayers instilled in me a renewed sense of confidence each time out.

There's a wonderful concept in the Bible that suggests that God resides in righteousness, in doing the right thing, and in the ways we carry ourselves and approach the challenges of each day, and I found that when I prayed about a situation I moved about with an extra bounce of confidence to my step. Whatever fears I might have had going in were somehow diffused. Obviously, I didn't think my belief in God made me bulletproof. It's not like I cloaked myself in an invisible shield, under His protection. After all, as the Good Book states, it rains on both the righteous and the unrighteous. But I was able to draw a measure of comfort and surety in knowing that I wasn't alone. It was like saying, *Hey, I need Your help on this one,* and drawing strength from that help, in exponential measure. Looking back, I can't recall a single instance in my FBI career when I was truly afraid. Back in Vietnam, with those shells raining down on us, my lack of fear had more to do with the irrational exuberance and invulnerability of youth than it did with any kind of studied faith, but as a churchgoing, Bible-believing adult male FBI agent it had everything to do with a belief in something bigger than myself—and in knowing I was on the side of right, and doing my part to make the world a better place.

I came to realize very early on that keeping God on your side is one thing, but that it isn't quite *everything.* You need to trust in yourself as much as you trust in Him, and to develop instincts and intuition that are deserving of that trust. Really, to survive and thrive as an FBI agent, you need to be part investigator, part minister, part psychologist and part Spider-Man—with a sixth sense that borders on comic-book supernatural. First time I noticed my own "Spidey" sense was in Rome, although back then I don't think I knew from Spider-Man and probably chalked it up to a hunch. Realize, I was new to both the FBI and to my first office. We had just moved to town, and I drove around in my Bureau-issued 1968 Ford, without air-conditioning or an AM radio, two features the FBI considered extravagant and unnecessary at the time. One of my first cases involved the interstate transportation of a stolen motor vehicle—an ITSMV, in FBIspeak. I got the call early one morning and was told to drive down to some small-town jail—without AC and AM, naturally—to interview a man being held on just such a charge and to present my findings to the local U.S. Attorney. Nowadays, in most jurisdictions, the drill is for visiting law enforcement officers to place their weapons, spare bullets, and handcuffs in a lockbox upon entering a prison, to ensure that an inmate doesn't overpower you, but I was new and the jail was old and nobody asked for my gun.

I walked into the cell of the captured car thief and our eyes met. He was taller and heavier than me, but there was something else about him that struck me as somewhat *off*. Something odd, almost diabolical. He seemed weirdly glad to see me. It didn't make sense and it didn't feel right. The hairs at the back of my neck stood on end, and a voice cried out in me that this wasn't a good setup.

I turned to the jailer who had led me into the man's cell. "Search him before you leave," I said, half asking, half commanding.

"We already done that when he come in here" came the contemptuous reply. Obviously the jailer didn't want some green FBI agent telling him what to do.

"Look," I tried again, trying to be nice, "do me a favor and search him again."

The jaded jailer shook his head, but he did as I asked, probably to humor me. He kicked the guy's feet apart and began to pat him down, and as he ran his hands around the subject's belt, he found a large folding knife tucked between the guy's belt and his pants.

"Why, this SOB's got a knife on him," the stunned jailer announced, more to himself than to me. He spun the subject around to face him and started barking out questions: "How'd you get that knife? What you think you were gonna do with it?"

The car thief looked straight at me, half nodded his head as if to point at me, and smiled—one of those Steven Spielberg, *Jaws*-type smiles, behind a set of dark, blank eyes that seemed to look right through you, like you were raw meat there for the taking—and I was overcome by two distinct emotions: the chill of what might have happened and the thrill at knowing I had somehow intuited a danger sign and reacted appropriately. And so I learned very quickly to trust my instincts and to take no one's word that my safety was assured—because if I ever did, I might only get one chance to be wrong.

At one point I looked up and realized I had arrived. I'd jumped through all kinds of hoops and survived all kinds of false starts and half-steps in the wrong direction to where I was finally living out my lifelong dream. To me, being an FBI agent was like being Peter Pan. I could fly . . . I could *really* fly. It was the only thing I ever wanted to do, and now that I found myself doing it I almost couldn't believe it. I had a devoted and loving wife, and a growing family as daughter Jenna and son Jonathan rounded out our family portrait, and a sustaining community of friends and neighbors, all of which was far more than I could have ever imagined—and yet, I *also* got to go to work each day and do something I truly loved. To be a kid from a steel town, who flunked out of college twice, who was looking at a lifetime of dead ends and dashed hopes, and to get to the point where the stuff of your dreams becomes the stuff of your days is a wondrous thing indeed.

What did I learn from all of this? Well, if I had to break it down to just one thing, I'd give the nod to a line from one of my heroes, Winston Churchill, who said, "Never, never, never, never, never give up." Words to live by, don't you think? Certainly, they're words I've tried to live by, and I'm reminded here of an old story that nicely illustrates the way I approached my life and career. It's an old story about a rich man in biblical times. He owned many acres of land and had many animals and many servants. One day a servant came running up to this man and indicated that an older work animal, a mule, had slipped and fallen into a deep, dry well. The rich man said that the servant could solve the problem by filling in the dry well and burying the old mule, thereby solving two problems at once. A number of servants were then called to gather around the well with shovels, to carry out the owner's command that they bury the old animal and fill in the well. But as the workers shoveled dirt into the abandoned well they noticed a strange thing. First, the mule's ears appeared at the top of the well, followed by his head, and eventually his entire body—until the mule was able to step from the hole and walk away from what would have been his grave. The mule would not allow himself to be buried; he took each hit, shook it off, and stepped up again until he somehow managed to climb out of the hole.

What follows is a collection of stories from the tip of the spear that comprises my life and career, and a reflection on what it means to be out in front, face-to-face with pure evil, when standing behind you is the love and support of friends and faith and family. Like I said, it's been the stuff of my dreams set against the stuff of my days, and I present the stories that follow in hopes of shedding light on one or the other.

SUICIDE BY COP

"NOTHING TO DIE ABOUT"

Rochester, New York. Early 1970s.

From Rome, Georgia, it was on to upstate New York for what would be the first significant, open-ended stop of my FBI career, which took me headlong into my first frontline hostage-barricade assignment to follow my initial training in hostage negotiating strategies, which left me looking at a second such assignment just a short time later—which in turn set me up for my first lingering professional disappointment. Altogether, it was a fascinating, devastating, and ultimately rewarding sequence of events, as I will attempt to make clear.

Let me first set the scene. There was a local organized crime (OC) family (long before *The Sopranos*), but other than one mob boss being blown up via car bomb outside a local restaurant by another OC faction, there wasn't a whole lot to Rochester beyond the snow—twelve inches of which dumped down on us on our second day in town, on our way to 160 inches in one year! Still, there was more than enough going on to suit me and my family. Good schools. Rich cultural environment. Nice community. Comfortable lifestyle. And, perhaps most significant, affordable housing on an FBI agent's salary. Our needs were modest, and Rochester met or surpassed most of them. Got me to thinking I could stay there for my entire career, and then the FBI announced a master's degree program that sounded too good to be true. If you were one of fifty agents accepted into the program, the Bureau would pay your tuition, provide time off from work to go to school, make secretaries available to help with typing papers and such, and generally offer the kind of far-reaching assist that made the pursuit of a master's seem more like a realistic goal than folly. In my case, it was a necessary goal if I had any hope of teaching at the FBI Academy, a long-held dream for which I needed my master's, so I put in for the program.

The good news here is that I was accepted, both in the Bureau's program and in the public administration program at the State University of New York—Brockport, where I would have the benefit of professors like Ed Downey, who recognized that working adults had a difficult time balancing family, job, and school. Dianne and I celebrated with a much-too-expensive dinner, something unusual on an agent's salary, but it was an especially welcome turn. The bad news was that it turned out to be one of those typical government-bureaucracy–type situations, because six months into it there was no time for me to go to classes during my normal workday, and no secretaries available to help me type my papers, and none of the other support systems in place that would have made all the difference, especially in the amount of time it ultimately took for me to complete the degree program. There was a generous and much-needed tuition subsidy, but that was about the beginning and the end of any FBI assistance in the master's program. It might have been too good to be true, but as it turned out it was also good enough, and I ended up going to night school, and typing my papers on the weekends, and spreading myself so thin that those five long years are just a blur. Our daughter Jenna was born during that period, and I think I missed the first three or four years of her young life—that's how crazy my schedule was, and at the same time how determined I was to get a leg up at work.

The work itself was routine: boring at first, but elevated soon enough to routine. I was initially assigned to work Foreign Counterintelligence, or FCI, which operated on the premise that Rochester was known for its technology-based businesses, and that there was always the potential for industrial espionage and things of that nature, so we spent our days developing information on potential sources of foreign counterintelligence, which I guess is a fancy way to say we were chasing down spies. It sounds high-tech and glitzy, and it might have been a justified line of pursuit, but it was tedious drudge work, with very little payoff. Plus, it wasn't a whole lot of fun. There might have been one coon up every hundred or so trees, but we had to go up a lot of trees. Checking records. Conducting spot surveillances. Running license plates. Monitoring who was talking to whom. And it didn't make a whole lot of sense to me. I worked alongside tremendous veteran FCI agents like Joe Cain and Joe Corcoran, but I lasted about a month before I sought out the Special Agent in Charge in Buffalo, who ran the Rochester office as well, and made my frustration known.

"I made a hundred arrests my first year in Rome," I told him, not really boasting about my stint in Georgia so much as offering a point of comparison and some context. "I'm very comfortable doing criminal work. I'm very comfortable doing hands-on, out on the street. But this FCI is bullshit. It's not what I joined the FBI to do."

I set this frustration out there as if it mattered. Well, clearly it *did* matter—to me, anyway—but as I heard it back it didn't seem to make a whole lot of difference to the gray-haired gentleman sitting across from me. How could it? I was a smart-ass kid, fresh from Vietnam and college, with one year in the FBI, telling an SAC with twenty-five years of experience that this type of work was beneath me. By rights, he could have sent me packing, or consigned me to an even less desirable fate just for spite, but to his great credit (and my great good fortune) he cut me some slack. Told me to stick it out for six months, after which I would be free to come by to discuss some other options.

Six months to the day, I was back in the SAC's office, pleading my case yet again. "Remember what you told me six months ago?" I said.

He nodded.

"Well," I said, "I still hate it."

The SAC was good to his word, and reassigned me to the criminal squad in the Rochester Resident Agency, which for the most part meant pursuing federal fugitives and working bank robberies and extortion cases. That was the meat of it and I couldn't have been happier. All of a sudden it was exciting to get up and go to work each day. I could feel like what I was doing made a difference. The best part of the job, to me, were the chess-match aspects of it, the constantly trying to outthink and outmaneuver your adversary. Some of these fugitive types, they'd go to all kinds of lengths to disappear and keep from being found out, but the challenge for me was to go to these same lengths to trip them up. As often as not, school records would be a bad guy's Achilles' heel. If he had a son in first grade and a daughter in third when he skipped one town, for example, he'd have a son in first grade and a daughter in third when he alighted in another. He could change the names of his children, but he couldn't change their ages, so I was frequently able to track them down through school district records. And if it wasn't school it was something else, some other paper trail. A doctor's prescription, a love of racetracks . . . there was always some way to unravel each mystery, and that was one of the things I loved about the job, the endless puzzle of it, chasing down each mouse trail to find the elusive mouse.

Another great thing: there was no better feeling as an FBI agent than testifying in court, putting together a good, solid criminal case and sitting in that witness chair while a defense attorney tried to make you look like a blithering idiot so he could save his transparently guilty client from going to jail. It was another part of the same chess match, played out in a court of law, and it was always a special thrill when I could withstand the withering questions and still manage to get in my testimonial evidence. At the end of the day, that was what counted. You could chase guys in the street. You could knock them down. You could put handcuffs on them and drag their butts off to jail. You could write the best reports and cover every other angle, but if you fell on your face in court, one-on-one against the defense, you were useless. I was fortunate in that I never lost a case in court, probably owing more to the great federal prosecutors who worked with me than to my own finite investigative skills.

At around this same time, I began taking some courses in hostage negotiation—theory and practice—a relatively new discipline that had its roots in the New York Police Department following an infamous hostage-barricade crisis at John and Al's, a New York City sporting goods store. The sketch version of that standoff is that an NYPD lieutenant took a bullet in the head while standing beside his vehicle across the street from the store where the bad guys held hostages at gunpoint. Struck this poor lieutenant dead, and struck everyone else on the side of the law that the thing to do in this particular situation was to talk it out instead of to shoot it out. This was a huge leap in thinking. Up until this time, the idea of a "talking cure," as negotiating has come to be known at the FBI—or "law enforcement's most effective non-lethal weapon," according to a journal article I wrote during this period—was anathema to most folks in law enforcement, but here it seemed to make sense, and during the course of the long, impromptu negotiations that followed at that sporting goods store it became clear that the hostages had been left alone in a second-floor storage area. Police were able to keep the bad guys distracted and talking while the hostages discovered a false wall that they were able to break through, which led them to a stairwell to the roof—and to safety. With no hostages, the bad guys had no choice but to give up. NYPD officials like Captain Frank Boltz and Lieutenant Bob Louden took the casework to the FBI and the two agencies began to develop their separate hostage negotiations programs—the first dedicated efforts in the country, and the precursor to the more scientific, field-tested approach to hostage negotiations deployed today.

I found that I was drawn to negotiating. I had a talent for it, an appreciation for it, and a great respect for it as well—and the more I learned about it, as negotiation strategies and tactics began to morph from theory to science, the more I wanted to be a part of it going forward.

It was into this mix and mind-set that I took my first real test as a hostage negotiator—and it just happened to work out that the hostage-taker was a guy I'd sent to jail a couple years earlier. In a relatively small town like Rochester, I guess, it was only a matter of time before I started running into these same bad guys a second time around. I happened to catch a report on an armored-car hijacking down in Kentucky. An all-points bulletin had been issued by local and federal authorities. One million dollars in cash was reported missing. This much was known: two armored car drivers had drawn down on a third driver and left him bound and handcuffed and stuffed into the back of the armored car, making off with all that money. The police in Kentucky were up against it. The two men and the money had seemed to vanish without a trace. The armored car company had given the names of the two drivers, Howard D. Kelly and Howard Kalsbeck, and I stared at the teletype and couldn't believe my eyes. I was still new enough to law enforcement that there weren't all that many names for me to keep straight, and these names just popped right out at me. Howard Dennis Kelly was someone I'd put away just a couple years earlier for stealing cars and altering the vehicle identification numbers. He was one of those guys who always wanted to be a police officer, but there's a fine line sometimes between the crooks and the cops. I can't tell you how many times I ran across a crook who thought he would have been a good cop—or vice versa. In any case, the crooks always thought they were smarter than we were—and Howard Dennis Kelly thought he was all kinds of smarter than me. Howard Kalsbeck, I remembered, was his father, which left no doubt in my mind that these were the same characters, now having moved from cars to cash.

I called down to Kentucky and introduced myself. "I know these guys," I said. "I think I can help."

And we set about it. Clearly, the armored car company missed the fact that Howard Dennis Kelly was a convicted felon in its background investigation. When I checked in, the local authorities had no real leads on these two guys, but I had a hunch we could track them through Rochester—and, sure enough, I got a line on Kelly through one of his old girlfriends. Where else were these two characters going to go? They were from Rochester, so it made sense they would land in Rochester once this armored car job went down. Anyway, it made sense to at least look around in Rochester to see what we could turn up.

As I tracked Kelly and his father to the house where they were reportedly holed up, I reminded myself that I had treated him right the first time around. Some law enforcement officers, once they get a guy in cuffs, they hold him up like some kind of dead deer, showboating to their fellow officers and anyone else who happens on the scene: *Look at this animal I'm slaying. Look what I caught.* That sort of thing. I was never about that. I didn't care to show up these bad guys. I didn't care to strut or rub their nose in anything. Folks were still calling us pigs in those days—a holdover term from the sixties that took a couple years longer to fade in Rochester than it did in, say, San Francisco— but I laughed it off. I didn't care that Kelly had bullshitted me and dodged me all those weeks when I was pursuing the stolen car case. And I didn't care to bullshit him or feed him some line about the charges he was facing. I gave it to him straight. He was a human being, after all, and that's how I treated him, the same way I tried to handle every bad guy who crossed my path. My body language was plain and simple and pretty much reflected what came out of my mouth: *I got you. That's all. Case closed.*

For some reason, this struck me as significant at just that moment, and I suppose it was as I scoped out the house where Kelly and his father had barricaded themselves, along with two handguns and a shotgun—and, as it turned out, a couple of potential hostages. We didn't have any details on the hostages just yet, although we assumed they were the homeowners. The house was big and difficult to secure, so we called in the Rochester Police Department to throw an outer perimeter around the outlying street, to divert traffic from the area. Then we threw up an inner perimeter and tried to initiate contact with Kelly and his father.

By this point I was a freshly minted graduate of the FBI's freshly hatched hostage negotiation program. I was out there on the edge of negotiating theory—and now practice. I had myself thinking there was no agent better qualified to handle this situation. Really, I had this routine *down,* and in my rookie thinking it was just a matter of time before the two Howards were laying down their arms in peaceful surrender.

Yeah, right.

The way it actually happened was this: I kept calling and calling the house on the telephone from a house across the street that a good citizen allowed us to use as a command post, but I couldn't get an answer. When I wasn't placing the call myself, there were members of the Rochester Police Department going through the motions on my behalf. Police could hear the phone ringing through the windows across the street, so it's not like we weren't sure the lines were even working, but try as we might we couldn't get anyone to pick up. I thought, *How in the world am I supposed to conduct negotiations with these guys if I can't even begin a dialogue?* For an hour, we kept trying. For the rest of the afternoon, we kept trying, until finally daylight drifted into twilight and we were no further along than when we started.

It was turning out to be a hot summer night, and folks began to spill out of their homes to see what the continued fuss was all about. We were in a section of town that had a pretty high density of lower-economic and working-class people, and after a couple hours watching a bunch of cops surround a building and cordon off a street, I guess folks got a little curious. Like it or not—and on this point I checked in on the side of *not*—our standoff was the neighborhood entertainment for that particular evening. There were news crews on the scene from the local radio and television stations, and half the cops in town were trying to keep some sense of order about the place. It became a real happening—only there wasn't a whole lot happening.

Unfortunately, these neighbors weren't exactly concerned citizens. They were clamoring for a good show—it would have made a great episode of *Cops*—and before long folks were hooting and hollering and making a plain fuss. It was terribly distracting, but I didn't see that there was anything I or my colleagues could do about it, other than continuing to try to raise one of these Howards on the phone to initiate contact. And so we kept at it, hoping we could keep the crowd in check—a crowd that had me thinking I was at a minor league hockey game on a bad night, constantly ready to duck the rubber chickens that were thrown into the rink.

After what seemed like hours, a captain in the police department told us he was concerned about the growing public nuisance. People were milling about in housecoats and bathrobes like it was an after-hours block party, and the mood of the crowd was restless. It was a surreal scene. There were sirens sounding and red lights flashing and neighbors reconnecting—a combustible mix on a hot summer night.

"Five more minutes," the captain said, "and we're going to flood the house with tear gas."

At some point there appeared to be a general concern that we were cutting into the police overtime budget—which, for my money, wasn't much of a concern. My only concern was defusing the situation and seeing these hostages out and safe, and to this end I was able to persuade Gene Walsh, one of Rochester's truly dedicated federal prosecutors, to come out to the scene to offer the insight of his office. He had prosecuted Kelly with me that first time around. "I'll cut any deal you need to get them out," he said, trying to give me the room I needed to talk these guys out without gunfire.

Trouble was, I still couldn't get these guys to talk, and the police were watching the clock. I thought, *We flood the house with tear gas and these guys start shooting and the whole thing goes south on us real quick.*

I sought out the police captain. "Give me one more try," I found myself saying. Then I ran from our command post and hunched behind the front tire of a marked police car with a PA system. I positioned myself with the engine block between me and any shot the Howards might try to take, and with the PA microphone in hand I prayed in silence: *Lord, let them hear me, and let them come out peacefully.*

"Howard Kelly," I called out. "This is Clint Van Zandt with the FBI. Pick up the phone."

Look in the dictionary under *backfire* and you might see a description of what happened next. Turned out this wasn't such a bright idea, me using the PA system like that, because it got the crowd going big-time. These folks had been relatively quiet until I opened my big mouth, but now they were all over it, and all over *me,* shouting "Don't pick up the phone, Howard!" or "Screw the feds, Howard!" or whatever they could think of to get this guy riled up and disinclined to cooperate. Let me tell you, it transformed the outlying scene from a sideshow to a zoo—and I suppose it would have been funny if it wasn't so serious, if it wasn't my butt on the line as the leader of this stalled hostage negotiation about to turn to tear gas, knowing all the while that we'd probably wind up victims of the tear gas ourselves.

The Rochester police didn't think it was all that funny, either, and I guess they were wondering about the rookie FBI agent handling the negotiations, because after a couple minutes more I got another report that they had reached a breaking point. I was still crouched behind the police car, microphone still cupped in my hand, when a cop crawled over to me and said, "Chief says we're running up overtime and losing the crowd and that we're going to gas the house now."

There we were, busting our butts to negotiate through this impasse, still uncertain how many hostages were inside the home with Kelly and Kalsbeck, and I had the police chief worried about running up overtime and losing the crowd. I didn't see how the one had to do with the other, but there it was. Then I thought back to how I'd treated this Howard Kelly character the first time around, and figured I'd give it one more try—for old times' sake and for the hell of it, both. "Howard Kelly," I shouted out. "This is Clint Van Zandt. I didn't bullshit you last time. Do you remember that? I didn't hang you out to dry or string you up, and I'm not out to do that here. We can talk about this, and we can be straight with each other. I never lied to you then, and I'm not lying to you now. We can come out of this okay, but we need to talk about this." I poured it on pretty thick. Whatever I could think to say to this guy, I said to this guy, and I didn't mince words or worry about appearances or protocol. Most FBI agents wouldn't have used a word like *bullshit* over a PA system in front of such a large crowd, and they certainly wouldn't have beseeched the guy in such a public way, but I didn't care because I knew that if we gassed that house we would have lost—and our "situation" would have become a full-blown "crisis."

Finally, a beat or two after my desperation appeal, one of the cops came loping over to me. "Somebody in that house just picked up the phone," he said. "They want to talk to you."

Sure enough, the police had continued to call from our makeshift command post, hoping someone would crack and finally pick up the phone—and now that someone finally had, I raced back into the CP to hold up my end. "Howard," I said into the receiver, trying not to sound out of breath.

"Hi, Clint," I got back, in a voice that struck me as a little too cheerful for the situation. "How you doin'?"

"Okay, Howard," I answered. "How you doin'?"

"All right, I guess," he said. "Looks like we got ourselves a situation."

"What's going on in there?" I wanted to know.

"Well, we're doing pretty good right now," he said. "I've got my dad with me, and we've got the owner of the house, and we've got his wife in here too. We're all doing okay. How about you?"

"We're doing okay out here," I said, "but we've got to talk about how we're going to get out of this mess. We've got to talk about getting all four of you out of there."

This was the first confirmation any of us in law enforcement had had regarding the number of people being held in that house against their will, and it signaled all kinds of alarms—and yet, I was careful not to react too strongly until I could get a good read on this guy's state of mind. I didn't want to say or do anything to set him off, at least not just yet.

"Nothing to talk about, Clint," he said. "I'm not going back to jail. You're going to have to take me here and get it over with."

As a hostage negotiator, this was about the last thing I wanted to hear. Realize, this was my first hostage-barricade situation and even I knew this much. The comment echoed in my head, and I thought, *Van Zandt, this is not good.* Here was a guy making up his mind that he was going to die, and he had indicated that there were two hostages inside that he might choose to take down with him. That, mixed with a neighborhood crowd egging him on to do just that, put us all in a tough spot, and I found myself wondering if there might be some textbook somewhere could tell me how to negotiate my way out of such as this.

"Nobody's going to die today, Howard," I said, reaching into my fresh bag of negotiating tricks and trying to play it cool. "Nobody's going to get hurt. We cut our losses right here, you're not looking at a lot of time."

"I don't think so, Clint," he said. "I'm not going back to jail."

"You did a couple years last time," I said, doing my best to diminish what this guy had already been through and what he was now facing. "It was no big deal. Worst case here, that's what you're looking at. I'm not gonna bullshit you on this, Howard. A couple years, that's all."

We went back and forth on this for a while, but I couldn't get Kelly to move off the notion that there was no end to this standoff, that we would have to take him out in order to resolve the situation. This was a dangerous place for us to be, him feeling desperate and backed into a corner, and I struggled for a way to steer him toward a more open-ended outcome. I asked to speak with his father, thinking I could maybe get the senior Howard to talk some sense into the junior Howard, but Kalsbeck wouldn't get on the phone. Every now and then we'd break off conversation for a stretch of time, with a promise to reconnect a short time later, and I tried to follow the basic negotiating strategies I'd learned in class and set them in some kind of sensible motion. My focus was on keeping a line of communication open, on minimizing the crimes Kelly may or may not have committed, on getting him to see some light at the end of his dark tunnel, and on doing all these things with some measure of credibility. If I'd just come out and told this guy he wasn't facing any jail time, or that there might be some way for him to walk away from this scene, he'd have seen right through me. And if I'd come down hard and told him we were going to put him away for good, he'd have never surrendered. So I straddled the fence, and gave him some time to kick things around, and kept the pressure on in what ways made sense.

Things went on in this way for a couple hours. We'd talk for a few minutes, leave off for a while, then talk again. When twilight finally disappeared, a SWAT officer shot out a transformer to "kill" the lights for one square block surrounding the house, thinking this would eliminate some of the crowd and the attendant distraction, but the darkness only made the scene appear more dramatic, especially when set against the flashing red lights of the couple dozen police and FBI vehicles that were strewn about the scene; plus, now we had no way to quickly turn the street lights back on. The neighbors continued to make quite a racket, which turned out to be an unexpected good thing. Why? Well, in the middle of all the noise and disorder and back-and-forth communication the two hostage-homeowners managed to slink out the back door. Took us completely (and, happily) by surprise, but there it was. And it was the most remarkable turn—not at all the sort of maneuver we might have endorsed if we had known about it. Kelly and his father were preoccupied by the phone and the crowd noise to such a degree that the homeowner was able to turn to his wife and say, "To hell with this, let's get out of here." And that's just what they did. Managed to run clear across the street to our command post without being detected, and we were even able to debrief them and learn what else was going on in that house before Kelly and his father had any idea that they had gone.

Next time I had Howard Dennis Kelly on the phone, I put it to him plain—with just a side of relish. "Howard," I said, "tell me again, how many people are in that house with you?"

"There's me and my dad and the two homeowners," he said. "Four of us in all."

"You're sure about that?" I said, pushing him a little.

"I'm sure," he said.

"Well, then you better count heads again," I said.

The phone went silent for a couple beats, and when Kelly came back on the line he said, "Son of a bitch!"

"Don't go blaming me for this one, Howard," I said. "These people up and left on their own. I guess they caught you napping." I was careful not to rub his nose in it, while wanting to rub his nose in it at the same time.

He calmed down and seemed to think about this for a moment. "I guess so," he finally said, resigned to it.

"There are only two of you now," I said, "and I guess you know that changes things a little bit."

"I guess so," he said.

"Changes things a lot, actually," I said.

"Yeah, yeah, I get it," he said, cutting me off, his tone essentially flat. "It changes things. So what do you want me to do?"

"I want you to come out," I said. "I want you to walk out the front door. It's the only smart move. It's how everyone wins."

Of course, I didn't expect Kelly to lay down just because I asked him to, but nevertheless I felt I had to ask. I should mention here that negotiators don't use the word *surrender,* because it somehow rubs the bad guys the wrong way, so we talk around it or come up with euphemisms. We all know what we mean, though. It's the word itself that seems to cut against the grain. The notion of it can be okay—and sometimes the bad guys just don't think of it themselves. You see, the word *surrender* is what I call a "bullet word," a red flag of a term like *give up* or *jail* or *courtroom* that could have a negative effect on negotiations, so I tried to avoid them.

"Let me think about it," Kelly said, and then he hung up.

In all, it was an unexpected, astonishing development—and as thrilled as I was that the homeowners had somehow managed to escape without injury, that's how frantic I was that I might have lost the confidence of Howard Kelly and that he himself might now be at risk. Those worries were confirmed a short while later when one of the Rochester cops came careening into the command post area to report that some unidentified individual had bailed out of the barricaded house by the same back door used by the homeowners. Again, it was the most remarkable thing—the *second* most remarkable thing in a relatively short stretch of time. After hours and hours of nothing doing, the two hostages ducked out a back door, and after that they were quickly followed by one of the hostage-takers. You could work twenty years on the job and never see a hostage stage his own escape, and another twenty without seeing a bad guy slink off into the night past a police perimeter, but it was one of those unlikely nights. Apparently, Howard Kelly had hung up the phone, fisted about a quarter million dollars in cash into an old suitcase, and decided to make a run for it. How he got past the police department SWAT guys, I had no idea, although it wasn't long before there were enough theories on it to pass for legitimate excuses. It was dark. All the lights were out. The police were not anticipating a sudden escape at just that moment. Kelly zigged when everyone thought he would zag. Best theory of all: as Forrest Gump would later tell us, shit happens. All the time, shit happens—and every now and then dumb luck is enough to help a bad guy skate past a couple dozen cops who just happen to be looking left when he runs right.

As this particular shit happened, though, Howard Dennis Kelly's dumb luck only took him so far. As a matter of fact, it took him just past the fence to a neighbor's yard, where a clothesline had been strung up and now hung almost invisibly in the night air. (Thank goodness for that time before clothes dryers!) Poor Kelly ran full tilt across that yard, making his getaway, probably congratulating himself on how he had outsmarted us, until he collided into that clothesline with his neck. Evidently, he was sent reeling like a wide receiver cut down across the middle of a football field, and as his body continued forward with momentum and his head snapped back and he eventually landed with a thud on the hard ground below, the handle on his apparently cheap suitcase somehow broke loose in his hand. Kelly scrambled to his feet as quick as he could, and continued on his break, gripping the suitcase handle as if it still might be attached to the suitcase itself, and he managed to hop a fence and sprint another couple hundred feet until he ran smack into about 250 pounds of Rochester police officer—just kinda bounced off the cop's chest and slumped to the ground—and before Kelly knew what hit him he was in handcuffs, wondering what the hell had happened to the rest of his suitcase and all that cash, and how that huge cop happened to alight in his path.

Kalsbeck, meanwhile, was back in the house, thinking Kelly had been shot and killed. The man was inconsolable, and determined to take his own life before seeing us send him to jail. "You've killed my son," he wailed into the phone, "and now you're going to kill me."

"No, Howard," I assured, "we haven't killed your son. He's alive and well. He's in custody, but he hasn't been harmed."

"I'm not going to jail," he said again. "I'm too old to go to jail."

"Let's talk about this," I said. "Nobody's been hurt. You can still return the money. Maybe it won't be so bad."

Of course, I knew better, but I didn't want him thinking his circumstances were too bleak to get past. I didn't want him thinking he was better off dead. And I didn't want him to come out shooting. That was my biggest worry, that he would be too cowardly to point a gun at himself and would start firing on us good guys instead, knowing that one of our snipers would then be forced to take him out. This last was not a scenario I cared to consider, and at the time we weren't really trained to consider it anyway. It was off the map of our case histories and experience, even though that would change in the months ahead. For the time being, though, it fell to me to talk Howard Kalsbeck down from his despair, so I played the legacy card. I reminded him that he had another child, and that he had grandchildren with that other child, and that he had an obligation to those grandchildren. "These kids have a right to know their grandfather," I said. "You have a responsibility to be there for them when they're growing up."

"I suppose," he allowed.

"What happened here today, this is nothing to die about," I said. "Far as we know, this is the first wrong thing you've ever done, and it's not too late to undo some of it. You borrowed some money, that's all. You can return it. Nobody's been hurt. It's no big thing. Nothing that means those kids have to grow up without a grandfather."

The phone went silent on the other end, which I took to mean he was thinking things through. I didn't want to push too hard, or come across as insincere, so I let these thoughts hang for a couple beats—until, finally, he came back on the line. "What do you want me to do?" he said.

Surrendering to a local police department and a SWAT team and a bunch of FBI agents is no easy task, because we all have our little routines and assurances and paces we like to put the bad guys through. I told Kalsbeck he needed to leave the guns in the house and come out with his hands on his head. Then he'd have to drop to his knees with his hands remaining on his head, which was the way the SWAT guys wanted things to go, only Kalsbeck bristled at the treatment he was about to endure. "Bullshit," he barked into the phone. "You're not going to treat me like an animal. I'm just going to kill myself right now."

I had set the hook and was reeling him in and thought we were home free, but this SWAT surrender nonsense had set him off yet again—so I went at him a second time. "Tell you what," I said. "I'll talk to the SWAT guys. I'll talk to the chief of police. Just come out with your hands on your head, then wait for instructions from the officer who greets you in front of the house. He'll tell you what to do."

I caught this great look of disdain from the SWAT guy next to me, who looked like he wanted to cuff me for changing his surrender terms, but I was going on feel here.

"I can do that," Kalsbeck said.

"Yes, you can do that," I said.

"I won't be down on my hands and knees?" he asked, making sure.

"You won't be down on your hands and knees," I said, only I couldn't make such a statement with absolute certainty because I wasn't going to be part of the tactical team to take him into custody. Basically, the drill is you do what you're told. Some of these SWAT guys, they want you out, they want you down on your knees, they want your legs crossed and your head between your legs and every which way. Other guys, they'll just slap the cuffs on you and move on to the next thing. Sometimes, it's a heat-of-the-moment, seat-of-the-pants– type deal.

Here, Kalsbeck must have sensed my uncertainty over this one issue, because he asked me to personally meet him in front of the house. He wanted to surrender to me, not to some SWAT guy he'd never dealt with before. That was his comfort level—to have the agent who had been decent to his son and who had so far been decent to him be on the one to take him into custody—and the way I looked at it, it was still my job to keep him comfortable and cooperative until we had him in custody. At first I only agreed that I would talk him through the surrender once he got out the door, thinking I could keep out of sight and still be good to my word; but he wanted to see me, which presented a problem. A lot of times, in what we negotiators call the "surrender ritual," the bad guy wants to see you for these legitimate comfort-level–type reasons, but a lot of times they have it in for you. Since you've been the guy talking them through the stalemate, they might hold you personally responsible for their situation, and they might be looking for ways to take you out before they're taken down. We teach negotiators not to go face-to-face with their opposite numbers, because that's how you get killed. I knew as much, but I set what I knew aside. This had been my first full-blown hostage negotiation, which made this my first full-blown hostage negotiation surrender, and I was determined to see it through. I was also determined not to be stupid about it, so I got with the police sniper team before I crossed the street to the house in order to work through a plan of action in case things went sour—which, I knew full well, sometimes happens. (In this line of work, Murphy and his law are always lurking out there somewhere.) The deal was this: if Kalsbeck emerged from the house with a weapon of any kind, I would dart sharply to my right to give the snipers a clear shot. It was essential that these guys be able to focus on their target and not have to worry about which direction I might run to get out of their way. They needed to concentrate, and I needed to live, so it was in our shared best interests to get the choreography down.

Turned out, Kalsbeck didn't have it in him to fight. He was done—hands on his head, routine all the way—and as soon as our guys had him safely in cuffs, I felt this huge weight being lifted. From me, from the scene around the house . . . it was like a giant collective sigh. For hours and hours people had been talking about taking their own lives, about killing hostages, about taking down cops, and now that it was suddenly over, there was this great, overwhelming silence. I needed to decompress, so I just took off. It would become my own little surrender ritual: I put as much distance between myself and the scene as I could while still keeping myself available to tie up any loose ends. Always, at the resolution end of these standoffs I'd find myself disappearing into my own quiet reflection, and here I headed out into the streets and kept moving—away, away, away—like I was on some inner-city walkabout. Like I said, it would become a habit as each new situation resolved itself, but this was the first time I needed to unwind in just this way, and as I walked past the scene it struck me once again as utterly surreal. There were television crews breaking through our now redundant perimeter. Rochester police retreated to their vehicles. Bathrobed and slippered neighbors returning to their homes, disappointed perhaps that they hadn't seen more of a show. (There wasn't even any gunfire, which seemed a great disappointment to these folks, who probably would have been better off staying inside watching television.) And to top it all off, there was now a mist of rain that had turned up as if on cue.

I took in the scene and willed myself away, and as I walked I thought about what had happened—specifically, about my role in what had happened. There had been so many lives hinging on my ability to talk these two guys out of that house, and it struck me full in the face that I had put myself in a position where people would live and die by how I did my job. In a classroom setting, this negotiating business can be an interesting intellectual exercise, but out here on the street I realized it can also be tense and nerve-racking as hell. It's life and death. It's everything. And for the first time I knew what it meant when negotiators said, "If you're right, you're right. If you're wrong, you're dead."

I walked for about three blocks, hands in pockets, my head pretty much all over the place, when a police car sidled up to me. The officer slowed and rolled down his window. "Agent Van Zandt," he said, "Kelly wants to talk to you. You want me to run you back there?"

"Sure," I said, and hopped in the car, thinking there would be time for my self-indulgent walkabout later. Headed back to the command post area, where Howard Dennis Kelly sat in handcuffs, looking a little wet and bedraggled and beaten. *Caught.* That's really the best word to describe it. For all his father's worry about being treated like an animal, that's the image that bounces into your head when you see one of these guys in cuffs at the resolution end of one of these ordeals, which I guess is why some law officers have a hard time treating people decently once they've got them in cuffs and a situation has been defused.

Anyway, we had a good talk, Kelly and me. Went over a bunch of things that I was able to use in the next negotiation, and the one after that, and it reinforced for me how essential it was to treat these bad guys decently, honestly, respectfully. Each time out. No matter what. Trust is key. The line in the classroom is that the only lie you should tell in a hostage negotiation is the last lie: the lie you need when all else fails and you must get the bad guy to step in front of the window to give your snipers a clear shot. The lie you'll never have to answer to: the final option. Short of that last, necessary lie, we allow ourselves what we might call "tactical expressions," which basically means we layer in some wiggle room. We might tell someone there's only one arrest warrant out for him, when in reality that lone arrest warrant might be based on a twenty-five-count indictment. It's okay to sometimes stretch the truth, or possibly even obscure it a bit, but there better be some truth in every claim and promise you make, because you'll see these guys again. Absolutely, the Howard Kellys of the world will get spit back out by the criminal justice system and return to haunt you—and if *you* don't happen to see them, then it'll be some other cop, somewhere down some other road, who'll have to deal with him, so we'll all do well to take the same honest, straightforward approach. Doesn't always work out that way, but that's the way it should go.

One final footnote to the Howard Kelly saga, filed under Yogi Berra's classic line "It ain't over till it's over." With the two Howards in custody, we recovered the money and took it back to the local FBI office to count it. As I wrote earlier, there was never a whole lot going on in Rochester to begin with, and there wasn't a whole lot going on this particular night other than this case, so most of the local agents were on hand to help with the counting: Hugh Higgins, Dick Foley, Tom Carney, Hal Thomas, Ken Olson, Pete Jacobson, Andy Manning, Gene "Stats" Anthony, the two FCI Joes (Cain and Corcoran), along with a few others. We counted the money twice and came up with two different totals.

Finally, Hugh Higgins, the senior FBI agent, told everyone to go home. "We'll get a count in the morning," he said.

I put the money back in the bag and stowed it in a safe place, under my desk.

The next morning, the armored car company called, wanting to collect their cash. At this point we finally had a count just shy of the original $1 million. The two Howards had spent a couple thousand dollars, but otherwise it was all there. When the armored car representative arrived, Huey quite reasonably suggested that the guy do his own independent count and sign our receipt for it, but the guy refused. "We'll count it later and get a receipt out to you in the mail," he said.

I chimed in that we should just put the money in the bank and draw interest on it until we had their receipt, after which the armored car representative gave in and accepted our total, and I mention the back-and-forth here for the way it reminds us how money becomes just a lot of paper when it's not yours.

A couple months after the Howard Kelly standoff, I was faced with another hostage-barricade situation—and during this one I would once again be made to confront the frightening concept of how to handle such a crisis when there was nothing at stake but life itself. Typically, a hostage-taker will have demands of some sort: money, justice, media attention, a means of escape, clemency, freedom for an oppressed people . . . As a result, we would approach each standoff with an appropriate set of bargaining chips and a preset notion of how things might go.

But that was all about to change.

Following the Kelly case, I had become the de facto hostage negotiator for the Rochester FBI office. We didn't get a whole lot of hostage-barricade calls, mind you, but what few we did catch came to me. I also handled a lot of the bank robberies in our office, and this next combined my two areas of expertise. It was a reasonably warm Rochester day, and I was at a small Italian restaurant where I had just sat down to a get-acquainted lunch with a new agent, about to bite into a great sandwich, when my portable radio went off. In those days my call sign was Roger Four, and I heard, "Roger Four, bank robbery in progress, Security Trust Bank, corner of Thurston and Sawyer, possible hostage situation as well."

I thought, *So much for this great sandwich.* I also thought, *Better hit the head before heading out, because you never know when you'll get another chance to use the bathroom.* In this one respect at least, we FBI agents were pretty much like the Boy Scouts: always prepared.

The Security Trust Company Bank was located clear across town from the Italian restaurant, so we slapped the emergency light on the roof of my FBI car and ran a bunch of red lights to hustle over there double-quick. Instead of going directly to the bank, which had been a frequent robbery target, we went to a command post that had been set up in an office building down the street. I popped the trunk, slipped into my bulletproof vest, and grabbed a special hostage phone I had jerry-rigged to allow me to record conversations, or to allow a third party to listen in: once again, always prepared.

The lay of the land was this: one or possibly two individuals had gone into the bank and taken an uncertain number of bank employees hostage. There may or may not have been some customers among the hostages as well. Shots had been fired. Two police officers had already been hit. The extent of their injuries was not yet known. Pedestrians had also been shot at up and down the street. In all, not the most pleasant situation to enter into, but these were the cards we were dealt on this day, and now I had to put them in play.

One of the wounded officers had come under intense shotgun fire as he rolled his police cruiser up in front of the bank. The officer was hit while in the driver's seat and again as he crawled from the passenger side door as the bank robber bounced rounds around and under the police car. The officer was struck in both his arms and legs and was pinned down. Some other brave cops commandeered a city dump truck and raised the truck bed to form a bulletproof shield, and then they backed the truck up the street to the wounded officer to carry him away to a waiting ambulance. In all, a dramatic scene that fairly set the somber mood for the ongoing hostage situation, one with a gunman who clearly wasn't afraid to shoot it out with the police.

The number of hostage-takers or bank robbers or whatever we would start calling these particular bad guys was a vital piece of information, and it was just beyond our reach. Some witnesses had reported seeing one, and others had reported seeing two, and the space between those two numbers was staggering. (Note: eyewitness reports always yielded the least reliable information, so we were careful to corroborate every detail before acting on it.) If there was one bad guy, our snipers could take him out and effectively eliminate the threat and end the standoff. If there were two, we couldn't take out one without simultaneously taking out the other, because as soon as one went down, the other could start shooting and we'd have a bloodbath on our hands—which meant that we had to proceed under the assumption that there was more than one bad guy until we had firm information to the contrary.

First order of business, while we attempted to confirm the number of hostage-takers in the bank, was to stabilize the situation in what ways we could—which meant placing a tactical or SWAT team around the bank, establishing an outer perimeter, clearing the civilians from the surrounding streets, and rescuing and administering aid to the two downed police officers. And while all this was going on, it fell to me to initiate contact with this bank-robber/hostage-taker–type person and to find out who he was and what he wanted. The bottom line, at just that moment, was to get him talking, to make a connection and get a dialogue going. That was my job: to keep him talking instead of shooting, because at the very least it's hard to talk and shoot at the same time. The only problem with this strategy was that I once again couldn't raise anyone on the phone. I kept calling in and calling in, and each time a bank employee was evidently instructed by the robber or robbers to pick up the phone and then to hang it up. Every now and then I'd get out a few words before I heard the click on the other side of the line: "Clint Van Zandt, FBI. . . . I need to talk to one of the people in charge. . . . I'm an FBI agent. . . . I need to talk to the guy with the gun. . . . Tell him it's urgent. . . ." And every *other* now and then, someone on the receiving end would slip in a couple bits of information before I could hear someone in charge bark out orders to hang up the phone. "No one has been hurt," I heard on one call. "He doesn't want me to talk to you now. . . . There are three of us in the back room. . . . I've only seen one guy with a gun, but I think there might be others. . . ."

Note: if you have a gun, you're in charge.

Who knew what these people heard from me before they hung up, or what they passed on to the guy with the gun? Who could tell how valid their observations actually were? Indeed, there was no way to know what was being passed along, if anything, but I kept calling and someone kept answering, and after a couple dozen hang-ups and call-backs we were able to piece together a more complete picture of what was going on inside that bank. Not a full picture, mind you, but a whole lot more than we had to work with going in.

As a negotiator, this brick wall I kept running into on the phone was a bad sign. Whenever you can't get the hostage-taker to talk to you directly, you leave yourself open. If you wind up communicating through a third party, there's room for misinterpretation: a tone could be easily misread, a message not properly conveyed. You lose a lot in the translation. And that's the best-case scenario. Worst-case is when there's no communication at all, which was pretty much what we were facing here. All we could hear, out at our command post, were a few snippets of unauthorized and who-knew-how-reliable informa-tion, punctuated by random shotgun blasts coming from inside the bank. Whoever it was who had taken these hostages, he had soon enough shot and killed the copy machine and blown away a couple windows . . . on his way to firing his shotgun more than one hundred times during the standstill, making this one of the most dangerous and volatile situations I'd ever encounter.

During the course of these going-nowhere negotiations, a police officer approached me at the command post with information regard-ing another incident elsewhere in town: a report of a double homi-cide with a third person critically wounded, just a few blocks away.

"Do I need to know about this?" I shot back.

"I don't know," the police officer said. "Just came in on the radio."

"You'll let me know if anyone thinks there's a connection" I said— asking and telling, both.

"I'll let you know," he said.

And I moved back to what I was doing, little knowing how critical this last piece of information would turn out to be in this case.

A couple hours in, we had our first real break when the hostage-taker finally revealed himself to us. His name was William Griffin, and he had taken the time to write a note, which he wanted one of the hostages to read to the police over the telephone. We thought it might be a list of demands, or a statement of purpose, but instead we got reports of a rambling diatribe from Griffin, going on and on about his life and the various wrong turns he had taken, and the wrongs that were in turn visited on him. Inexplicably, he included a phone number for the U.S. Marshals Office, and for the sheriff's office, and another few numbers we couldn't place right away. The message was so long and unfocused, and the message bearer was so nervous and distracted, that the note was never read in its entirety—and this would prove to be another critical gap. It turned out there was a significant line toward the end of Griffin's note, where he used the phrase *after the police take my life* . . . Clearly, that was a key indication of this guy's state of mind, and had I heard that line I would have started to think, *Okay, this is not a bank robber we're dealing with. This is not some guy seeking reparations. This is someone who wants to die.* But the woman reading the note never got that far. If she had, it would have placed an entirely different spin on the crisis going forward, while instead we just continued to spin in our familiar direction, trying to negotiate our way through it—and to hope for the best.

Unfortunately, the best was not to be—not today, not in this case.

See, in virtually every hostage situation, there are four possible outcomes, or "tactical alternatives," from the law enforcement perspective: You can use tear gas and drive the bad guys from the barricaded area. You can use a sniper or a team of snipers and shoot the bad guys. You can order a direct assault on the barricaded area, where a SWAT team pours through all the doors and windows and puts an end to the standoff by force. Or you can contain, isolate, negotiate, and attempt to get the bad guys to surrender. In this instance we couldn't use tear gas because we had a report that at least one of the bank tellers had an upper respiratory problem and that one might or might not have been pregnant. We couldn't use snipers because we were still unable to determine if there was more than one hostage-taker. We couldn't storm the bank because it was a fortified area and—get this!—nobody in the bank's management chain could locate a spare set of keys, and the only way to enter the building was to batter down the doors and windows, which would have left our tactical team easy targets as they stepped through the shattered glass.

And so we were left with negotiations as our only available strategy. The problem with this last, as I have indicated, was that William Griffin and any partners he might have had inside the bank with him were thoroughly unavailable to negotiate. We kept calling, and calling, and collecting whispered snippets of valuable information, but there was no real communication beyond that rambling note—until finally, about three hours in, one of the tellers came to the phone and said, "He's got a message for you."

It was about two-thirty in the afternoon, and I thought, *It's about time.* "Good," I said. "What is it?"

She said, "Either you come to the front entrance doors of the bank at three o'clock and have a shootout with him in the parking lot, or he's going to start killing hostages."

Then the line went dead.

I thought, *What are we dealing with here?* It was like something out of the Wild, Wild West—a shootout in the parking lot?—and something so completely foreign to our admittedly limited experience. Still, back at the command post, we felt it was something we had to consider. We kicked it around and tried to figure how it might go. We wondered what, exactly, this guy was asking for. It made no sense, and we went back and forth on it for a good few minutes. A shootout? Who asks for a shootout in this day and age? And for what purpose? Our prevailing thought was that Griffin must have seen this as a way to take out another police officer—this time an FBI agent. You have to realize, at the time we all thought we were dealing with a trapped bank robber, which is how it usually happens when someone takes hostages in a bank. We figured it was a bank job gone bad and that this was the only move left for the guy that would allow him to possibly save face and take the money and make a run for it.

The deadline troubled me. Frankly, the shootout in the parking lot troubled me a good deal more, and there was no way to justify putting myself or anyone else at such obvious risk, so we focused on the deadline. As a negotiator, we deal with deadlines all the time. Best way to treat them is usually like an ultimatum from a petulant child, like something we have to get beyond before we can move on to the next thing. If a hostage-taker tells me he's going to hurt someone by a given time unless I meet this or that demand, I look to keep him talking until we pass that deadline. It's a simple strategy but generally effective. It doesn't matter if you're arranging for food to be brought in, or for a phone call from the bad guy's mother, or whatever, as long as I can keep the guy's mind off the clock. Once you slip past the designated time and he has been unable to act on his threat, the advantage in the negotiation tilts mightily in your favor—and any subsequent deadlines carry a lot less weight.

Here, though, I couldn't get Griffin on the phone. We kept calling and calling. At about 2:50, I managed to get through to one of the tellers. "I need to talk to him," I said. "We need to get some food in there to you people." But there was no response. At 2:55, I reached someone else and implored them to get Griffin on the phone. Again they hung up. The clock inched toward 3:00 p.m.—2:57, 2:58,

2:59 . . . We kept calling and calling and the phone kept ringing and ringing, but we were getting nowhere. In the back of my mind, I kept thinking that Griffin would pick up at the last second to tell me how serious he was and we could finally start a dialogue, but I never got that chance.

At precisely 3:00 p.m. there was a huge commotion across the street, just as a report came over the police radio. I was standing next to the PD SWAT commander at the time, and we flashed each other looks that said, *What have we got?* What we had, sadly, was a female hostage dragged to a glass-enclosed vestibule in front of the bank and shot three times through her midsection with a twelve-gauge shotgun. The poor woman was basically cut in half by the blasts and blown through the glass. Her name was Margaret Moore, a bank teller and the mother of a young child. Later we would learn that she was sitting on the bank floor with other employees as Griffin looked them over one last time. The hostages were black and white, male and female, young and old—and yet, for some reason, in his sad state of mind, Griffin pointed to Moore and told her to get up. He then forced her at gunpoint to walk to the lobby doors as she pleaded for her life, where-upon he sent these heavy shotgun shells crashing into her body; as we spilled from our command post a short while later, you could see her slumped on the ground beyond the bank doors, her blood staining the pavement around her lifeless body. It struck me as not unlike the chalk outline silhouettes you see on television, only here it was drawn with blood and the poor woman was dead and it was all too real.

We were all stunned, and devastated, and momentarily silent. I suppose everyone who works in law enforcement is eventually faced with a maddening, frustrating, confounding moment when nothing makes sense and you're left to wonder if you could have done anything differently, and this was one of those moments for every one of us in that command post, as well as everyone outside on our tactical team. It was such a brutal, senseless, startling development that we were all shaken—

and, I'm guessing, most of us are still shaken by it. But it was a moment we didn't have to spare, so we set it aside and looked to our next move, even as we knew our minds would own that image forever.

"We're not going to get this guy out of there," I said to Del Leach, the new Rochester chief of police, a good cop who came up through the ranks, and to Hugh Higgins, once again the senior FBI agent on the scene. "He shot police officers. He's just killed a teller. We can't talk him out. We're going to have to take him out."

As it happened, Chief Leach and Huey were way ahead of me on this one. There were a couple nods of assent and the order of a "green light" to the sniper team outside. The plan was for a sniper to shoot Griffin at the first available opportunity, after which the tactical team would assault the bank, looking for a second subject. And it was put in motion immediately. After Griffin shot Margaret Moore in the vestibule area on one side of the bank, he crossed to a plate glass window on the other side. The window overlooked a church across the street, where a police sniper was positioned at a second-floor window. (A sniper in a house of peace and worship? That was just one of the sad realities of the job.) Griffin was aware that our sniper was so positioned, because earlier in the day he had shot at the same sniper and demanded his retreat. Now, though, he merely pressed the side of his face against the glass and offered an easy shot for a high-powered rifle. The sniper across the street caught Griffin in his scope and fired and Griffin slumped to the ground, dead from a head shot.

"It was an easy shot," the sniper would later tell me, "almost like he wanted to give me a good target."

At this point the tactical team stormed the bank, just as bank manager Ernie Lofton began to walk gingerly across the bank lobby to where Griffin now lay dead. His idea was to pick up Griffin's shotgun and to carry it outside the bank to indicate to the surrounding police that there was no longer a threat, but our guys were looking for a second shooter, so such a move would have put him in a very tenuous situation—this alongside witness statements suggesting another black bank robber was still on the scene. (Lofton, too, was black.) Mercifully, Ernie Lofton thought better of his plan and ran toward the door instead. He later told us there was a voice, something like God talking to him from inside his head, saying, "Ernie, don't pick up the gun."

When they came across Griffin's body, our SWAT team discovered he had been wearing earmuffs—not the kind you wear to protect against the cold, but the kind you wear at a shooting range to muffle the sound. It was another telling detail we all wished we'd had earlier. We could see all along that Griffin had something on his head, but even with our binoculars it appeared it might have been a headset of some kind, which we had assumed he could be using to communicate with a coconspirator. But no, they were sound-deafening earmuffs, under which he wore earplugs, which meant he must have been oblivious to our persistent phone calls and deaf to the entreaties of his hostages—not that it would have made any difference if he had been able to hear perfectly well. The telling piece, in my estimation, was that the earmuffs and plugs suggested this guy didn't want to hear anything outside his own thoughts. Sure, they muffled the sound of his own shotgun, which he fired constantly, but they also prevented anyone on the outside from talking him down from his mission.

And just what was William Griffin's mission that day at Security Trust? Well, as it turned out, he went there to die—and he enlisted the help of the Rochester Police Department and the FBI to accomplish his goal. This much became clear just a few moments after our tactical team had taken the building when a connection to that double homicide down the street was finally established. The murders had taken place at Griffin's home—and as connections go, I guess, it doesn't get much more transparent than this right here. William Griffin had woken up that morning and walked down the creaky, worn wooden stairs to the living room of his mother's residence, where he shotgunned his mother and a wallpaper hanger to death, and when his stepfather stumbled on the scene he shot and critically wounded him as well. Then he walked out of the house and down the street to the bank to commit these terrible acts.

The earmuffs, the double homicide, the random and rampant shotgun fire, the refusal to talk, the absence of demands of any kind, the rambling third-party message that was never delivered in full—these were all clues that would have presented a clearer picture of what we were facing, if we had thought to look for them. Pieces of a puzzle never completed. If we had known what we were looking for— better, if we had even thought to look outside the box from a fresh perspective—we might have been able to resolve the situation differently. And that's why this case was so incredibly important: infuriating, and tragic, but also useful in helping us to develop strategies and approaches to help prevent such an outcome in the future.

Instead of my now-customary walkabout following the stabilizing of a hostage scene, I walked the few short blocks to Griffin's middle-class urban home. I needed to put some space between myself and what had happened, but I was also desperate to understand this guy, and how we had missed so much, and the thought of waiting for an investigation to play itself out was an abomination. I happened to find Griffin's diary, before the place had been picked clean by the homicide cops; as I thumbed through the worn pages I came across an entry dated about thirteen months earlier in which Griffin pretty much detailed the events of this day. The takeover of a neighborhood bank. The plan to have the cops take him out because he was too cowardly— or too psychotic—to do the job himself. It was an eerie thing to see these horrible events all written out and thought through, to see me and my law enforcement colleagues so coldly and, apparently, easily manipulated by a desperate man unable to end his own life but unwilling to continue living.

As a result of this one incident, the study of a phenomenon known as "suicide by cop" began to take shape, and the standoff at Rochester's

Security Trust Company Bank became the first documented case in the country where a hostage-taker started killing hostages on deadline, simply to bait the responding officers into killing him. Now, incidents such as this one may have indeed happened before in the annals of United States law enforcement history, and I'm afraid I know for a fact that it has happened since; but at the time it had yet to be identified in just this way—and this last, we all knew, would make all the difference in keeping it from happening again.

It was probably the lowest moment of my entire career—certainly the lowest to that point. An innocent young mother had been killed on my watch. It's not supposed to happen like that. For a while in there I even thought about giving up negotiating and leaving this kind of killing frustration to someone else in our office. But then I realized we need to find some good in every situation, and here I took it on myself to conduct a sort of psychological autopsy of Griffin and to subsequently write and lecture about this "suicide by cop" scenario all across the country: to police departments, FBI field offices, and eventually, once I completed my master's, at the FBI Academy. I never wanted another FBI agent or police officer to come across another William Griffin and not recognize the signs that he or she was being manipulated by some wannabe "dead man walking."

The more I learned about Griffin, the more the pieces seemed to fit. He had been raised by his maternal grandmother. He had one failure after another in his life, running from his job to his marriage to his financial situation, to where he eventually retreated to the inside of his bedroom and his own mind, only to resurface on this fateful day. Neighbors said that he wore winter clothes in the summer, sat in their yards in a lawn chair and refused to talk or move, and became lost in his own twisted thoughts. A psychologist might have labeled him a paranoid schizophrenic, but no one called any social agency about him; after all, they were to tell me, he wasn't their responsibility. And in the end Griffin changed the course of hostage negotiations forever, wounding and murdering innocent people in the process. I thought about Margaret Moore and prayed for her then-young son every time I presented this case, and I still wish like hell we could have done a better job of it that day—for both their sakes—but Griffin had another plan.

This situation might have been prevented if we had known to guard against it—even better, if we had known to anticipate it. We learned a lot from this case. We learned not to approach every apparent bank robbery as a bank robbery and not to approach every hostage-barricade situation as a standard hostage-barricade situation. We learned that when a hostage-taker won't talk to you, won't present a list of demands, doesn't indicate any desire to escape, and won't reveal himself to you in any way, the thing to do is come at it from a different angle. When bits and pieces of a case don't add up—like the earmuffs, the wild shotgun blasts, the double homicide just a few blocks away, the confusing statement read into the phone by a terrified third party—it's usually because our frames of reference are off and they will never add up. It's said that there is order even in chaos, but who would tell Margaret Moore's young son that his mother died because of some shotgun-wielding mental case? How do you explain to someone so young a concept that none of us even understood?

The Kelly/Kalsbeck standoff planted the first seeds of doubt that sometimes a hostage-taker is after something we can't begin to negotiate, while the Griffin case saw those seeds grow into full-blown uncertainty. As a result, I teach negotiators to imagine every conceivable worst-case scenario in every hostage-barricade or suicide situation. Assume the worst, I tell them, and pray for the best. And live and work in the curious space between.

THE ARM OF THE LORD

"THERE WILL
BE ANOTHER TIME"

This one comes with a backstory. Actually it comes with *two* backstories—mine and the criminals'—and a couple digressions just to keep things interesting. I'll hit the personal notes first, before easing into the sidebars and the case file—because, as usually happens, my frame of mind at home and at work helped to frame the ordeal in the field.

There I was, assigned to the FBI office in Rochester, New York, liking the work a whole lot, liking the office a whole lot, liking the community a whole lot. True, it was God-awful cold in the winter months, but I was warmed by the fact that I was working interesting cases, alongside interesting people, and getting more and more involved with the endlessly interesting negotiating strategies and tactics we were putting into place in more and more situations: taking courses to learn the latest psychological theories and generally embracing the sudden acceptability of the "talking cure" as a viable—and peaceable—

weapon in our arsenal. Let me tell you, it was exciting to be out there on the edge of such profound change in the ways agents went about their business, and the ways we looked to defuse uncertain situations—and encouraging to see how quickly our theories on "suicide by cop" situations were adapted around the country. Really, it was a great, good thing to make a difference beyond our sleepy upstate town, and to know at least that the tragic standoff at the bank that day had helped to effect some positive change.

On the home front, Dianne and our three kids were happy, which went a long way toward seeing me happy. Oh, I went through the motions to advance within the Bureau, applying for supervisory jobs around the country, but the truth was things were okay for a good stretch in there. More than okay, they were just right. Like many other agents at my level, I put in for promotion every now and then, because that's how the FBI works. Agents were always looking for a bump in grade, with a corresponding bump in pay, and I was no different. I also took courses here and there, and kept plugging toward my master's with what I could scrape together of my diminishing free time, but for the most part I was content with my lot up in Rochester. I was fat, dumb, and happy, with a low mortgage payment on a nice house, about as far removed from Bureau politics as I had any right to expect.

Life was good.

There was, however, one wrinkle to nearly upset the easy balance I had achieved between work and community—and the first indication that Bureau politics might chase me from my contentment after all. Dianne and I had become quite active in our local church, the Grace Covenant Church. I had been elected a legal trustee of the church, and one of our most important initiatives at the time was the establishment of a Christian day school in our church building. We Van Zandts were particularly interested in the school, because we planned to send our three children, Jeff, Jenna, and Jon, as they became age-appropriate. Unfortunately, the town building inspector weighed in that we couldn't locate a day school in our facility, a decision that struck us as some-what arbitrary, and so I joined with church pastor Rod Jones and other active parishioners to protest the ruling. The church was actually located in Chili, New York, a small town just outside Rochester, and at one point the town leaders made it clear that if we went ahead with our plans to open the school they would shut us down and arrest Pastor Jones and anyone else who had openly challenged the ruling.

I discussed the matter with Hugh Higgins, still our local senior FBI agent, and he put it to me plain: if I got myself arrested in this case, I'd probably also get myself fired. I thought, *Principles are principles,* but was this something I wanted to risk my job over? Dianne and I kicked it around all that night; we even talked it over with our children. The day school was important to all of us, and so we decided as a family to keep pushing for what we felt was right. If I lost my job in the bargain, we all thought, I'd just go out and find myself another line of work. And so we took a stand, letting the chips—and my job—fall where they may.

I set this out as a reminder that sometimes we must put our values ahead of our careers, and that at all times we must put our family first. Anyway, that's how it had always been with me, and that's how it would be going forward. The planned school at Grace Covenant Church would provide an enriching, nourishing Christian-based education that my children would not be able to find anyplace else in that part of the country, so it was worth fighting for. Plus, it was a fight we all felt we could—and should—win. Trouble was, we didn't exactly have the kinds of deep pockets at church to hire an attorney to represent our interests, so it fell to me to do a good chunk of our legal work. I was writing all of our legal briefs, and filing all of our motions, and cracking the archaic town building code in what ways I could, and at one point during our preliminary efforts Dianne and I found ourselves at a party at the home of U.S. Marshal Dan Wright, engaged in conversation with U.S. District Court Judge Mike Telesca.

Judge Telesca let on that he was aware of our legal battle with the town and inquired about our lawyer.

"You're looking at him," I said, with equal parts pride and embarrassment.

"Where did you go to law school?" he wondered.

"I didn't," I said.

The judge smiled back at me, and I got the distinct impression that he thought I was crazy. I also got that he saw our little church on the side of right and wanted to do what he could to help. He handed me a piece of paper with the name and phone number of his law clerk. "From this moment on," he said, indicating the name on the paper, "he'll be your lawyer and I'll cover the costs."

I thought, *What a saintly man! What a gift from heaven!*

And, indeed, it was. Of course, we had to keep our arrangement just between us at the time, because we couldn't let it be known that an esteemed local judge had thrown in as a supporter of a church in a legal battle against the town, but it was a most welcome and unexpected turn.

In the end, owing mostly to the work of Judge Telesca's lawyer friend, the Grace Covenant Church prevailed in the New York State Building Code Board of Appeals, the highest level in the state. We had our school, my children had the opportunity of their young lifetimes, and I managed not to get arrested or lose my job, reinforcing an all-important point that bureaucracies frequently get in the way of our smooth sailing. That, or you can fight town hall.

Bureaucracy came calling again just a short while later, this time in such a loud, loathsome tone that it begged the question whether or not some FBI functionary put the *bureau* in the term. It also made that long battle for our church day school seem somewhat moot, at least in our house, because it suddenly seemed we wouldn't be staying put in Rochester after all. In some higher-up's infinite wisdom, it was determined that all FBI agents should have to endure an extended tour of duty in one of the Bureau's fifteen largest offices, despite the fact that there had historically been more than enough agents who actually sought those positions to see that those offices were always fully and competently staffed. It was called the 10-1-69 program, because it applied to all agents who signed on after October 1, 1969—which meant, of course, that it applied to me, which in turn meant that I'd have to start taking some proactive steps regarding my all-but-certain reassignment. The move made no sense to anyone who was affected by it, and yet there it was, a capricious hoop we agents now had to jump through just because some bean counter at FBI Headquarters thought it a bright idea to put us through the same miserable motions and transfers and chaos he had undoubtedly been put through.

Now, I'd bounced around some, at this point in my career. I'd worked in Atlanta, and Buffalo/Rochester, as I've detailed, but neither one of these was among the Bureau's fifteen largest offices, so neither one qualified, and I was faced with the not-too-pleasant prospect of being reassigned to some big-city outpost where the cost of living would be just out of my reach and the daily hassles of commuting and slogging through all the big-city nonsense would be killer. Take somebody who's sitting in our Columbus, Ohio, office, for example. Say he's been there for ten years. He's got his house, he's got his kids in school. Maybe he coaches Little League or serves as a deacon in his church. He's got his whole life worked out in a way that makes sense for him and his family, and all of a sudden he's told, "Okay, you're being reassigned to L.A." Boom, just like that. Los Angeles, where the same house in the same type of neighborhood is going to cost him four times as much, where his commute is going to be five times as long, where his headaches will multiply exponentially. I wasn't an L.A. kind of guy. We weren't an L.A. kind of family—and, for that matter, we weren't too keen on New York City or Chicago or Miami or Newark or San Francisco or Detroit or anywhere else we now seemed likely to land. Nothing against those great cities; it's just that we were cut a little differently, and with three kids and a salary of about $50,000, I didn't think I could afford such a move. That kind of money in Rochester was enough to get by on; that kind of money in New York or L.A. was barely enough to leave me scrambling.

(Not incidentally, unlike most police officers, FBI agents were forbidden from holding a second job to make ends meet; we were expected to live on loyalty to the Bureau instead of dollars and cents.)

Keep in mind, Dianne and I were prepared to move, if it meant moving to a better job at a better salary. That's the deal we had made with each other and with our kids. It's just that here we were told to prepare for a lateral move that had more to do with pushing paper than advancing my career, and this last rubbed me the wrong way and set me on edge. I was able to put the move off for a year or so on account of my graduate school studies, but eventually the FBI was going to take its pound of flesh from me, just as it would from other members of the ill-fated "10-1-69 Club."

Not knowing what else to do, I put in a call to a friend of mine in the transfer unit at FBI headquarters, Roger Nisley, looking for any kind of leg up. "I'm really getting screwed here," I said.

"Tell me about it," he said. "You and everyone else."

Apparently, this 10-1-69 initiative had set off a firestorm of protest in smaller offices around the country. Folks were not happy. There was this massive reshuffling of agents about to happen, for no good reason that anyone could figure, and a great disruption to a great many families, and it wreaked a particular kind of havoc in the Transfer Unit because you could bet I wasn't the only agent looking for a leg up. Everybody had a buddy they could call—only mine was about to come through for me, big time. "Where do you want to go?" he said. "Tell me and I'll see if I can send you."

"I don't know," I said. "I don't want to go anywhere. I like it right here up in Rochester."

"What about Philadelphia?" Roger said. "It's the best-kept secret in the Bureau."

I thought, *Philadelphia?* I thought of that old W. C. Fields line, about how he'd rather be dead than in Philadelphia, and the endless jokes I'd heard at the city's expense. Granted, I'd heard some of those same jokes about Buffalo/Rochester before moving there, and that had turned out fine, but Philadelphia? "What else you got?" I tried.

"No really," he insisted. "Philly's where I'd look to go if I were you. Good office. Good work. Always something going on. You live over on the Jersey side. Homes are affordable. Commute's not bad. That's the move."

"Okay," I said. "What the hell. Send me to Philadelphia."

Of course, it wasn't any kind of done deal. I still had to wait on an opening, and there was process and paperwork, and I filled the waiting checking out every "Places Rated Guide" I could find in the bookstore. Nowadays you can research all of this stuff on the Internet, but back then I had to dig out every guide or almanac I could find and check out things like the cost of living, and the seasonal temperatures, and the schools and churches in each area. Quality of life was key, and in every resource I consulted, the New Jersey suburbs outside Philadelphia kept checking out okay. Even so, compared to Rochester, I'd have to spend about twice the money for half the house, but given my options it seemed like the most viable next move.

So that's where we went. My friend Roger in the Transfer Unit came through, and Dianne and I found a great house on a tree-lined street in a small town called Medford Lakes, New Jersey, about an hour's drive from the FBI Philadelphia office. It was a long commute compared to my twenty minutes in Rochester, but the trade-off seemed worth it, with a nice house in a more relaxed environment— and a nearby lake, where Jeff, Jenna, and Jon would swim most warm-weather afternoons. And I could have made a good go of it, too, if I hadn't been assigned first to an applicant investigation squad, and then to Jim Payne's drug squad working black organized crime. The first assignment was boring; the second, a little out of my wheelhouse. I knew nothing about drugs. I knew nothing about black organized crime. Everyone else on the squad was single, or separated, or at the tail end of a second or third marriage, and they lived for this stuff. All they wanted out of life and work was to come into the office and chase bad guys, and kick up some dust, and then to go out at night and drink and raise hell and chase what seemed to them to be a good time.

Let's just say it wasn't me. Let's just say it wasn't a good fit. There was one hostage barricade situation in my first few months on the job, in a downtown bank, but there was nothing remarkable about it. No heavy lifting. Talked the bad guys into surrendering and we all moved on to the next thing. But other than that, the work wasn't all that exciting to me. It was more routine than anything else, and I wasn't much for routine. I loved the thrill and surprise of not knowing how each day would go, and here each day started to look pretty much the same. The other agents were nice enough—they were good guys—but their interests were far different from mine. Despite the nice house and the nice neighborhood over in Medford Lakes, the work itself was a drain, and since I tended to spend most of my waking hours at work, this was not a good thing.

I was hardly in town a couple months before I was desperate to get out, so I jump-started my efforts to land a supervisory position elsewhere in the Bureau. I figured, as long as I've got to be in a place I don't like, I should at least get a raise out of the deal. I put in for everything. At some point I took a long look at a position at the FBI Academy in Quantico, Virginia, in the hostage negotiations unit. Talk about a good fit. I'd studied that kind of work. I enjoyed that kind of work. And I seemed to be pretty good at that kind of work. So I called down to Conrad "Con" Hassel, the Special Operations and Research Unit (SOARU) chief, to check it out. Con was about as gracious as could be. He knew I had some experience in this area but told me he didn't anticipate any openings anytime soon. It was a teaching position, primarily. There was some limited active fieldwork you could be called on to perform from time to time, but for the most part you were training other agents in what was still a relatively new area for the Bureau, and at just that moment there happened to be three veteran agents filling those positions and none of them appeared to have plans to give up their gigs anytime soon. So I thanked Con for his time and continued casting about for another position, because I really couldn't see myself on the drug squad of that organized crime unit for too terribly much longer.

I applied for this job and that job and every job in between, and what I was finding out, much to my dismay, was that I was being bigfooted out of every damn one of them by either more senior agents or by agents junior to me who were applying straight from FBIHQ. I might have known. That's how it worked at the FBI at the time, and for all I know that's how it still works. It's like a high-grade game of musical chairs, and it seems the seats are always filled by higher-ups. You have to make your bones up at headquarters for a couple years in order to pick and choose your career opportunities going forward, but that hadn't been my game plan, and I hadn't paid my FBIHQ dues, so to speak. Actually, I didn't seem to have a game plan. I had been content to keep doing what I was doing up in Rochester, but that ridiculous 10-1-69 program set me off course, and now I was just short of desperate to move on.

And then, six months into my unhappy tour in Philadelphia, I took an unlikely call from the chief of the hostage negotiations unit at Quantico. Same guy who told me just a few months earlier that all his positions were filled, only now Con Hassel was calling back to tell me that one of those three guys, Jim DeSarno, was moving on to another position (he would eventually become an assistant director of the FBI) and that now there was an opening.

"You should put in for it," he said.

So I did.

Tom Strentz, the senior member of the unit, checked in with the same message, after I had presented the "suicide by cop" case in his negotiations class, recommending me to Con Hassel at the same time.

About three months later, and nine months to the day from when I first reported to work on the Philly drug squad, my orders came through for Quantico, and I couldn't have been more delighted. And yet, underneath that excitement was the usual frustration at how things go in the FBI and what I was about to put my family through, yet again. I may have been unhappy in my job in Philadelphia, but my family was just loving the house in Medford Lakes, and the schools, and the neighborhood, and now I was about to uproot everyone and start all over again in some other town after less than a year, and for mostly selfish reasons. Plus, it was such a maddening waste of time and effort and energy, not to mention a substantial waste of money. It cost the Bureau about $25,000 in relocation expenses to move me and my family from Rochester to Philadelphia, and now, just nine months later, it would cost another $25,000 to move me to Quantico, all because of a stupid policy that made about as much sense in theory as it did in actual practice—which is to say it made no sense at all.

(Just as an aside, I can't tell you how many great agents quit the FBI because they couldn't live on the money they made once the 10-1-69 guidelines forced them to move. Whoever sold that policy to FBIHQ sold a lot of good agents down the drain.)

One of the reasons I went off in pursuit of my master's degree in Rochester was to qualify me to teach at the FBI Academy, which had a tremendous program set up through the University of Virginia (UVa), and here I was about to realize that long-held goal. I could even call myself a member of UVa's adjunct faculty, which was actually pretty cool, although the coolest piece was that I would now be in a position to influence young people who had chosen or were considering law enforcement as a career. That sounds like a line, but that's God's honest truth about how I felt. It was an awesome responsibility, and a great privilege, and I did not take it on lightly, so I rolled up my sleeves and set to work as one of three instructors in the SOARU hostage negotiations unit, determined to make a difference. The SOARU also taught SWAT, observer/sniper, tactical air operations, crisis management, and major case management, so we really covered the waterfront.

I was also determined to make it up to my family for this constant moving around—or, at least, to make it as painless as possible—so Dianne and I deliberately avoided the northern Virginia suburbs, where most agents tended to live, and settled instead in the quiet and quaint town of Fredericksburg, Virginia. I was now a GS-14–grade employee, with a reasonable bump in salary, but it turned out I would lose my take-home car in the bargain, on the then-sound theory that an agent who worked primarily as an instructor was not in need of an emergency response vehicle around the clock. Weighed against the raise, it was probably a wash, because now I needed a second vehicle for the drive to work each day. If we'd chosen to live north of Quantico, like most of my colleagues, I could have probably arranged for some sort of carpool, but I made a decision with this move that I would not follow the typical career path at the Bureau. The routine, for the most part, if you wanted to really rise through the organization, was to come back to headquarters, seek reassignment out in the field, return to headquarters, and then go back out again, inching up in grade with each move. But that wasn't for me. A lot of guys—good friends of mine, actually—looked at me like I was some kind of radical for cutting against the grain in just this way, but I couldn't see putting my family through these motions again so soon. No, sir. In fact, one of the agents in the office at the time of this move really pressed me on this, so I pressed right back.

"How many times have you moved in the last fifteen years?" I asked him, pulling no punches.

He fumbled for a bit in his response and then guessed that he had moved about nine or ten times.

"And how many times have you been married?" I continued.

"I'm on my third," he said.

I thought, *Man, here's a guy been through two tough marriages, working on his third time around, with alimony and child support payments coming out of his ears, and buckets of money lost to some badly timed real estate transactions, and yet he'd probably do it all over again if given the chance.* I looked across the desk at him and realized that, to him, each move had been a good career move. And as far as the FBI had been concerned, each move *had* been a good career move, but mostly to the Bureau's benefit. I'd seen so many guys who had constantly put their careers ahead of their families, ahead of what was really important, to where they'd look up one day and realize they didn't know their wives and they didn't know their kids and they couldn't see that their whole world was coming down around them. They had a ten-year-old picture of their kids on their desk, their families were miserable, and for what? Dianne and I sat down and talked this through one night over the kitchen table, even though it was essentially a no-brainer. We talked about how this was as far as I'd go in my career. I wasn't going to run an office as a Special Agent in Charge or become an Assistant Special Agent in Charge (ASAC). I wasn't going to make any more money, other than my cost-of-living raises. I wasn't going to let the FBI keep moving us around. So, instead of going up the trunk of the tree, I decided to step off onto a branch, and I would have to hold fast.

Fredericksburg was an easy decision—and the commute to Quantico was certainly easy enough. Finding a place to live was another matter, although after four months in a hotel room with three kids and a dog, and a false start on a custom home, we finally found a functional house with a mortgage we could handle. On the day of the closing, Dianne was actually ripping the hideous wallpaper from the dining room walls when the previous owners stopped by to pick up a few things—a potentially embarrassing situation were it not for the indisputable fact that their taste in wallpaper was truly dreadful.

The great kicker to Fredericksburg was the wonderful Fredericksburg Christian School, run by our equally wonderful Christian friends Andy and Gary Foss. Dianne and I especially liked that the school represented no one single religious denomination, which we felt would present our children with a balanced worldview. Incredibly, there were over fifty different churches represented among student families, so that gave the place a real nice balance. Actually, we decided on the kids' school first, before we settled on Fredericksburg, which was—and remains—a nice little Civil War town, where the prices of homes were still somewhat reasonable, especially compared to the suburbs of northern Virginia; and as we settled in, we looked forward to a long, happy life in our new community. We had no plans to move anytime soon.

At work, I was aided and abetted by my new colleagues in the Special Operations and Research Unit. We actually called ourselves the SOARS unit, even though the acronym didn't quite match the name; our thinking was, it looked good on a T-shirt, and we all looked pretty good in those T-shirts. Our guys taught FBI Special Weapons and Tactics and other macho pursuits that had our agents running from, jumping over, and shooting at all kinds of stuff. There were three of us on the cerebral side—Tom Strentz, Fred Lanceley, and myself—and we taught the still-developing art of hostage negotiations. We were instructors, first and foremost, but we were also there to do research and to develop and implement our training program.

The only real drawback to this new gig was that I wouldn't be out in the field all that much, and for a guy who had sought a career in "active" law enforcement, this was going to be a significant shift in gears. I couldn't imagine teaching hostage negotiations without also having an opportunity to go out and put that teaching into practice— and in the beginning those opportunities were few and far between. One exception to the general rule of thumb turned out to be a real agent of change. In March 1978 there was a massive standoff in Washington, D.C., wherein a group of Black Muslims calling themselves the Hanafi Muslim sect took between one hundred and two hundred hostages in three downtown buildings along Embassy Row. Two days into the siege, foreign ambassadors helped to resolve the situation peacefully, but one hostage was killed and another wounded (Washington's controversial future mayor Marion Barry). The upshot was that the Department of Justice was made to realize that there was no dedicated unit to handle a high-risk hostage rescue mission at the federal level. Yes, there had been a SWAT team from the D.C. police force, but that was only a half-dozen guys who were reasonably accurate shots; certainly, they weren't trained to handle multiple situations of a complex nature. And the FBI had SWAT guys, too, but they were pulled from a working pool of field agents, and they only practiced their special weapons stuff a day or so each month.

In the aftermath of that D.C. standoff, then-president Jimmy Carter created Delta Force, the U.S. Army's secret counterterrorism team that has carried out missions around the world that team members don't talk about and the rest of us don't hear about. Two Delta Force operators later gave their lives attempting to rescue the pilot of a downed UD-60 Blackhawk helicopter in the ill-fated 1993 operation in Mogadishu, Somalia, to arrest warlord Mohamed Farrah Aidid, as depicted in the movie *Blackhawk Down*. There's a great scene in this movie about sacrifice, duty, and honor in which an Army major, in the middle of a fierce firefight, tells a wounded soldier to drive a truck out of the kill zone in an attempt to save the lives of his fellow soldiers. The young soldier briefly protests. "But, sir," he says, "I'm wounded." To which the major replies, "Son, we're all wounded. Get in the truck and drive." I look on at that scene and I'm reminded of the sacrifice of these soldiers and the not-quite-conflicting notions that we are all somehow wounded in life and that we must find a way to shoulder those wounds and press on.

The FBI would eventually put together its own hostage rescue team, or HRT, under then–FBI director (and former CIA director) William H. Webster. As it was originally conceived, the HRT was to be the civilian counterpart to the U.S. Army Delta Force and to the U.S. Navy SEALs, owing to the little-known Posse Comitatus Act that prohibited the use of military forces for civilian law enforcement tasks without the express direction of the president.

The HRT took shape in 1981 under the command of FBI agent (and attorney at law) Danny O. Coulson. To most folks, "Doc" Coulson was one of those people you either hated or respected, but you had to be on one side of the fence or the other; there was no straddling or ambivalence. Over time, I grew to like and respect Danny and would have followed him through the gates of hell—a situation that nearly presented itself on more than one occasion.

A couple of not entirely irrelevant asides seem in order here. The first: an early training exercise, with HRT, Delta, and ST6 (the Navy SEAL counterterrorism team), in preparation for the 1984 Summer Olympic games in Los Angeles. Tom Strentz and I were assigned as the hostage negotiators in a simulation that would include the takeover of an airliner by terrorists, and in the interests of verisimilitude Tom had recruited a couple dozen United Airlines flight attendants to play supporting roles in the training scenario, as stewardesses and passengers. The two of us shared a room in a seedy motel in a lousy section of South Central Los Angeles, which also served as a makeshift dressing room for the flight attendants, who stowed their purses and compacts and such in our room for safekeeping. After one particularly long shift, I returned to our room to catch up on some sleep, setting down my Smith & Wesson .357 Magnum on the nightstand by my bed, as was my custom. As I slept, the training exercise came to an abrupt end on Tom's shift, and he escorted the flight attendants back to our room to retrieve their possessions.

This was where the fun started—at least as far as Tom Strentz was concerned. As he approached the door to our room, he quietly told the women to all jump into bed with his partner, realizing full well that the thought of two dozen stews in a motel bed might have been the dream of every young male FBI agent but me.

Sure enough, the girls crashed through the door and leaped onto my bed and startled me awake. I instinctively reached for my gun as I faced the inexplicable rush of people coming toward me and attempted to assess the "threat." You never saw so many women stop so quickly in your life—or a young male FBI agent so embarrassed by his hair-trigger response.

The moral of the story? Never wake an FBI agent from a sound sleep if he has a gun nearby—*even if you've got a couple dozen United Airlines stewardesses in tow!*

In a later ST6 exercise at sea, I was again assigned as a negotiations adviser. This particular scenario featured a ship at sea hijacked by terrorists, and the plan called for the SEALs to retake the ship. I flew to the scene with the SEALs on Blackhawk helicopters a few feet off the Atlantic in the middle of a pitch-black (read: moonless) night. As we arrived at the ship—a U.S. Navy sub tender used to simulate a cruise ship—a fast rope was dropped from the helicopter to the pitching deck, whereupon the SEALs quickly and effortlessly slid down the rope to the deck below. When it was my turn to descend, I could only pray for two things: *Lord, don't let me embarrass the FBI* and *Don't let me die.* Those prayers were mercifully answered, only to be replaced by two more, at the other end of the exercise, when we had to depart the ship by the reverse route. The U.S. Navy captain who led ST6 told me he saw no use for negotiations in such an event—that is, until the "terrorists" had the hostages in the ship's boardroom, hand grenades in their hands, pins pulled. The terrorists' message: shoot us and we all die. Now, at last, it was time for negotiations.

The helicopter again appeared over the still-black deck, with only small chemical light sticks to mark our way. A metal caving ladder unrolled from the chopper and rested on the deck, with one SEAL anchoring the thing by sitting cross-legged on the deck while holding the ladder's bottom rung. The other SEALs, as usual, scrambled quickly and effortlessly back up to the chopper, while I lapsed once more into prayer mode: *Lord, don't let me embarrass the FBI* and *Don't let me die.* This time the answer was a little longer in coming, because as I reached the top of the ladder I found myself suddenly spent and unable to continue. One of the SEALs kindly grabbed me by the belt like I was a toy and swung me over the bay of the Blackhawk, from where I hung perilously until someone else thought to haul me the rest of the way inside.

The moral of this second story? I'm not entirely sure, although I would have much preferred being awakened in a seedy South Central motel room by a couple dozen lovely stewardesses to hanging with my butt in a sling over a raging black sea.

In any case, the FBI's Hostage Rescue Team was up and running, and very early on in this new setup we were faced with our first real crisis: a tense standoff in a remote corner of Arkansas that captured national headlines and occupied our full attentions for a stretch of weeks in April 1985. It would have been a far bigger story but for how it ended—which is to say peacefully, and without incident, other than the incident itself. In many ways it was a precursor to another tense siege, in Waco, Texas, a number of years later, which ended far differently and sounded a national alarm we might have anticipated, given this earlier showdown.

Here's the background: in 1970 about one hundred white supremacists formed a survivalist group known as the Covenant, the Sword and the Arm of the Lord (CSA) on a farm in Elijah, Missouri. By 1976 the founder of the group had pooled the meager resources of his followers and purchased a 225-acre farm in rural Marion County,

Arkansas, from the Campus Crusade for Christ; the farm was located about seven miles southwest of Pontiac, Missouri, and the group switched its operations there, and from their new base CSA members began to stockpile food and weapons and to train themselves in paramilitary and survival procedures. CSA leaders began to speak out on behalf of the Christian Identity Movement, espousing their racist and anti-Semitic beliefs to all who might listen, and the group attracted a following throughout the region.

Throughout the early 1980s, as their buildup continued, several individuals associated with the CSA were implicated in a number of violent crimes and acts of terrorism, including the firebombing of a homosexual church in Springfield, Missouri, the firebombing of a Jewish community center in Bloomington, Indiana, and the bombing of an interstate natural gas pipeline in Fulton, Arkansas. And yet, despite the suspicions of law enforcement agencies investigating the group, no arrests were made among CSA leadership, and it was subsequently decided to go after the group on weapons charges in hopes of shutting down their operation.

By the spring of 1985, in cooperation with then Arkansas governor Bill Clinton, Arkansas state troopers, local police, and the Bureau of Alcohol, Tobacco and Firearms (ATF) began a full-scale investigation of the CSA with a special focus on the converting of semiautomatic weapons to fully-automatic weapons, either for resale on the black market or to add to the group's stockpile. The general thinking among ATF agents assigned to the case was that the weapons charges were their best shot at putting these guys out of business and letting some of the air out of their cultlike operation. That's how it works when you're dealing with a cult such as the CSA. If you allow the thing to take root and take hold and take charge of individuals' lives, it becomes more and more difficult to derail. If you cut it off at its source, if you can remove the leadership and put them away even for a short time, you can really sap the group of its momentum and focus, and that's what we were after here. Despite the looming threat they posed, the CSA was still a relatively small outfit, and we meant to weaken their ranks to where they were smaller still.

At the time, the CSA was led by a right-wing extremist named James Dennis Ellison, who had somehow managed to create the impression among his Arkansas neighbors that he and his cohorts were relatively harmless, despite their avowed hatred of Jews and blacks and the mainstream American government. They ran around their compound in military garb, and saluted each other, and took themselves and their mission very seriously. There were a lot of intermarriages within the group, and to a casual observer they might have appeared just a little more threatening than any other group of right-wing neo-Nazi religious survivalist nut jobs. A lot of the CSA members held blue-collar–type jobs in the neighboring communities, so it's not like they were holed up and hiding out in their compound, even as their stores of illegal weapons grew. They moved about fairly freely, as if our laws somehow did not apply to them.

In the months leading up to the siege, ATF agents set up surveillance around the CSA compound and began monitoring the group's comings and goings. Their reports indicated that there were approximately one hundred men, women and children living on the compound, and that everybody had guns. It was a real nightmare. Even the kids were armed. The women made some attempt to home-school the children, and there seemed to be a loose, commune-type atmosphere about the place, but the central focus of the group was the buildup of weapons and ammunition, all leading toward some kind of vaguely articulated showdown with government or establishment forces. There were a number of reasonably nice homes built around the property, all of them built by the CSA members and their outside contacts, and funded by the renouncing of each other's worldly possessions and a pooling of resources. There were group marriages and communal living arrangements all around. It was a real cultlike operation, a foreshadowing of what we would find in Waco with David Koresh and the Branch Davidians, and it seemed to begin and end on the impulse of one powerful individual with a powerful personality able to persuade dozens of lonely, disaffected paramilitary types to throw in on a lifelong campaign against the establishment. Indeed, cultlike movements like this one tend to attract the disenfranchised by offering them love and a sense of belonging and purpose—not unlike the United States military, some CSA members might suggest.

At some point the ATF, led by agent Bill Buford, one of the best and brightest in that agency, who would be critically wounded in the initial shootout at the Branch Davidian compound in Waco, realized they might need some help on this operation, so they reached out to our Hostage Rescue Team. I guess they figured there might come a time they would actually need help in dealing with these guys if things didn't go as planned. Realize, the HRT was the only team of its kind in the country, and it was their job to deal with high-risk hostage barricade situations that municipal police and FBI SWAT teams simply weren't trained for or weren't large enough to handle: hijacked planes, trains, ships in harbor, that sort of thing. HRT was housed in a separate facility at the FBI Academy in Quantico, although my SOARS office was across the road a piece at the Academy, where I did most of my training, teaching, and research.

As I've written, the HRT team leader or commander was Danny "Doc" Coulson, who at that time I knew only to shake hands. Unlike almost every other HRT agent, Coulson did not have a specialized military background, but he was a lawyer—something that probably had not gone unnoticed when he was appointed—and he had been a damn good street agent in New York City, with a number of high-profile arrests to his credit. The man had *Been there, done that* written all over him. Doc's focus was all the way on the tactical side of our operation. He was a real fireball, and he brought tremendous energy to the team. Indeed, he helped to build it and breathe life into it, so this was very much his mission—and HRT's first real test on any kind of national scale. At the outset, though, Coulson didn't seem to have much respect for the skills I brought to the task—or he didn't have much patience for those skills, which I guess is a better way to put it. The behavioral science of negotiating was a little out there for a hard charger like Danny Coulson, and he wore his distrust on his sleeve. The first time I came over to address the HRT, he introduced me by saying, "Watch out for Van Zandt, guys. He's from Quantico, the other side of the street. Be careful what you say around him."

I let the comment slide, but it rankled—and set off a couple of red flags. It struck me like a father telling his daughter that her new boyfriend was from the wrong side of the tracks and was therefore unworthy of her attention. I couldn't have these HRT guys thinking I was some kind of bureaucratic enemy. Yes, Coulson outranked me, but we were all on the same side, and if he built up a divide in the minds of his team, I'd have a tough time getting past it.

The next day, I crossed the street for another briefing and I got more of the same from Coulson, so this time I asked him to step out into the hall for a private talk. "Look, Danny," I said, "this can't happen."

From the look on his face, it was clear Coulson had no idea what I was driving at. "What the hell are you talking about?" he said.

"I mean this 'Watch what you say around Van Zandt' crap," I said. "We'll never get anywhere if that's your attitude. I'm an FBI agent, same as everyone else here. I'm looking to take down and disarm these white supremacists, same as everyone else. We're going to have to count on each other. You can't get your guys thinking it's a them-against-me type thing."

Doc folded his arms across his chest and faced me full on. "I'm listening," he said. And he was, so I kept at it.

"My first responsibility is making sure all your guys come home alive," I continued. "And I guarantee you I won't lose sight of that responsibility. My second job is to talk everybody else out of that compound and to see that nobody gets hurt. But again, my primary goal is to bring FBI agents home alive, and it doesn't help for you to undermine me and suggest that I'm some kind of enemy."

He got it—or at least he pretended to get it—and we moved on from there.

One of the great rallying points of our months-long preparation for our move on this massive compound was our shared disdain for the CSA and its purported mission. We all took turns choking on their mouthful of a name—the Covenant, the Sword and the Arm of the Lord—and we couldn't understand the mentality that would leave these guys wearing baseball caps with *CSA* printed above the bills. It became a real haunting concern, especially when we brought in one of these CSA followers on a minor charge for questioning and this guy went on and on about how the Jewish people were the true enemy of the state. "You don't realize who runs this country," he kept saying. "The Zionist Occupational Government. They're pulling all the strings. They control all the banks. There's a nationwide conspiracy to funnel all our money back to Israel."

It got to where this guy's rant about the Zionist Occupational Government became the talk of the team, leading up to our siege, and after it was all over some agents went out and had these baseball caps made up with *ZOG* printed above the bills, just to bust these guys' chops a bit and to knit our group together and to remind ourselves that when you're dealing with crazies, it sometimes helps to have a sense of humor.

FBI investigation revealed that in December 1983, CSA leaders Jim Ellison and Kerry Noble, along with other CSA members and gun nuts like Richard Snell, had plotted to kill a federal judge, an FBI agent, and local Assistant U.S. Attorney Asa Hutchinson. The group never carried out its plot, due to an accident that Ellison took as a sign from God to back off. Less than a year later, however, Snell would become involved in a shoot-out with a black Arkansas state trooper after being pulled over for a traffic stop. The poor trooper never knew what hit him as Snell rolled out of his van and began pumping rounds into him. Snell was finally captured in Oklahoma after another shoot-out with law enforcement officers, who by this time knew what they were up against. The ATF had established a firm link between Snell and the CSA, increasing our knowledge base and further suggesting the threat this group could pose, even as we tracked its weapons and ammunitions buildup.

During our surveillance of their compound and activities, we learned that some CSA members were in the habit of taking target practice with silhouettes of blacks and Jews hung from the trees—which they referred to internally as "End Times Over-comer Survival Training," a chilling tag to be sure. Word was that it was only a matter of time before they took their foolish hatred into the streets and started shooting up innocent people, and what had started out as an ongoing background investigation all of a sudden had some real urgency to it.

The FBI had a great setup with the U.S. Air Force Reserve to fly its Hostage Rescue Team anywhere in the country on one hour's notice, so we all met at Andrews Air Force Base southeast of Washington, D.C., and deployed from there. HRT drove its trucks right onto the waiting aircraft and took off. When we arrived in Arkansas, we met with the state troopers and the ATF agents in a movie theater located several miles from the CSA compound, careful to be as inconspicuous as possible, which isn't the easiest thing in the world when you're looking to hide a couple hundred agents in broad daylight in a remote area. Although we rented older cars from miles away, we would have stuck out like a crowd in an open field if anybody cared to notice. Clearly, we couldn't twiddle our thumbs indefinitely, now that we were in town, so the plan was to meet that day and take the compound the next.

We still needed a cover to account for the large presence of men and equipment in this rural area, so we came up with the story that we were businessmen on a fishing sabbatical—a kind of a white-collar Outward Bound. We went to great lengths to cloak our movements and keep our operation secret, but there was soon enough a snag. (There's always a snag, I'd learned by this point.) The CSA was put on alert when a ragtag member of another survivalist group known as The Order was pulled over by two Missouri state troopers, again on an apparent traffic violation. David Tate, like Richard Snell before him, opened fire on the two troopers, killing Trooper Jimmie Lingar and critically wounding Trooper Allen Hines before escaping into the Missouri Ozarks, leading many in law enforcement and the media to conclude that he would be headed for the CSA compound. Ellison and his followers were all of a sudden at all kinds of attention—a kind of DEFCON 1, dug in and buttoned up and refusing to leave the area, denying us the hoped-for chance to arrest the group's leaders away from the compound and their store of weapons, not to mention the dozens of women and children who would almost certainly turn up in harm's way. Really, these guys were so primed for our assault, they could not have been more ready for us had we called them on the phone and said we were coming in. So much for the element of surprise.

The ATF had procured federal arrest and search warrants against the CSA leadership, almost all of them relating to weapons violations, but we weren't about to stroll up and knock on the door to serve them. The strategy was to go in under cover of darkness, by land and water. The air cover would be provided by the FBI's Nightstalker aircraft, a whizbang airplane with FLARE (forward-looking infrared radar) capability, which allowed us to fly long, lazy circles over an area with almost complete stealth. The Nightstalker itself was a closely held secret within the Bureau until it was photographed by a news photographer at an Arkansas airport, but we were still able to use it to advise our tactical teams on the ground and to help them establish the lay of the land. The CSA compound consisted of about thirty individual buildings, all set along the shores of Bull Shoals Lake at the center of the property. As survivalists, the CSA members had built many of their residences with shooting slots or portholes cut into the ground level of each building. In addition, the compound was said to be booby-trapped, with claymore mine–like devices hidden throughout, and all CSA members were assumed to be heavily armed, running to automatic weapons and hand grenades. There were even reports of at least one LAW (light armored weapon) rocket in the group's arsenal, and an armored car with a machine gun mounted on it.

We were ready to go on April 19, a date we would come to mark on our calendars in future years with the fire at Waco and the bombing of the Oklahoma City federal building—an unsettling reminder of the significance of anniversaries to a fringe personality. We had about two hundred agents positioned in a 360-degree perimeter around the property, with the idea of overwhelming these survivalists into submission. The plan was to announce ourselves in a great show of manpower and force—and then to hopefully have an opportunity to talk the group out before going to guns. As ever, the talking cure was our preferred course; anything else could have been a disaster.

Anyway, it was *my* preferred course. I'd have to see how it fit with Danny Coulson's strategy.

The whole thing was run like a military operation: camouflage and heavy armor and helmets and night vision goggles—the works. At one point early on, I looked around at our tactical teams moving into position—ATF, FBI SWAT and HRT—and realized that I was the only negotiator on the scene. Hundred of guys armed to the teeth, and me flapping my gums. Fortunately, FBI Special Agent Jerry Adams and other negotiators were en route, so there was hope for us yet, but at just that moment the odds appeared to be stacked against any kind of peaceful resolution. There was no doubt in my mind that my fellow agents were more than prepared to use their military might. Either they would scare the CSA into surrendering or they would prevail in a firefight, and I would be left pissing against the wind, hoping against hope for a nonviolent outcome. I'm sorry, but I just don't like going to guns against American citizens, no matter what these people had done in the past or might do in the future. The line I used to use was "We can always kill 'em tomorrow"—meaning that we can try to talk things out today, and if that doesn't work out we can take them down tomorrow. I truly believed that negotiation was our most effective nonlethal weapon, and yet, this was our first opportunity to put that belief to the test on any kind of grand scale. This was not one bank robber barricaded in a vault with a handgun. This was a hundred or so heavily armed zealots, in a fortified compound, operating on the shared belief that their government was their enemy and that they were in the "end days" of a perilous endgame to which they seemed to have the only set of rules. In a way, it set up as a kind of self-fulfilling prophecy, because there we were, about to move against them, just like their leaders had foretold.

In the days and weeks leading up to our assault, I had spent an inordinate amount of time researching Ellison and the CSA. I wanted to know what we were up against, from every possible angle and scenario. The intelligence on Ellison was troubling. I learned, for example, that he had once told his followers he had escaped arrest by the U.S. Marshals by turning himself into a mouse and scampering away, so I knew we were facing a flock of the truly faithful and a charismatic leader who fell somewhere between Jim Jones and Mickey Mouse. Ellison's number two guy, Kerry Noble, was probably the most intelligent of the group, so right away I figured he'd be a key to our negotiating strategy. If I could get to him, I thought, I could get to Ellison. The only problem with this plan, I soon realized, was that the profile I created for Ellison suggested he was not the type to engage in ordinary conversation with an ordinary FBI agent. He saw himself as a military commander, a World War II General Erwin Rommel–type figure, and he would want to negotiate with his General George Patton–type equivalent. Granted, Ellison was just a poser, having never served in the military, but he cut a proud figure in his own eyes. He saw himself as a commander, a true leader of men, given to military-style fatigues, snappy berets and an ever-present sidearm that left him looking like some survivalist G.I. Joe action figure.

Up against this type of personality, I knew that Danny Coulson would need to stand in as the Patton figure in any negotiation, so I spent a number of hours with Doc discussing tactics and strategies, paying specific attention to his body language and choice of words. You see, Danny Coulson was not the sort of guy to back down from any encounter, least of all a run-in with the potbellied doomsday bigot we all knew Ellison to be.

"You're going to have to talk to him face-to-face," I said to Danny, "and that breaks all the rules. It puts you in danger, and it puts him in danger, and it puts this entire operation in danger."

"What about the field phone?" Coulson wanted to know.

"That's a place to start," I allowed, "but ultimately you're going to have to meet with him. That's the only way to establish any kind of trust."

Already we had built a kind of trust with our decision to simply announce ourselves at the approach of the two CSA guards several hours earlier. We could have taken those guys out, but we chose instead to begin a dialogue, and I had to count on that decision serving us well in these negotiations.

One of the keys for Danny Coulson in communicating with Jim Ellison was to get him to stop using colorful language. "This guy is a religious survivalist," I reminded Doc. "He believes in the Old Testament. You've got to stop swearing."

"You're shittin' me, right?" Coulson said—and I couldn't tell if he himself was shittin' me with his response, or if he truly didn't get it.

"It won't fly," I said. "You cannot use profanity in front of this guy, because he will write you off as a non-believer, or a non-this, or a non-that. So you have to think before you speak, or he won't talk to you."

"Well, damn," Coulson said. "I don't know if I can do that."

"Well, damn, you're gonna have to," I said, and we went over it a bunch of times more until I felt confident in Danny's ability to bite his own tongue. I also worked with him on his body language, on approaching this guy with a truly open attitude and demeanor. Coulson was in the habit of standing with his arms crossed and his torso turned to whoever it was he was talking to, but that sent the wrong signal here. He needed to face Ellison when they spoke, and he needed to have his hands out and open so the guy could see he wasn't concealing a weapon—and, as important, to see that he was approachable.

It took a couple hours to bring Coulson up to speed to where he could talk to Ellison without fracturing the trust we were trying to build with him and the other CSA leaders, but Coulson was a smart guy and a quick study. He was also something of a reluctant customer, not at all comfortable with the idea that negotiations alone could resolve a standoff of this magnitude, but to his credit he was willing to hear me out and give it a try. Really, he'd done a complete about-face from our not-at-all-promising opening encounter back at Quantico to where he was now prepared to talk this thing through to a peaceful solution, but I didn't know if that about-face alone would be enough to get the job done.

There's an old saying among negotiators: "Negotiators don't command and commanders don't negotiate." I was reminded of it here because I couldn't reasonably expect to teach a crash course in negotiations to a tactical commander, but we had no choice other than to hope Doc could pull this off. It wasn't the best position, but we all felt it was our only position. As a negotiator, it's always helpful to be able to lay some responsibility elsewhere on your chain of command. If an incident commander or tactical commander also assumes the role of primary negotiator, he or she has no one to blame, no one to consult with prior to meeting a demand, no way to stall or put off an answer or decrease the subject's anxiety level. It's a tough spot all around, because it puts you in the difficult spot of trying to run the incident and negotiate with the subject, bringing two very different skill sets to two very different tasks with two very different agendas. In this case, though, Danny would have to take the lead on both fronts, and I felt it was up to me to see that he didn't drop the ball on the negotiating end.

And so, at about two or three in the morning on April 21, 1985, we set out to surround the perimeter of the compound. We had the Nightstalker for support, a black-painted aircraft in a black sky, with its infrared signature capabilities circling above the area, poised to pick up any movements we didn't make ourselves. And our own guys weren't moving too swiftly, I should mention. We had a whole group of agents in Ghillie suits—full camouflage garb with nets and leaves and branches stuck to it—advancing on their bellies toward the CSA compound and looking like tiny trash heaps. We had another group moving in by boat, crossing the lake George Washington–style and taking in water along the way. And we had our observer/snipers poised along the cordon, ready to take out a gnat at a hundred yards.

In all, it was a very efficient maneuver, and as far as we could tell, our men were soon enough entrenched without being noticed. Realistically, though, it was damn near impossible to move that many men into position without making at least *some* kind of noise, and I imagine we rustled enough branches to get the folks inside the compound to wondering if something was up. Shortly after our men were in place, we got a report over the radio from one of our Ghillie-suited agents on the ground that two men had departed one of the main CSA buildings and were crossing the field with rifles in hand. They moved like they were on patrol or making an inspection. Must be they heard some rumbling in the brush surrounding their dwellings, and these guys were dispatched to check things out. I suppose it was a little much to expect that we could move a couple hundred agents into position without rousing some suspicion, and here it was.

There was a long pause as we figured a next move, and after a couple heartbeats Danny Coulson leaned over to his number two in command, Jeff Wehmeyer, and let it be known that he intended to instruct his men in the field to jump these two CSA guys and take them into custody. I thought that was about the worst move we could have made at that point, and I said as much.

"Bad call, Danny," I said.

"What do you mean?" he shot back, and from his tone I could tell he didn't particularly like being second-guessed. No doubt, he'd heard more than enough from me by this point.

"Well," I said, "there's no telling how those guys might react. What if they start shooting? Next thing you know, we're in a full-scale shoot-out, middle of the night, right here and now. Is that how you want it to go down?"

"What else you got?" Coulson said.

"We've got a better chance of getting out of this thing without any shooting if we simply announce ourselves to these two guys," I suggested. "Tell them to go back to their compound and return with Ellison so we can talk to him."

Coulson seemed to think about this for a moment, and in that moment he tried to understand how it was that we had these guys outmanned and outgunned and outmaneuvered and he was still being pressed to let two potential shooters go. I got the distinct impression it was against his nature, but he wanted to win as much as anyone, and none of us wanted bloodshed if we could avoid it.

Before Coulson could decide one thing or another, the Ghillie-suited HRT agents on the ground came back on the radio. The CSA guys were walking right toward them and they needed some direction. "They're going to step on us," one of the agents whispered in measured frustration. "What do you want us to do?"

All eyes (and ears) were on Danny Coulson, but I spoke before he could respond. "Trust me on this one, Danny," I said. "Tell them to announce themselves and tell the CSA guys to go back into their compound and tell Ellison we want to talk to him."

Coulson took one last second to think this through, and then he went with my recommendation and his own gut: told his men exactly what we'd discussed. And that's just what they did.

"FBI," came the voice of our agents just a couple beats later, carrying out Coulson's orders. "Go back into your compound and tell your leader he needs to talk to us!"

There were multiple piles of leaves barking out orders to these two CSA scouts. Must have scared the plain crap out of these guys. They had no idea who our men were, or why they were there, or what type of strength or force they had backing them up. But, thank God, their first reaction was to retreat back to the compound, and another beat or two later, from our position, we could see lights coming on in all the buildings. The alarm had been sounded—and the men, women and children of The Covenant, the Sword and the Arm of the Lord were on full alert.

The game might have been "on" as we moved on the compound, but this was where it truly began. . . .

Our forward command post was just a couple vehicles parked along a slip of dirt road immediately beyond the compound area. This was where our "braintrust" had gathered: Coulson, Jeff Wehmeyer, HRT team leader Larry Bonney, HRT sniper team leader Steve Wiley, a commander from the Arkansas state troopers, a lead agent from ATF . . . and me. Once again I was the primary voice on behalf of any kind of talking solution, but for now my words would travel through Danny Coulson. Everyone else was poised and primed to go to guns at the slightest provocation, and at first light you could sense that we were up against it. There had been all kinds of movement and commotion from the compound, while our men on the perimeter had remained stock-still, and yet, all kinds of time had passed without any further contact with anyone from the CSA.

It was one of those still and beautiful spring mornings when the mist started to come up off the ground, and you started to realize that under other circumstances this would be a nice area to talk a walk in. It really was a picturesque scene, but instead we were looking at a tense stalemate, with hundreds of men and women on either side of the law, guns at the ready, everybody waiting for somebody else to make a next move. We were at that point where everything could go into the crapper in a blind instant, which is the worst-case scenario I always tried to look at during these standoffs. One wrong move, one wrong statement, one misstep, and everything unravels. Plan for the worst and you can deal with anything else.

Finally, Kerry Noble, Ellison's "executive officer," strode toward us from the main building. He was dressed out in full combat gear, with a pistol at his side and a white flag in his hand. Coulson spoke briefly to Noble, who agreed to carry our field phone back into his compound and to ask Jim Ellison to come down to where we were for a chat. A handshake later and he was gone.

Coulson returned to our forward position with a look that suggested he was proud of himself. "See," he said to me as he approached, "I didn't say one cussword the whole time."

"It's early yet," I shot back good-naturedly. "I'll still have to pull your chestnuts out of the fire."

We moved quickly from banter to business, addressing what we all believed would be an imminent showdown with Ellison. Coulson, like most of us, indicated that he had never knowingly confronted a federal fugitive and allowed him to walk away, but we both agreed that this might be a good time to break the rules. Besides, we were making up the rules as we went along, so it really didn't make any difference. Ellison, we both knew, would expect Coulson to come on strong; he might even expect our push for a dialogue to be some kind of trick.

But we would fool him and not arrest him, sending the distinct message that we were the good guys, that we were taking our time, and that we were here to win.

Ellison wasn't so easily fooled. He insisted on talking first on the field phone. He wanted to know who we were, why we were there, what we wanted, who we planned to arrest, where we were going to search. He subsequently agreed to a face-to-face meeting, on the condition that some of the group's women and children be allowed to leave the compound. We promptly agreed to this last, and set the women and children up at a local motel, where Steve Wiley and I would later interview them to develop information on who was left in the compound, including various outside "guests" we had yet to identify. In an uncertain standoff such as this, information can be a tremendous source of power, and I was out to collect as much of it as I could get my hands on—as quickly as I could.

A couple hours later Kerry Noble returned to our mobile command post—an HRT Chevy Suburban—and he and I engaged in small talk. The idea was to keep him busy for long enough to put our next tactic in place. I had already suggested to HRT team leader Larry Bonney that we conduct a shift change of tactical agents in full view of Noble, to let him see what he was up against. Bonney liked the idea and sold it to Coulson, and as Noble and I talked we put the shift change in effect. What was interesting about this "staged" conversation was that, as Christians, Noble and I shared a great many beliefs, but we parted sharply over some of his outrageous Aryan Nation–type ideas. Still, I was a ready listener and kept him talking as our parade of tactical agents began. About one hundred of our biggest, best, and brightest marched past his sight-line, all dressed in full body armor that included Kevlar vests and helmets and all carrying automatic weapons and sidearms and enough ammunition to start or finish a war, depending. They looked like giants who had all eaten snakes for dinner. Even I was impressed by the show—and, most important, so was Noble, whose eyes seemed to pop out of his head. And yet, just as he seemed most intimidated, he flashed a sudden look of indignation and disgust. The shift was alarming, and I couldn't begin to understand it.

"That SOB," he yelled, indicating one of our agents crossing his path. "He tries to enter our compound, we'll kill him."

I spun on the rock on which I was seated and tried to follow his gaze, and as I did so my eyes locked on one of our biggest, beefiest agents, Ben Clary, who also happened to be black. Ben was one of the kindest, most professional agents you'd care to meet, but Noble had picked him out of our lineup and revealed the full extent of his racial bias and hatred.

Damn, I thought to myself. Careful or you'll snatch defeat from the jaws of victory. *I should have seen that one coming.* And then I kicked myself for not thinking more like Kerry Noble, even as I realized the differences between us were greater than I could imagine.

Ellison followed Noble a short while later, looking very much like the general in charge, and like he would sooner go out in a blaze of presumed glory than surrender without a fight. But there he was, ready to talk as opposed to spoiling to fight. As a negotiator, I took this as a tremendous positive, because it meant that Ellison, too, held out hope that this deadlock would come to something other than a violent end, otherwise he could have chosen that route and we would have delivered, period.

Now that I had seen Ellison and the way he carried himself—most particularly, the way he dressed: in full battle gear—it was clear he would only talk to his presumed equal in Danny Coulson. Doc had guts, I'll give him that. It's never a good idea to meet face-to-face with one of the bad guys in this type of situation, because too much can go wrong in no time at all; but here we all felt we had no choice, so Danny went down to meet Ellison one-on-one alongside a ditch just inside our perimeter, away from the CSA buildings. Coulson wore a wire so we could listen in from our command post, but the way the meeting played out, it was difficult to figure out exactly what was going on just from the audio, and it took Coulson's later account to fill in some of the blanks for us.

Here's what happened. The two men met and grunted to each other in greeting. Then they sized each other up for a bit, like two short sumo wrestlers, neither one wanting to reveal his hand or his next move. Then Ellison reached over and grabbed a sprig of poison ivy from beneath a log near where they were sitting and popped it in his mouth. Started chewing on it like it was a piece of beef jerky. It was the strangest thing. Coulson was intuitive enough to get that Ellison was trying to get a reaction from him, and he was careful to give away nothing. He kept a poker face throughout, until Ellison finally said, "You know why I do that?"

"Nope," Coulson said.

Ellison said, "It's because when I eat it I'm able to build up a resistance to it, so it doesn't bother me."

"Okay," Coulson said.

I didn't know what the hell was going on as I was listening in, but when I heard Coulson's account later it seemed to me he'd played it just right. Clearly, Ellison was trying to test his counterpart with this opening move, trying to get some sort of reaction, but Coulson played it cool and flat, as if he'd seen folks pop sprigs of poison ivy into their mouths every day of the week—but of course he was wise enough not to eat any himself.

Ellison didn't cut such an imposing figure. He looked to be in his midforties, shorter than he was tall, and fat around the middle. Our intelligence indicated that he was "married" to two different women in the group: he lived with one, who had carried six of his children, but had worn a path between his house and a nearby dwelling where his second "wife" and their child lived. Despite his tubby appearance and his apparent willingness to negotiate, Ellison was no pushover. He let it be known in this first face-to-face meeting with Danny Coulson that his people would not give themselves up under any circumstances. He would not allow the FBI to arrest the women and children who remained in the compound. We would have to go in and take them by force if we meant to accomplish our objective.

Still, here he was, talking.

I had encouraged Coulson to try to get Ellison to agree to a follow-up conversation if this first one didn't end in surrender, and he was able to push the CSA leader to keep the lines of communication open, which we counted as another small victory in this early going. String together enough of these, I thought, and we just might have something.

Over the next two days we continued to meet with Ellison or Noble at least once every few hours. Sometimes Danny Coulson went alone for another one-on-one session, and sometimes Larry Bonney or I accompanied him, if Ellison had Kerry Noble in tow. I was careful at all times to match Ellison and his entourage with members of our team of comparable rank and stature, because I knew he was the type to pay attention to such things. I dressed in camouflage gear instead of a sports coat and tie because that's what this guy responded to. In between meetings there were phone calls on our field phone, and that's where I did most of my talking. At some point we made a deal that none of us would carry long guns to these face-to-face meetings. They could carry sidearms but no rifles, and here again it was another small victory. As a practical matter, it didn't mean all that much from our position of strength, because our snipers were primed to take these guys out if they went for their guns, but I wanted to make things a little bit more difficult for them. When you carried a handgun, you had to reach for it in its holster and bring it back up again before shooting. When you carried a rifle, it was already in hand and good to go, so this cut into their element of surprise a little bit and gave our guys a bit more time to react if someone made any kind of fool move.

Most important, it was a concession on their part, and it was a learned truth in the negotiating game that one concession frequently led to another; the nose of the camel was now under the tent, and what followed was yet to be known.

In the meantime we had to deal with the matter of feeding our own people and keeping them fresh and relatively comfortable. We could have done this by the book, but we set the book aside in the interest of team morale. We had a secret weapon in Special Agent Ron Kelly, an FBI supervisor from Little Rock whose job it was to scurry around our perimeter taking food orders. Pizzas and Cokes, mostly. This guy was like a pizza god to our tactical agents out in that field. Or a McDonald's god. Whatever these guys wanted, he arranged for it to be sent in, and if it weren't for his extra efforts on this one we would have been eating MREs—military meals ready to eat—for a stretch of a couple days, which if you'd asked any of us would have been a couple days too many.

The standoff shot right through its second day like nothing at all, and we were looking straight down the barrel at a third, and I could tell that Danny Coulson and his tactical colleagues were growing impatient. These guys were primed for some kind of action. We could stand out in this field forever, talking things through and through, and still never get anywhere, and as each tense hour passed we seemed to move ever closer to some kind of tipping point. It got to where I would consider almost any kind of strategy, proven or otherwise, as long as it made any kind of sense.

Despite their willingness to talk and to concede on various small points, there was no substantive movement in the CSA's overall position. They would not lay down their arms and surrender the compound. But at least they were talking, and it fell to me to keep the conversation going. I set it up so that each conversation, on the phone or in person, had some sort of agenda—like my ill-fated desire to show Noble our troop strength. I also set it up so that each conversation led naturally to some sort of follow-up meeting. Typically, in a hostage-barricade situation, there'd be an ongoing discussion about sending in food and other essential supplies to the hostages and the hostage-takers, but that wasn't the case here: these CSA guys had stockpiled provisions to see them to the other side of Armageddon, so they had everything they could have possibly needed. Instead, we'd leave an open point that needed to be discussed, or promise to bring in someone to answer a specific question or concern. When I got the feeling that Ellison needed to confront a Washington bureaucrat on some matter or other, for example, I drove Tony Daniels, then the SAC of Oklahoma City and a real agent's agent, to a local Wal-Mart and outfitted him with a pair of slacks, a shirt, a tie, a belt, and a snappy sports coat and brought him back down to the ditch where we usually stood for these face-to-face meetings so that Ellison and his men could feel they were talking to "a D.C. suit."

(Tony, like all of us, had only packed soft or tactical clothing for this deployment, so the $100 or so we spent on his "makeover" was essential. Of course, that didn't stop me from dummying up an invoice some weeks later, from the United States government to SAC Daniels, demanding that he repay the amount on his expense account that had been listed as "civilian clothing." When he called to rail about the relentless and mindless bureaucracy, I zinged him good: "Gotcha, Tony," I said.)

Appearance was key. Every day or so, we'd take turns running back to a nearby hotel to shower and change, on the theory that it's not enough to talk a good game: you've got to look good too. If I'm in a long, open-ended negotiation, I don't want to look like a bum or give off the impression that I've been beaten down in any way. I've got to have my game face on. I've got to have clean clothes. I've got to be clean shaven. And I've got to grab a little sleep, here and there. Over the years I'd become expert at the art of catnapping, and here I managed to steal an hour or so of sleep in the back of one of our trucks, and that was enough to keep me fresh. Coulson, for his part, was a master at this sort of thing, able to recharge his batteries after just a few minutes of sleep.

It was also important for us to substantiate our claims to these guys, in whatever ways we could manage out there in that field. When the conversation turned to what kind of time CSA leaders might be facing, on what kind of charges, I wanted to be able to address the matter from a position of authority, so we flew in the Assistant U.S. Attorney on the case, an easygoing but brilliant federal prosecutor named Asa Hutchinson, who would go on to become President George W. Bush's number two man in Homeland Security and a candidate for Arkansas governor, and he was able to tell Ellison and his henchmen what they were up against. I didn't want these guys thinking we were going to put them away forever, because that certainly wasn't going to be the case, but at the same time I didn't want to sugarcoat the pending charges to where they might see through a line. About the last thing I wanted was to get caught in an out-and-out lie. Jim Ellison and Kerry Noble and the rest of these guys seemed completely nuts, and their belief systems were all out of whack with mine, but they were still smart guys and I had to figure they knew a little something about the law, so we were careful to treat this line of our ongoing conversation as if they knew what they were talking about. It's okay to snow your opposite number a little bit as long as there is no chance they'll ever know they're being snowed, but the cardinal rule in these negotiations is to never tell a lie unless it's going to be your last lie, the one you tell to set up "the final option."

There was also the matter of music. CSA leaders took to playing contemporary Christian music through loudspeakers directed at our inner perimeter. The music was loud, and clearly intended as a distraction of some kind, but we couldn't let them see it as such. During a phone conversation with Noble, I reminded him that I, too, was a

Christian and that I enjoyed many of the same tapes at home. I even offered to send in some music from my collection for them to sample, which I guess was about the last thing they wanted to hear—not unlike the turnoff experienced by a petulant teenager when his parents embrace the rock or rap music he blares through the speakers in his bedroom at home. Sure enough, the music stopped. Evidently, Ellison's attempt at psy-ops (psychological operations) had fallen on deaf ears, so to speak.

It turned out the music was the least of their worries. Gradually, Ellison and Noble came to understand what they were up against and that they had no choice but to lay down their arms. However, there were a number of outsiders holed up in that compound with them who didn't quite see it that way. David Tate, the freelance nut job from The Order who had shot those two state troopers, hadn't made it to Bull Shoals Lake, but there were several other "guests" from outside the core CSA group, including Randall Evans, Tom Bentley, Jeff Butler, and Jim Wallington—names that were all known to us following our interviews with the released CSA women and children. These four men in particular stood against Ellison in his decision to resolve the situation nonviolently, and Ellison indicated to us that he needed some help convincing these radicals, the fringe of the fringe, to surrender peacefully. Specifically, he wanted Robert Millar, founder of the Christian Identity group Elohim City in Oklahoma, to be brought in to help broker some kind of truce among the conflicting radical factions. Tony Daniels, our Oklahoma City SAC, knew enough about Millar to weigh in with his caution, calling him "another gun nut and neo-Nazi," and indicating that this guy was probably even more "out there" than any of the nuts jobs and neo-Nazis already on-site.

The back-and-forth reminded me of those old *Batman* serials in which all the bad guys banded together to defeat the Caped Crusader and conquer Gotham City—and here we were, with the Joker and Riddler and Penguin at loggerheads inside their compound, thinking about flying in Mr. Freeze to talk some sense to them. It was a ridiculous, dangerous proposition, but we were forced to consider it.

I had been uneasy about sending Danny Coulson in as a tactically oriented negotiator, and now we were thinking about sending in a potentially hostile third party to do the same job. I didn't like it at all, but I didn't see that we had any choice in the matter. Plus, I convinced myself that I had used outside negotiators before, with some success, and we had long since thrown the book out the window on this case. I suppose I could editorialize here and suggest that we were "thinking outside the box" on this one, although in truth we were simply winging it.

The Millar maneuver had to be cleared through Tony Daniels, and ultimately Oliver "Buck" Revell, the FBI assistant director in charge of all criminal matters—and a good friend of Coulson's. Buck determined that he either had to give us enough rope to hang all of us or let us tie this whole thing together and end a siege that could cost dozens of lives. Daniels arranged for an FBI plane to fly Millar to the CSA compound, where I first met him. The man was indeed a sight. As he walked up the dirt road to our location, the sun to his back, I had to marvel at his getup. Oklahoma cowboys dress alike, apparently, whether they are gun-loving, Bible-thumping survivalists or would-be John Waynes, and Robert Millar was no exception. He struck me as a small man in big clothes: cowboy hat and boots, white suit, black tie, with a transparent distrust for the establishment and a big-time hatred for blacks and Jews and anyone who seemed in any way different. I took one look at this guy and hated that he held the key to resolving this entire matter—someone who didn't like the government, who mistrusted the FBI, and who could easily throw in with his CSA comrades in one last, grand showdown.

I handed Millar a cup of coffee as we sat in a dusty FBI truck and talked. "Mr. Millar," I said, "we need your help."

"Why should I help you?" he shot back.

I thought, *Okay, so far so good.* I said, "Mr. Millar, the whole world is watching to see how this works out, and only you can make it work."

I didn't know how else to play it but to pump this guy up and send him off with an inflated sense of importance. The risk, of course, was that he might enter the compound and report back on our strength and strategy and whatnot. The reward, for a guy like Millar, was the chance to be a power broker between the federal government and a survivalist group with similar leanings to his own, the chance to be a real hero in the eyes of his own disaffected community. It fell to me to push him through those extra paces. I told him he held all the marbles. I could see his eyes light up at this, calculating how he might play this unlikely position to advantage, and I figured the thing to do was to help him along in his thinking.

"This gets resolved without going to guns," I said, "and you're the one the media is going to want to talk to."

I kept at it: "You're the one who'll be the peacemaker.

"You're the one who's going to dispel the notion that groups like yours are only looking to violent solutions to our problems.

"You're the one who can show that your biblical and religious beliefs can also accommodate peace."

I laid it on as thick as I could—only here again it wasn't a line. All of these things were true, in their own way; it's just that I made them sound a little bit more true and a little bit more important than they actually were.

Finally, when I couldn't put much more of a full-court press on this guy, he turned to me and said, "What exactly do you want me to do?"

And I thought, *You son of a gun, I've got you!* Hooked him but good, and set about reeling him in. Next I introduced him to Asa Hutchinson, the federal prosecutor who would be handling the case, and stressed that the only violation we were seriously interested in here was the illegal conversion of weapons from semiautomatic to fully automatic. There were other offenses listed on our warrant, but these were the biggies. We spent a couple of hours together before I let Coulson know that I believed in this guy and that I thought he had too much to gain to screw things up. Danny concurred, and we sent Millar into the compound to meet with the CSA leadership and their four wild-card guests, after making certain that Millar understood our position on the points that I knew would be meaningful to Jim Ellison and his followers. We would not storm the compound and desecrate their homes. We would not arrest their women and children. We would search all homes and outbuildings for weapons, but we would do so methodically and return everything to its proper place. We would not confiscate their vehicles. If it became necessary to remove the women and children from the compound, we would place them in area hotels at government expense, as we had done with the group that had already left the property. We would pay for their lodging and meals. We would only arrest the individuals named on our warrants, and the most likely scenario was that these individuals would appear before the U.S. District Court judge assigned to the case the following day, whereupon bail would be set. In all likelihood, I suggested, these guys could be returned to their homes in a matter of days.

"You've got two hours," Coulson told Millar at the end of our session. "If for some reason you can't come back out in that time, you need to call me. Are we clear?"

Millar indicated that we were on the same page, and it fell to him to sell Jim Ellison on our agenda. Anyway, that was the plan. I had no idea how it would go, and after two hours had passed he picked up the field phone and checked in, right on schedule—another good sign. "I need some more time," he said.

It was about 5:00 in the evening, and I wanted him out of there before nightfall, but I felt we had no choice but to give him some more rope. Coulson agreed.

An hour later Millar called us back. He was still making progress, he said, but he wasn't ready to come out just yet. He needed more time.

Danny Coulson was listening in and shaking his head to indicate that he didn't want to give this guy any more time, but I was inclined to allow it. I didn't see that we had any choice.

An hour later Millar called us back again, this time reporting that he would need to spend the night. At this, Coulson was apoplectic. There was no way he was letting this guy spend the night, he said, or giving him all that time to mount some sort of counterattack with Ellison and the CSA leadership. And yet, we had backed ourselves into a corner. If we insisted that Millar come back out immediately and he refused, we would lose face because we'd demanded something we couldn't carry through on. So I turned to Danny Coulson and said, "I'd rather not make any demands on this guy just yet. We're better off telling him we need him out at eight o'clock in the morning, and getting him to agree to that, than insisting he come out immediately."

Once again Coulson reluctantly signed on, and I understood his concerns. I had plenty of my own. I worried that I no longer had a good handle on this situation and that the decision to send this guy in to meet with Ellison in the first place was ready to backfire, but I could see no other way to play it at this point. We were in too deep to turn back.

The following morning, Millar came back out to our appointed meeting place to make his report. Ellison was ready to surrender, he said, but there was a hitch. The seventy-five or so remaining members of the Covenant, the Sword and the Arm of the Lord were of one mind with Ellison and Millar to end this peacefully; the four Aryan Nation wild cards wanted to remain holed up in that compound. I heard this and wondered if they had some sort of exchange program going.

After a tense little back-and-forth, we managed to get the number one Aryan Nation guy, Randall Evans, on the field phone. Coulson handed the call over to me, saying, "I do the political negotiations, you talk to the criminals."

"Randy," I said, "we need to talk."

"So," he said. "Talk."

I fumbled for a bit for a way to get through to this guy, and he was basically telling me to go screw myself, but at some point I hit on the notion of trying to relate to him on his own terms. I thought, *What the hell. I'm on the phone. He can't see me. I can give myself a little leeway here.* And so I convinced myself it would be a good strategy to identify with the Christian Identity Movement—for purposes of this one conversation. It was worth a try, right? "We haven't met," I said, "but I'm a blond-haired, blue-eyed white Anglo-Saxon American male. Same as you." (As you can see from my author's photo, I'm really black-haired and brown-eyed, but he couldn't see me and I needed to identify with him.)

"Yeah," he said, "but are you a Christian?"

"Actually, I'm a born-again Christian," I said, never once thinking such a claim might come back to bite me, which it very nearly did.

"Yeah, well, if you're born-again, that means you believe the Jews are God's chosen people," he said, "and that means you and I have nothing in common and nothing to talk about."

He went to hang up the phone, and I thought, *Damn, Van Zandt, there you go again. You were* this close *to making some kind of connection with this guy, but you reached just a little too far and now it appears that you've blown it.*

"Wait a minute," I said, scrambling to keep Evans talking. "Just tell me, who are the worst people in the world?"

"What the hell you talking about?" he shot back.

"The worst people in the world. The least trustworthy. The cause of all of our problems."

He thought about this for about a heartbeat. "Well, that would be the niggers and the Jews," he said.

"Damn right," I said.

"Don't need you to tell me I'm right," he said back, his voice flat.

"What I need is for you to back off. We still don't got nothing to talk about."

And yet, there we were, talking, and it got to where he decided we would settle our differences in a kickboxing contest between the two of us. I wasn't quite sure how Evans had made the leap in his thinking that left me and him going toe-to-toe in a kickboxing battle to determine whether he and his Aryan brothers would surrender to my authority, but once he let the idea take shape, there was no talking him out of it. Not at first, anyway. So I went with it. My head was swirling, but I went with it.

"Okay," I said, improvising, "let's say we do that. Let's say you and I meet on that little hill they've got, a couple hundred yards past the compound. You know the hill I mean?"

Evans indicated that he knew the hill I was talking about.

"Well," I continued, "there's this great old oak tree on that hill."

"Yeah," he said, sparking to the scene I was laying out for him. "I've seen it."

"Good," I said. "That's as good a spot as any, wouldn't you agree?"

"That's a good spot," he allowed.

"Okay," I said, "so let's say we meet there and you and I have a fight, and it's such a bloody, cutthroat, all-out kind of fight that we wind up killing each other. Could happen, right?"

"Right," he said. "That could happen."

"And let's say that it's somehow decided that the two of us are to be buried beneath that great oak tree. Could happen, right?"

"Right," he said. "That could happen."

"And let's say that over our graves there will be two markers. One for you and one for me. And on each it will say, 'Here lies an Aryan warrior who died for what he believed in.' Words to that effect. You can see something like that, right?"

"Yeah," he said. "I can see it."

Danny Coulson and the other negotiators were listening in to my end of the conversation and couldn't understand what I might be getting at—and, frankly, I didn't have a clear idea where I was going, either, but I kept at it. Evans, too, was sounding more and more confused at the other end of the field phone, but I definitely had his attention, using what psychologists call visualization, in this case a kind of verbal paintbrush in my hands, with Evans there to critique my artwork.

"Stay with me on this," I said, to buy myself a couple beats more of this guy's thought process. "Now, tell me again. Who are the worst people in the world?"

"The Jews and the niggers," he repeated.

"That's right," I said. "We're agreed on that, but do you know what I see underneath that great oak tree, at those two graves?"

He mumbled that he had no idea.

"I'll tell you what I see," I said. "I see a black guy and a Jew. One's standing over my grave, and one's standing over your grave. And they're laughing. And do you know what else they're doing?"

My colleagues were looking at me like I had gone crazy on them, like they couldn't believe I was actually talking like this, but I felt I had figured this guy out. And from Evans's anxious response, it appeared that I had.

"What?" he said excitedly. "What? What are they doing?"

"They're pissing on our graves," I said, driving home my point. "They're pissing, and laughing, because these two supposed Aryan warriors were so stupid they couldn't work out their differences and instead came to blows and killed each other. Because we had a common enemy and we killed each other instead." I let this last thought hang for a bit before following through. "We're not going to let that happen, are we?" I said.

"No," he nearly yelled. "No, we're not."

Right there, I knew I had turned this guy around, and that we could now turn our talk toward resolving our impasse. And that's just what we did. The nearby agents were still looking at me like I had sprouted horns and should probably be written up on some impropriety or other, but I'd softened this guy up and spun him around to where we could now talk about the manner of the CSA surrender and how we might handle the Aryan Nation members who happened to be present. It was all downhill from there.

The manner of Ellison's surrender was somewhat complicated. He wanted to come out only after he and his group had bathed and changed clothes. Coulson obviously wanted him to come out immediately—but here again we didn't feel we could press the issue. If we had insisted that the group surrender straightaway, and if Ellison refused, the progress of the past couple days would be essentially erased. None of us on the side of law enforcement wanted to pass another hour, wondering what these CSA whack-jobs were doing inside that compound, what kind of last-ditch plan they might be hatching. There could be a mass breakout. They could come charging from those buildings and running in all directions, waving guns and flamethrowers and lobbing grenades every which way. Plus, there was also the thought that the group could pull a Jonestown-type mass suicide and start drinking poison Kool-Aid in the heat of the day. I ran through every worst-case scenario in my head and tried to figure out how we would counter it, and at the other end we were still wanting. There were too many things that could still go wrong; Murphy and his law hung over us like a dark rain cloud.

But once again we felt we had no choice but to concede the point. And so we waited. And waited. And waited. I paced and paced. I walked around in the woods, trying to clear my head and keep my focus. I was exhausted already, running on fumes and adrenaline after three long nights in these woods—and, frankly, running low on each. If I had had toothpicks, I could have used them to prop my eyes open. One of the things we talk about in our negotiating sessions is sleep deprivation and how we can sometimes be driven to bad decisions when we're overtired. Here, even though I knew better, I worried I'd be off my game. I had started drinking massive amounts of coffee, just for the caffeine. I'm not a coffee drinker, but in the middle of a long, tense situation, trying to keep sharp after three days and nights without any real rest, I was a regular Juan Valdez.

There was a moment during those long, restless few hours as I waited for some other shoe to drop on Ellison's surrender when I thought back on the past several months, on the transition from Rochester to Philadelphia to Quantico, on reaching the point in my career when I could finally put into practice some of the theories and strategies I'd studied over the years, on my ability to develop new ones on the fly, on the front-row seat I would now occupy in one way or another at virtually every hostage-barricade situation confronting the FBI. I hadn't meant to be a full-time instructor, but this CSA standoff told me that I wouldn't be spending all of my days behind a desk or at a lectern. I'd be out in the field, making a difference, and helping to bring about nonviolent resolutions to standoffs and conflicts that on someone else's watch might play in other ways entirely. I knew going in it was an awesome responsibility, and here I was, at the hopeful end of my first major test—and it was every bit as awesome as I had imagined. I allowed myself a long, purposeful sigh, prayed to God once again that all would continue to go well, and settled back in for the long day ahead.

As morning turned to afternoon, there were still some aspects of the matter to be resolved. One of the final sticking points to the CSA surrender was the order of retreat. Jim Ellison wanted the women and children to come out first, and Danny Coulson had initially agreed, but once I heard that that's how it was going to go down I didn't think it was such a good idea, so I argued the point with Coulson.

"Do you even have any idea what you're talking about?" Coulson said. "You've been on me the whole time we're here. That's what Ellison wants. And that's how it's gonna go."

"But it's a bad idea, Danny," I pressed.

"Every idea's a bad idea, according to you," he responded, more than a little miffed.

"And have I been wrong yet?" I said.

Coulson thought about this for a couple beats and then he seemed to shrug his shoulders in resignation, and I knew he would listen to my recommendation this final time. "Give me a reason," he said. "Tell me why it's a bad idea to let the women and children out first so I have something to tell Ellison when I go back on my word."

I explained how in my worst-case-scenario handbook there was the possibility that these CSA guys, knowing their women and children were safely in custody, might either refuse to come out or start shooting up the place, whereas if the men came out first with the women and children left behind, they would be less likely to do so. Coulson couldn't argue the logic in it. "Fine," he said, "but we still need to sell it to Ellison."

Turned out it wasn't such a tough sell, and we set it up so that the men came out first and stood beside our agents as the women and children were escorted from the compound. Out of respect to the women and children, the men were not handcuffed or manacled or restrained in any way beyond the two SWAT guys we had standing on either side of them. That's how we set it up, two of our guys for every one of theirs, just to give these right-wing supremacists a little dignity in front of their families—and to show their women and children the same respect. We searched them, of course, but after that they stood freely.

Still, it was an anxious procession, because we were dealing with individuals who could go south on us real quick, although the moment I saw Jim Ellison I knew that wasn't going to happen. He was wearing street clothes, which was huge. I took one look and thought, *Thank God*. He had undergone a complete transformation, from a military commander to a noncombatant—and the same was true for the other CSA members as well. In fact, all of the men had changed into civilian clothes, which I took as part of their surrender ritual. It was a laying down not only of their weapons but their military artifacts as well. The clothing. The aspect. The identity that had fueled their arms buildup and their master plan to topple the American government and to rid the country of blacks and Jews and any other group they deemed undesirable. The "surrender ritual," as we called it, was about complete. The fear, of course, was that the CSAers might have changed clothes to die in their Sunday best, but I didn't think so. Not this time; not in this place; not today. And so it went.

In the end, FBI agents seized an enormous cache of weapons from the CSA compound, including countless automatic assault rifles, a fully operational LAW rocket, C-4 explosives, land mines, hand grenades, a Lewis machine gun, hundreds of handguns and rifles, thousands of rounds of ammunition, and a thirty-gallon drum of cyanide—this last, as one CSA member told me, to have been used to poison the water supply of a major U.S. city to kill minorities, notwithstanding that whites drank from the same water supply as blacks: another example of their twisted logic.

And yet, it was a relatively quiet standoff, as I indicated earlier. Substitute David Koresh's name for Jim Ellison's—substitute Waco, Texas, for this remote corner of Arkansas—and you have a completely different story as far as the national media was concerned. Don't get me wrong: the CSA standoff was a big story at the time; but it didn't make the kind of splash it might have if it was shot through with death and destruction, and nowadays you'd be hard-pressed to come across someone who even remembers it other than the folks who were directly involved.

But there it was. And there we were, counting it a giant victory that no one was hurt and that the situation was resolved. Indeed, as we wrapped things up that morning we knew we had put the Covenant, the Sword and the Arm of the Lord out of business for the next while.

Jim Ellison and Kerry Noble and the others would be going away for just a few years on these weapons charges, but the group itself would lose steam and its members would drift back into the rest of their lives, their doomsday CSA compound destined to become a footnote, a forgotten artifact of another age that some future archaeologist might uncover in the Arkansas hills and wonder at its history.

Always, at the peaceful end of these tense standoffs, I looked for some way to close one chapter and move on in my mind to the next ordeal. And here I actually caught myself looking. There had been so many horrific images racing through my mind over the previous few days, out of fear that our negotiations would sour and there'd be an all-out shoot-out and dead bodies splayed all over the compound, but none of that had come to pass. Instead, there was this peaceful procession of men, women and children who only hours earlier had been armed to the teeth and shot through with hatred and poised to fight to the death, and here they were dressed in their Sunday best. It was an odd picture, one I'd hoped for at the outset but at the same time one I certainly hadn't counted on. And yet, the picture itself didn't offer the closure I sought. My eyes raced about the scene until they landed on a small boy about seven or eight years old. He was standing off to the side, by himself, several paces from a woman I took to be his mother and two little girls I took to be his sisters. His hair was combed, his face scrubbed, his clothes pressed neat and clean, and in his face I thought I'd found what I was looking for: the symbolic reminder of why we had gone through these tense motions in the first place.

Closure and me, we seek each other out, so I crossed to the boy to see if we might have anything to say to each other. Anything positive. Anything helpful. Anything at all.

I reached to shake his hand and said, "Son, I'm real glad everything worked out the way it did."

The boy looked at me without expression. He did not move to shake my hand. He did not move at all. After a long, awkward silence, he finally spoke. "We could have beat you," he said. His voice was cold, flat, menacing, and it struck me as the most incongruous thing, coming from such a sweet, innocent-looking face. Then he pointed his finger at Jim Ellison and said, "If God hadn't told Pastor Ellison to lay down his arms, we could have beat you. We could have beat you anytime."

I started to back away from this young boy, realizing our conversation wasn't going to take us anywhere I particularly wanted to go, and certainly nowhere positive or helpful, but he kept talking as I moved on.

"There will be another time," he said, shouting now. "We will meet again, and we will beat you."

I didn't realize it just then, but I guess this was the closure I was seeking. *There will be another time.* His voice hung in the air like a threat. Really, it was a chilling, haunting reminder that I was looking into the face of the next generation of individuals who will grow up hating other people simply because of the color of their skin, the strength of their religious convictions, and the power of their political views. In ten years I would see that face on the other side of yet another standoff and I would realize that there was no end to it.

There were two additional grace notes to the CSA standoff, and each stands as closure of a different kind. The first was a follow-up conversation I had with Jim Ellison after he was in our custody, after we had escorted the women and children to area hotels. I reached out to him the same way I'd reached out to that little boy. "I'm real glad things worked out the way they did," I said, once again offering my hand.

This time Ellison chose to shake it. Then he said, "We could have killed you at any time."

It wasn't exactly the response I was expecting, but I was curious to know what he meant. "What are you talking about?" I said. "We had the place surrounded."

"Go back and see for yourself," he said, and then he described the front bunker to the main building, which he and his men had laid out with sandbags and shooting ports—and a scoped rifled pointed directly at our makeshift forward command post.

Sure enough, I later walked over to the bunker and checked it out, and as I looked through the now abandoned scope rifle I had to admit that these guys had us dead in their sights for the entire three-and-a-half-day standoff. Absolutely, Jim Ellison could have killed me at any time. It would have set off an all-out firefight, and he and his faithful CSA flock would have undoubtedly lost the war, but he could have taken us out at any moment, for any reason, or for no reason at all. Me, Danny Coulson, Larry Bonney, Steve Wiley, Jeff Wehmeyer . . . any of us. We had been like sitting ducks.

The second story came to me electronically several years later, after most of the CSA guys had served their time and been released. Ellison, as I recall, was still incarcerated, but Kerry Noble, Ellison's number two guy, had been paroled. Noble had been flipping around the television dial when he saw me being interviewed on a cable news program, whereupon he looked up my company Web site and sent me an e-mail. (Ah, the wonders of our modern technology and our information age!) In his e-mail, he brought me up to speed on what he'd been doing with his life since he'd gotten out of prison, told me he'd seen me from time to time on television, and wondered if I could possibly introduce him to an agent with a speaker's bureau. It seems that that he was hoping to hit the lecture circuit to talk about his experiences as one of the leaders of a cultlike paramilitary group, which he thought might have special resonance in what even Kerry Noble now regarded as "our troubled times." I had to reread the e-mail a couple times, to make sure it wasn't some kind of goof or hoax, but it was Kerry Noble all right, and he seemed earnest enough. I thought, *What irony! To have been on opposite sides of a tense, days-long standoff, at a man-hour cost to the federal government of millions of dollars, against the kind of high stakes that could have meant the lives of dozens of federal agents and a*

hundred or so CSA survivalists, and to now get this e-mail asking for a refer-
ral, for old times' sake . . . Man, it was rich.

So what did I do? I sent a return e-mail giving Kerry Noble the
names, addresses and phone numbers of the three different speakers'
bureaus I used at the time. I also offered to stand as a reference, in the
event that any of the agents wanted to check him out before taking
him on, and as I clicked on the SEND icon on my computer screen, I
paused for a couple beats to relish the weirdness of what I used to do
for a living and what I do now for a living, and to wonder how it is
that we live in a world where the bad guys can ask the good guys for
career advice and where the good guys are inclined to give it—on the
faint hope that a second chance might take, after all.

SHOWDOWN IN SPERRYVILLE

"GOOD-BYE, KITTEN"

Fall 1986. Saturday night into Sunday morning. Midnight. Maybe one o'clock. The phone call from the HRT woke me up not long after I had fallen asleep. A hostage-barricade situation was going on in Sperryville, Virginia, about a ninety-minute drive from our home. Some guy holding a woman and a child at gunpoint. The case had been unraveling for several days, and the bad guy had only now been located, and I needed to be on the scene.

I listened to the sketchy details and thought how Sperryville was where we'd gone to pick apples with our kids. It didn't fit that a hostage-barricade situation would find itself in such a bucolic setting, but there it was, and as I hopped out of bed to meet it I thought about the stark contrast between what I'd been doing a couple hours earlier—I'd been off on a retreat with a men's group from my church—and what I was about to do. That was how it was for most of us in the Bureau; what we did for a living never quite fit with how we lived the rest of our lives.

First rule of thumb in the Bureau: always keep your gas tank full. It goes back to that old Boy Scout credo, and it applies as both metaphor and absolute: stand at the ever-ready, ever-charged and good to go. Anyway, never take your car home with less than a half-tank, because you just never know. Bureau car, your own car . . . it's much the same. It's a rule I always tried to follow, except on this one night when I got caught. I'd come home late from that church outing, thought I might bend the rule this one time, and as I hurried into my clothes I chided myself that *this one time* is always the time that comes back to bite you.

There were local FBI negotiators and Virginia State Police on the scene. Elements of the Bureau's Hostage Rescue Team had arrived and deployed. And there I was, heading west on Route 3 out of Fredericksburg in my old, tired Honda, trying to find a gas station. It felt like I was in the middle of nowhere. Pitch-black. No streetlights. No moon. No gas station.

No time to lose.

I pulled into Sperryville about an hour and a half after the call. I managed to find a gas station somewhere, an excursion that had ended up costing me more in worry than in time. There was a command post set up at the local firehouse, and from there someone escorted me to the scene. A rural farmhouse. Nice. Looked like someone had put some money into it not too long ago. It was dark, but not so dark you couldn't get the idea. The house sat by itself in the middle of an open field. It was a weekend place, apparently, and here it was, midweek, the center of all this great and heated attention. The state police had brought an armored vehicle out to the field, and that was being used as our forward command post. It was parked near a small bridge over a now-dry creak, a few hundred yards from the house where the woman and child were presumably being held. The thinking was that our agents and state troopers could find cover behind the armored vehicle, if cover was needed. At that point we still had no idea what kind of weapons the hostage-taker had in his current position—no clear idea, initially, where that position happened to be. There was a lot we didn't know as our team settled into the situation—a lot we wouldn't find out until later.

These were the details as they came in to me. A young mother and her child had been missing for several days from the mother's hometown in the northeastern part of the United States. New Hampshire, it turned out. The apparent kidnapping was reported by the woman's parents, who alleged that the child's biological father had abducted their daughter and grandson. Their whereabouts were unknown, until the tags on an abandoned car along a rural road in Sperryville turned up the father's name, Charles Leaf. FBI agents, state police, and U.S. Forest Service personnel began an immediate sweep of the area in the vicinity of the car, desperate for clues. The woman's parents had insisted that their daughter would not have gone off with Leaf of her own free will, and reported that Leaf had previously made threats on their daughter's life and the boy's safety, so our agents searched dozens of houses, each one much like the next—"farmettes," typically enjoyed by weekenders from D.C. and northern Virginia. Most of the houses were unoccupied—not abandoned, just unoccupied—which meant that with each unanswered knock on the door agents and troopers were faced with a decision: Do you move on to the next house, or do you kick the door down and wind up replacing all the locks for these second-home owners? Usually, a nickel-and-dime decision like that, it's a no-brainer: you kick down the door; but by the time you've kicked in a dozen doors you start to wonder. Already, agents had been up and down these country roads, in and out of a bunch of houses. They'd even been through the house that was now targeted as Leaf's hideaway and found nothing on the first pass; they'd subsequently been to an outbuilding on the property, a barn where stacks of hay seemed to have been moved around to form a kind of bunker, where open cans of food were strewn about, where all was not as it should have been, early Sunday morning, in these manicured parts. There was an electric meter running in the back of the house. Someone was clearly about. Someone who had no business being there.

Leaf had had a couple days to figure the house for empty. Tough to tell from the outside looking in, but over time the absence of activity gave it away. He'd pitched a tent in the woods off the field and tied the woman to a tree with a rope around her ankles so she couldn't run off, and for several days tried to figure his next move. It was unclear whether he restrained the little boy or whether he felt he needed to: to be sure, the child was unlikely to run off without his mother. With the woman and child back at the tent site, Leaf broke into various homes, scrounging for something to eat. There was a nighttime burglary of a local convenience store that our guys thought was connected and indeed later confirmed; Leaf had gone out to see about supplies, leaving the mother of his child tied to that tree. Finally, after a couple days of these feral conditions, the woman convinced Leaf to take her and her child into the nearest house so she could run some wash, get some clean clothes, and get a good night's sleep. She would have promised him anything, just to get her son in from out of the cold and maybe give them a chance to escape.

We learned later that Leaf was actually in an upstairs bedroom with his two hostages, listening through an open window to the law enforcement officers talking out in front of the house just prior to my arrival on the scene. He talked to the child's mother about making a run for it, confronting the officers below at gunpoint, and escaping with a police car. He weighed his options as more and more agents and officers descended on that farmhouse. He didn't like his chances to begin with, but with each moment of indecision he liked them even less. He talked the situation through with the woman as our SWAT team cleared the first floor of the house, and when our guys moved upstairs to clear the second, Leaf made his move. He sprang from a corner at the top of the stairs, the woman and the child in a shared headlock in front of him. Our SWAT guys are good, but they're not that good. Leaf had a rifle pointed at our tactical team as they ascended from the first floor, and he was hollering for them to "get back, get back, get the hell back."

As textbook situations go, this one's listed under positions to avoid. It's really a worst-case scenario for a tactical agent to have to back down from ground already gained; to have to do that backing down on a flight of stairs with a rifle pointed at you is even worse. Wayne Waddel, our local SWAT team leader, was halfway up the stairs with other SWAT agents behind him, and he had to turn from the hostage-taker and retreat due to the obvious threat to the woman and her child. The barrel of his CAR-15 rifle caught between the spires of the stair rail as he turned toward Leaf, and he had to slowly pull his rifle back toward him without provoking the bad guy to fire. While retreating, he had to shift from a tactical strategy—trying to take Leaf out—to a negotiating strategy—trying to keep Leaf from killing him or the hostages. Our SWAT teams are cross-trained in both disciplines, and Wayne was a trained negotiator, and he somehow managed to talk Leaf out of taking their lives right there on that staircase as the SWAT team reached the first floor and disappeared around the corner of the stairs.

I took the fact that Leaf didn't come out firing as a good sign, a hopeful sign. There wasn't much else to like about the situation, but the hostage-taker had our guys dead to rights on that stairwell and he held his fire, which told me this was possibly someone we could manipulate into a peaceful resolution. If we played it right, and if the bad guy stayed true to the form exhibited here, we might all be home for breakfast.

Our agents gave up the second floor, but they would not give up the first and Leaf didn't press the issue. At some point, though, he demanded that all the lights in the house be shut off. It was nighttime; we were in the middle of the countryside, in the middle of an open field, with no outside lighting. Tactically, SWAT wanted to keep some light on the situation—they felt, correctly, that it gave them an advantage—but when they resisted Leaf's demands, he stepped out into the stairwell and shot out a bulb in the ceiling. It was a cold, matter-of-fact act, and it told us a few things: this guy was willing and ready to use his weapon; his rifle was loaded and in working condition; and, he really didn't like lights.

It also told me that whatever good sign I had seen in that first impasse, it was likely an aberration. As soon as shots are fired in a standoff like this, whether or not they're fired at a human being, it ratchets up the pressure and raises the stakes, and as I stepped onto the scene both were running pretty high. That's how it usually goes for a hostage negotiator. Often, the rest of the tactical team is already in place, the drama already unfolding, and the dialogue with the hostage-taker already under way. That's how it was here in that farmhouse when I arrived. Our guys had isolated Leaf on the second floor. Leaf had shot out the lights. The standoff was deep into its second act. And now it fell to me to bring about a peaceful resolution, if there was a peaceful resolution to be had. Anyway, that was the desired course. Next best thing would be to get the woman and child to safety—and, if necessary, to take Leaf out if we had an open shot. Understand, this last wasn't our preferred option, but it was most definitely an option.

The first thing I did, after assessing the situation, was reach out for the available background information on Leaf and his hostages. I got on the phone and spoke to Max Howard, the FBI agent in New England who'd been investigating the kidnapping. These days, of course, you can pick up a lot of this information en route, on a cellular line, but in 1986 we were still in the Dark Ages in the Bureau as far as telecommunications were concerned. I made the call from a landline in our command post, but it was too important to leave to an intermediary. I wouldn't have known what questions to ask next until I'd heard the answers to the ones I'd asked before. As a negotiator, the more information I have on the person I'm up against, the better my chances for a successful outcome. The more I know, the more I can do. The more psychological hooks I can put out in a negotiation, the greater the likelihood that my adversary is going to reach for one of them. In life, information is power; in a hostage situation, it's essential.

The woman's name, I learned, was Cheryl Hart. Her son was four years old, the product of a volatile relationship with Charles Leaf. On at least one previous occasion Leaf had kidnapped the little boy—in the dead of winter, with little or no clothing for the boy. That one time, Leaf abruptly decided to let the child go, but he was fearful of being apprehended while returning the child to his mother so he instead directed the boy to approach a stranger on the street and ask for help, leaving the child to fend for himself. Leaf had a history of alcoholism, I learned from the investigator, and a possible history of drug abuse. He had recently lost a parent, and his best friend had been killed in an accident. He had been living in a cabin in the woods that he had built himself, but it had just burned down and he had no place to live. He'd also just lost his job—in all, a quadruple whammy he'd have a hard time overcoming.

Before we even said one word to this guy, I began to build a psychological profile in my head. The picture that came back was scary. I got a picture of someone whose life was going to turn on this incident. One way or the other, this would make him or break him. Everything that could have gone wrong in Leaf's life up until this moment had gone horribly wrong, and here I imagined he'd made a decision to set things right in what ways he could. Either he was going to force this woman to be his wife and force this child to stay with him, or he would die trying. He was looking for something, someone, to hold on to, and the only anchor within reach was this child, and this child's mother, who for her part had been so afraid of this guy she'd taken to sleeping with a knife wedged between her mattress and box spring. She even took the knife with her into the shower, like a reverse replay from the Alfred Hitchcock movie *Psycho*. The poor woman was convinced Leaf would come after her, in the dead of some night, and that's just what happened. In the middle of the night he kicked in the door of her parents' home, where she'd been staying. Then he dragged her through the house at gunpoint, with the child in tow. She didn't have a chance to reach for her knife. He simply loaded them into his car and the race was on.

I had a real bad feeling about this one. I played out every scenario in my head and couldn't see a good outcome. It was a lot like a stalker case where the bad guy gets to thinking, *If I can't have you, then no one is going to have you,* and I had the sick feeling that Cheryl Hart's life, and the life of her son, were very much in jeopardy.

Our small negotiations team tried desperately to get Leaf to let us send up a Hostage Phone Line—a hard-line, two-way phone that would allow us to communicate directly with each other without first having to place a call—but he refused, and right away we were moved from our desired position. We were already in the dark, quite literally, and now the only way we could get a dialogue going was to shout up the stairs or through an open window. I never liked to do that, because in trying to get your voice to carry it can sound angry. Leaf could possibly perceive an edge in our shouting when we were really just trying to make ourselves heard, so the negotiations began at some disadvantage. Also, and significantly, we always wanted to keep a buffer zone between our negotiators and the hostage-taker, and the dedicated hostage phone was the best way to achieve that buffer. Now, in order to make ourselves heard up the stairwell or through the window, we had to put ourselves a little too close to Leaf's line of fire. As a result, we found ourselves talking less freely, less frequently, than I would have liked, and there were long pockets of quiet in that dark farmhouse as each of us—negotiators, SWAT, hostage-taker, and even hostages—considered our next moves. Half hours went by when nothing was said at all, and that's a good long time, in that kind of setting, for nothing to be said at all. I didn't think we had that kind of time, against the ticking time bomb I'd pegged this guy to be.

These moments were so tense that I sometimes caught my heart beating so loudly, I worried Leaf must be able to hear it across the way, like something out of Poe's "The Tell-Tale Heart."

Unbeknownst to us at the time, Leaf put a gun to Cheryl Hart's head at some point during the long night and raped her. We were all downstairs, wondering what the hell was going on up there, and there was nothing we could have done about it, but it happened on our watch so in a way we all felt responsible. Sickened and responsible.

Once or twice we heard from Cheryl Hart during the night, but there was nothing in her voice to indicate the distress that she was feeling or the sexual assault that had just taken place. We also heard from Leaf when he felt he had something to say. We didn't hear from the little boy, but the mother assured us that he was okay. Frightened but okay.

There was very little in the way of back-and-forth dialogue for the first several hours. I was concerned about the shouting, and about putting myself or another negotiator into harm's way, and at the same time Leaf didn't seem to want to connect just yet. With daybreak, though, we began to hear from him a little more frequently, and we took the opportunity to press him on his needs. That's always a good way in, to find out what the hostage-taker needs. Not what his demands are, but what his *needs* are. There's a difference. Anyone in a situation like that has personal, emotional, physical needs. It might be something as simple as a roll of toilet paper, or something to eat, or a pack of cigarettes. At some point early in the morning Leaf asked if we could retrieve some belongings from his tent site somewhere in the woods near the house. Evidently he had allowed the boy to bring along some toy cars and trucks, and they had been left in the tent. I took the request as another hopeful sign and the basis for future conversations. It showed me that there was a human being behind the monstrous acts of the past several days, that he wanted us to get these toys for his little boy. And it gave us some common ground—our children, and the toys they were always leaving underfoot—and for a while we were able to talk about something other than this standoff.

In that same while, we dispatched some of our guys to search the area for Leaf's tent site, but they couldn't find it, and when they came back empty-handed Leaf was upset. Whatever ground we'd gained interpersonally I felt we'd now lost, but I knew to keep him on point.

"Draw us a map, Charles," I said. "If you really want us to get these things, we're here to help you, but draw us a map. We need your help."

It's always a good idea to bring the hostage-taker into whatever effort is under way on his behalf, to make him a part of your team, so that's what I was hoping for here. I didn't want Leaf to feel we had dropped the ball or failed to follow through on a promise. I needed him to trust us, and we needed to establish a basis for that trust, and for the time being at least this was all we had to work with. This way, if we still couldn't find the site after a second look, it would be on him as much as would be on us. This way, we'd have given it our best shot—a phrase we of course would not have used with Charles Leaf.

So he drew us a map and we eventually located the camping site and the little boy's model cars and trucks, and when we brought them back there was another basis for dialogue. We were still pressing Leaf to tell us how we could make him comfortable, to help us to help him. The situation was stable as far as we were concerned, and it wouldn't do for Leaf to start thinking he needed to move. One of the last things we wanted was for him to try to move with his hostages, to "go mobile" into a car, or a bus, or a boat, or—worst of all—a plane. When you go from a stable, contained situation to a mobile situation like that, it changes the whole equation, so I very much wanted to keep him in place, and a great way to do this was to keep him waiting for a series of deliveries, for these various things he might ask us to get, for him, and to use that time to possibly wear him down through personal conversation. We negotiators would rather bore a hostage-taker to death than kill him.

After the toy cars and trucks, Leaf wanted something to eat. Invariably the hostage-taker will ask for something to eat or drink before too terribly long, and I've always found these requests instructive. It could be for something inconsequential like a can of Coke, but it's a bit more complicated than dropping a couple quarters in a vending machine. It sets in motion a whole series of discussions. Really, there are so many layers of bureaucracy you have to muddle through, just to get this guy his can of Coke, so many man-hours of consulting and decision-making. The time and the skill sets involved in bringing back this one soda might run into thousands of dollars in man-hour costs. That's one expensive can of Coke! It can even get to be a power struggle or a turf thing among us agents, and between agencies, over which one of our people is actually dispatched to fetch the can of soda.

Sometimes there's a split between SWAT and the negotiators, and usually the one side jumps to conclusions about the other based on stereotypical assumptions. We negotiating types were always dismissing our SWAT colleagues as knuckle-dragging gorillas, and the tactical guys had us pegged as wimpy social workers. You know: one side would want to just shoot the bastard and get it over with, and the other side would find every reason to put the guy on welfare for the rest of his life. There never seemed to be any kind of middle ground.

Happily, on this early morning, both sides were at least somewhat in agreement on the food issue—principally because of the mother and child involved—at least initially. If Charles Leaf needed to eat, then so did Cheryl Hart and her son. The only problem with this was Leaf also started asking for a couple weeks' worth of food supplies—canned goods, boxed foods, provisions he could include in his getaway plans. The two requests got tied together. If we were going to get him something to eat, on the order of breakfast, we might just as well bring back these additional provisions. And, as it happened, we had an FBI helicopter parked in a nearby field, and he wanted to see us load the bird up with boxes of food, so we could clearly and dramatically demonstrate our good-faith efforts to meet his requests. I was all for it. I couldn't think of a better visual argument for how cooperative we were hoping to be than to load down our chopper with boxes of food. Of course, there didn't have to be any canned goods or other food-stuffs in those boxes, but we had to go through the motions just the same. We had to demonstrate to Leaf that we were willing to meet his demands and that we were taking him seriously.

I should explain here that in virtually every hostage situation that I worked for the Bureau, I was not the FBI Special Agent in Charge—a distinction that usually falls to the SAC of one of the FBI's then fifty-five field offices around the country. In this case the SAC was Terry O'Connor, another lawyer by training and a man who was always willing to hear a considered opinion in a crisis situation. And I always had a counterpart on the tactical side; here it was HRT Supervisor Steve Wiley, a tall, thin agent who would eventually be promoted to lead the FBI's Critical Incident Response Group, the successor to the HRT. Steve was a former HRT sniper, and we had worked together on the CSA standoff in Arkansas; he knew by experience that negotiations work, but he also knew the ability of HRT snipers, a good combination to have on this scene.

Final decisions, though, came down to the SAC, who had to listen to Steve's tactical presentation and my negotiating presentation about this not-so-simple breakfast issue. I felt strongly that we should feed this guy; for a while, though, Steve felt just as strongly that we should not. I believed that when you put some food in a guy's tummy, you can bring him down a notch or two emotionally. Realize, this guy hadn't slept for most of the night. Who knew when he'd last eaten?

He was tense, agitated, fatigued, and probably not thinking too clearly. I thought, with the light of day and some scrambled eggs in his belly, perhaps he'd see his situation a little differently. Maybe he'd fall asleep and the hostages could walk away. In any case, it might offer an opening to find a good way to end this standoff.

Hey, Charlie. No big deal. You haven't done anything that bad, not yet. It's not even clear you've broken any laws. All you've done is taken your kid and your common-law wife for an adventure, shown them a new part of the country. Maybe she wasn't that crazy about coming along, but she's here, isn't she? I don't hear her crying out for help, do you? Must be, deep down, she wants to be with you, am I right? And that convenience store in town? That's nothing. You borrowed some food when you were hungry, no big deal. And you needed to feed the boy, didn't you? Look, why don't you come outside and we can talk about it some more?

In a hostage-barricade situation, you always try to minimize what the bad guy has done. Minimize, minimize, minimize. Everything is no big deal. I'm repeating myself here, I know, but it's an essential point, getting the bad guy to think that nothing he's done is too terribly bad. Certainly, nothing is beyond repair and whatever he's facing can't possibly be as bad as it looks. You don't want the hostage-taker to feel he's crossed any kind of line to where there's no going back, because then you take a guy who's teetering on the edge of violence and send him over the top. No one wants to think of himself as a bad person—no one wants to see his situation as hopeless—so you reach for whatever good you can find in this bad scenario. You make it up if you have to. Or you put a positive spin on an obvious transgression. *Yeah, buddy, but you've only killed three people so far, and who's to say those three didn't deserve it?* I've talked out child molesters and found myself saying things like, "You know these little girls, five and six years old, walking around with those short dresses like they're asking for it . . ." I hear myself talking and I want to puke, but that's the drill. That's how it's done. You want to reach over and choke the life out of the guy, but you can't, and so you sit there and invite him to open up to you, and soon enough he leans forward and you can tell he's agreeing with you, everything about his body language has gone soft, and you think, *You bastard, I got you. You know I got you.*

We weren't getting any of that from Leaf just yet—and I didn't think we would, because I couldn't imagine us getting any time face-to-face, the way this standoff was playing out. Sometimes in a negotiation I've sat down with the hostage-taker, man-to-man, face-to-face. Other negotiators have too. It can be a very scary thing. In a fraction of a second, if the bad guy's got a gun or a bomb, he can kill you, kill himself, kill both of you. I didn't think so, but I had to consider the possibility that this would turn out to be another "suicide by cop" case, but I'd been there before too. The entire exchange is shot through with such in-your-face risk you can almost taste it if your mouth weren't so dry, but you do it for the advantage it can bring. You do it because there's no substitute for looking in the bad guy's eyes, for studying his body language, how he holds his weapon, how he wears his clothes or parts his hair. You do it because sometimes you can't *not* do it, if the opening presents itself. There are so many tells in the way we present ourselves, and that's one of the aspects we lose when we have to do our negotiating over the phone—or, as was the case here, shouting up and down a staircase.

But at least Leaf was talking, and we did what we could to keep the conversation going. Beneath the back-and-forth with Leaf there was also the back-and-forth between our tactical and negotiating teams about how to actually deliver the food, and when, and under what terms. The tactical team wanted to use the delivery as an opening to rescue one of the hostages. They had it all worked out in their minds. They'd place the food halfway up the stairs, in such a way that Leaf would have to come down to get it, or send someone to pick it up. Leaf probably knew better, and most likely the kid was too little to fetch a tray of food, so Leaf would probably send Cheryl, at which point our guys could stage some sort of snatch-and-grab, some sort of rescue. The thinking here seemed to be: if you can save at least one of the two hostages, that's a good thing—and it typically is a good thing, only in this case I didn't see that it made any sense. What mother would leave her child's side in this kind of situation? Even if she stepped outside her upstairs room to retrieve a tray of food, that wouldn't mean she'd want to be pulled from Leaf's custody, pulled away from her child. It's awfully hard to rescue someone who doesn't want to be rescued. I told the SWAT guys and the SAC that if they tried to pull this woman down the stairs, she'd be kicking and screaming and trying to get back to her child. Leaf would very likely be roused by the commotion and head to the top of the stairs with the child for cover and start shooting.

Again, to reinforce an all-important point: I always approached these standoffs from a worst-case perspective. Whatever could go wrong in a hostage situation, I expected it to go wrong. Whatever the parameters were between our best and worst outcomes, I expected the worst. Anything more I took as a bonus, but I never counted on anything more, so I laid out my reasoning to the SAC. I don't mean to make these tactical guys out to be evil, or anything of the sort. They're good guys, all of them, and I could certainly understand where they were coming from. I mean, if they can reduce the hostage load by 50 percent, that's a pretty good day, and I can see how they'd think that was a pretty good day, but I had a different perspective.

We ended up leaving the food on the stairs and agreeing not to make a move for the woman if she was sent to retrieve it. We were still hoping against hope that maybe Leaf would be stupid enough to step out for it himself, without his hostages as human shields. It was a long shot, but it wasn't without precedent. I once had an airline hijacker ask for a pack of cigarettes; we parked a car on the tarmac alongside the plane, and we put the cigarettes on the roof of the car and told the guy that's where they were, and sure enough he came down himself to get them. SWAT jumped him; case closed. (Thank God for nicotine addictions.) Sometimes these idiots make our job easy. Of course, Leaf wanted us to deliver the food right to his door, but we told him that wasn't happening. We told him there was no way we were sending one of our guys to the top of the stairs, where he could get shot, told him in such a way that he couldn't really argue the point, and so we agreed on this halfway deal. It was up to Leaf to figure out how to get the food the rest of the way. We'd keep him thinking, wear him out, and if he came down for it himself we could take him out, one way or another; if he sent Cheryl Hart for the food, we'd have to leave her alone and let her complete the delivery; if he sent the boy, there was still some thinking on the tactical side that we would have to pounce and somehow bring the child to safety, even if it put the mother in further danger.

Just to cover all angles, our agents prepared handwritten signs that they would hold out for Cheryl Hart to read if she was the one sent out for the food. *Are you okay? Do you want to run?* It was crude, and basic, but it would be the only way we could communicate silently with Cheryl on that open, vulnerable stairwell. As it happened, Leaf sent her down for the food, and she waved away our signs and retreated immediately to the upstairs room to rejoin her son. And as she did so I thought, *Of course: How could she do any differently? What mother would do anything differently?*

I knew the food would keep Leaf occupied for the next while—we'd also included a pack of cigarettes, as a further gesture of goodwill—so I took the time to get something to eat. It was late morning and I hadn't had a bite of food and hardly any sleep, and it was important for me to keep sharp. It's not just the emotional and physical well-being of the bad guys we have to worry about; we also have to take care of ourselves. We've all been in days-long hostage-barricade situations where if we didn't find time to eat or sleep we'd have been of no use. Sleep deprivation and empty stomachs make for poor decision making, something we couldn't afford. Anyway, there were other negotiators in place to handle anything that might come up, and the situation was stable, and we all assumed this standoff still had a long way to go before playing out, so I grabbed Steve from HRT and we headed back toward our command post at the fire station in town. It was just a two-minute drive, but we might as well have been a thousand miles away, because a call came in on the radio just as we were pulling in, telling us we needed to be back on the scene immediately. Leaf was flipping out. No one could tell us what had triggered the change, but he was all of a sudden threatening to kill the woman, kill the kid, kill himself, take out a few of our agents along the way. We had no idea what had set him off after such a point of emotional calm, but the feeling now was that whatever was about to go down was going down now.

"I thought you said he'd quiet down," Steve said on the ride back to the scene, taking the easy opportunity to needle me on my position regarding the food.

"I guess I was wrong," I allowed.

It was all about to hit the fan.

When we got back on the scene, Leaf was ranting and raging something fierce. So much for the full belly acting as pacifier. So much for the pause for each side to figure a next move. He wanted our helicopter to fly him out of there. He wanted a car. He wanted money. He wanted all kinds of things, and I became absolutely convinced that his threats against Cheryl Hart and his son were not at all empty. There was no talking to this guy. Whatever good faith we had established with the food and the cigarettes and the loading of boxes onto that helicopter, it had somehow gone out that open second-floor window with his shouting, and I moved from thinking we had a stable, contained situation to knowing that the only resolution would be to get these two hostages out of the house, to get Leaf thinking we would give in to his demands and get him moving in a direction we wanted.

It went against my preferred strategy, but the threat level was not what it had been just a half hour earlier. Leaf had ratcheted things up in such a way that Cheryl Hart and her son were now at immediate risk, so we needed to change tactics.

We came to the conclusion that the only way to save these two hostages was to create a diversionary situation to bring Leaf out of the house on false pretenses and set him up in that field so that the HRT snipers could get an open shot at him. Now, my HRT and SWAT counterparts weren't used to hearing such endgame scenarios from negotiating types like me. Remember, we were the wimpy social reformers. We were the ones who wanted to talk instead of act. I rarely made a case for the tactical guys to take someone out, but I felt Leaf had left us no choice. He'd made the case himself, really. My instinct had always been to resist, resist, resist; to talk things through until there was nothing left to say; to hold back until the last possible minute, seeking a peaceful outcome, withholding the final option. We still didn't know for certain whether Leaf was prepared to use force, but he had a loaded rifle and his emotions were high. He had nothing to lose and nothing to gain—a dangerous combination of negative outcomes. We couldn't afford to wait for him to kill one of the hostages in order to justify making our move to save the other. The only thing to do, really, was to make a preemptive tactical move on his life. When it comes to second-guessing, I'd rather second-guess myself on the decision to take a bad guy's life than on the decision to wait that bad guy out on the thin hope that he wouldn't take an innocent life.

Interestingly, it was a very unemotional process, talking our options through with SAC O'Connor, Steve from the HRT, Wayne, the local SWAT team leader, and a commander from the VA troopers, although the troopers knew it was our show to win or lose. The weight of what we were talking about—the taking of a man's life—didn't really register in the discussion, and looking back I've tried to understand how such a thing was possible. I mean, it's one thing for a police officer to encounter an armed bank robber and, in the heat of the moment, with lives on the line, make a decision to fire his weapon to save a life. It's either you or the bad guy. Pull the trigger, or you're dead. But there we were, standing on a dusty, dirty road in a small, picture-perfect town in Virginia on a beautiful fall day, discussing who was going to live and who was going to die in a very sterile, analytical, unemotional way. I made my case to my colleagues. I said I thought Leaf was a significant threat, fully capable of killing Cheryl Hart and her child at any moment. I reminded everyone that he'd already used his weapon, for no real reason at all, and that he had a history of violence against the mother of his child and a history of significant losses. I thought that if we didn't move him to another location, or give the appearance of meeting his demands, that people were going to die—not just the two hostages, but in the extreme some of our agents and/or troopers. And I felt confident that, through negotiation and guile, we could get this man outside, to where our snipers would have a clear shot at him. Our chances of reaching a peaceful conclusion had gone from slim to none. I didn't see another way out—and I didn't see that we would have another chance with Leaf.

Of course, I could have been wrong, and people have asked me over the years how I could have been so sure on this, sure enough to recommend the taking of another man's life. And I have no good answer. "What if you had waited?" people ask. "Maybe at the last minute he would have thrown his gun down and surrendered." Maybe. Maybe not. I'll never know. I'm not God. I'm some guy who grew up in a midwestern steel town, with a state college education, making life-and-death decisions based solely on my experience, on my gut, on what the situation calls for. I could be wrong, but I had to bet that I was right. And I had to bet the lives of others, because nothing less was at stake. We negotiators are like everyone else: We like to win. We want to be successful, to talk the bad guys into surrendering, slap ourselves on the back, high-five our colleagues, and go home. But winning takes all forms, and here it meant *not losing*. Here it meant negotiating Leaf into a position where he'd be the easiest possible target and to eliminate the dangers he presented to those around him. Here it meant getting Cheryl Hart and her son to safety, whatever it took.

It all meant something far different to Charles Leaf, however. He was not about to give up that woman and child. No, that much appeared certain. It was his child—and, in his mind, Cheryl Hart was his woman. Every scenario we talked about had him making his getaway with the two hostages in tow, to where they might start a new life as a shell of a family—this was his delusion, his fairy tale of a belief system—so I took that as a given. We moved from there and on to the next point of contention. In any negotiation you have to be prepared to give something up, to create the belief on the part of your opposite number that he has gained some sort of advantage. This is especially so in a life-and-death negotiation such as this, with good pitted against evil, and I had to look for ways to get Leaf thinking things were going his way. I had to give him an edge. It's just like a used-car deal: You want five thousand dollars for it, and I offer thirty-five hundred dollars. How much am I willing to give? How much are you willing to take? Somewhere in the middle, that's the selling price, and in this particular situation the selling price was whatever it was Leaf had to hear in order to get him to come outside. That was the deal. And, no matter what, Leaf could never feel like we were jerking his chain. As a negotiator, I never believed in lying to people—or, at least, never lying in any kind of transparent way. Like I always said, I didn't want there to be any surprises but for the last surprise. We told the bad guy what he was going to see, what he was going to hear, what was going to happen next. And we told him why. We had to get him to trust us, to bond, and we had to use that trust to manipulate him into whatever position or situation we needed him to be in. That was our job, what we called the tactical role of the negotiator, and we meant to do it well.

Leaf made the obvious request. He wanted the helicopter to take him, Cheryl Hart, and the boy from the scene, and he wanted only one pilot in the chopper with them. I could see his point, but I showed him mine. We told him it was FBI policy to fly only with two pilots, pointed out to him that FAA regulations demanded a second pilot as a safety precaution: in the event of an injury or a heart attack, there'd be another pilot on board to take over the controls. Naturally, we could have promised Leaf anything, because there was no way that helicopter was taking off with Leaf and his hostages on board. That was just not going to happen. But we still had to get him to leave the house and cross that field to the chopper, and in order to do that we had to make him feel like he had some kind of control; we had to make him a believer. We had to offer credible resistance, or he would never have bought my concession. We argued the one-pilot, two-pilot issue for the longest time. Leaf quite reasonably felt that a second pilot put him at risk; he must have seen too many bad television movies and figured the one pilot would fly the bird and the other would attempt to overpower or shoot him in midair. It was a real sticking point in his mind, while to me it wasn't an issue either way except in how Leaf perceived it. Ultimately, we gave up on the second pilot, but we gave up *hard*. We needed him to think he'd won something, to be so caught up in this one small victory he developed a kind of tunnel vision about everything else.

Make that one critical error in judgment, Charlie. Just one.

The helicopter was a great visual stimulus. Charles Leaf could see that bird parked in the field all morning long, and he could see us loading those boxes of food, per his request, and at some point I asked pilot and FBI agent Tom Kelly to get the rotors spinning. Actually, I spent a long time with Tom, telling him why I wanted him to take off, and when I wanted him to take off, and at what angle—in such a way that it might disorient Leaf and take him by surprise while providing some element of protection for Tom and his bird. Remember, I didn't like there to be any surprises in a tense negotiation such as this, but for that last deadly surprise, the one that came so fast Leaf wouldn't be able to react. Here I wanted to be dead certain that if Leaf made it as far as the chopper, he'd be in for the surprise of his life. We rehearsed the whole thing and hoped like hell Leaf would respond in predictable ways—and in order for that to happen, each twist and turn had to be logically connected to the twists and turns that preceded it. The chopper had been still and silent, but the notion of firing up the engines and getting those blades spinning had a kind of integrity to it. It made sense, if Leaf was making to leave. Of course, he was never going to reach the helicopter—and, in the unlikely event that he did, it would never leave the ground. It just wasn't an option. To let an armed man on a helicopter—it was too ludicrous to even think about; but here was Charles Leaf, and that was all he was thinking about. To him, it made perfect sense, and it followed that those rotors should be spinning too.

Next, we had to make another key decision—and the tactical and negotiating sides were once again split. The only way I could get Leaf to come downstairs was to get our tactical guys to give up the first floor of the house, and they were not in the habit of giving up ground. As in a military operation, you don't give up ground that you've taken. You just don't. It's like we'd taken Pork Chop Hill and I was asking them to give it back to the North Koreans. Once they backed out, Leaf could have moved downstairs and changed his mind, and then where would we have been? He'd have the whole house and we'd have to start all over again.

Still, I pressed the matter, because there was no other way to move Leaf from the house to the field. We had to invest in one outcome or another, to let all the chips ride on one spin, and I didn't think he'd back down at this point from his desire to move. I didn't think he was going anywhere but toward that helicopter. Really, he was like a moth to a flame. His attention had been drawn to it for hours. It was his focus, his center, and eventually even the tactical guys were able to see this and they backed away from the house. Now it was up to Leaf to make his move, and I stood about a hundred yards away, along the fence line to the property; one of the local tactical agents tried to bet me ten dollars that Leaf would never come out that front door, and I told him I wasn't in the habit of betting on such things but that if I was I would surely take that bet. "He's coming out," I said, out into the cool air of the Virginia autumn, which was being whipped into swirls by the spinning rotors. "He's coming out."

I'd never been more certain of anything in my entire negotiating career—and at the same time I realized that you just never know. In my line of work, you can be certain and still have no idea. There were no crystal balls here. There never are..

For a long time we waited for the front door of that farmhouse to burst open. Our agents were out of the house and in places of cover in and around the field and into the surrounding woods. Our observer/sniper teams—with the radio call signs Sierra (for *Sniper*) One, Sierra Two, Sierra Three—were in position. I stood at the edge of the clearing, leaning against a fence post, listening to our tactical radio, waiting for something to happen. The plan was for several members of our tactical team to retake the house from the rear as soon as Leaf cleared the front door; another group would seal the perimeter; as soon as he crossed the threshold, there'd be no place for him to go—nowhere to run, nowhere to hide. And yet, we all had a terribly uneasy feeling. Charles Leaf might have been outnumbered and outflanked—and he was about to be outmaneuvered as well—but he still had the hostages; in this one regard, at least, he was still holding all the cards.

And so we waited.

Finally the door swung open and Leaf stepped outside with the two hostages held close. His son was sitting on his shoulders, like he was taking the kid to the mall or lifting him for a better view at a ballgame. The boy's legs were tied to Leaf's neck and shoulders with the sash from a bathrobe so he wouldn't topple over. Cheryl Hart was out in front, Leaf's arm around her neck with a knife to her throat. In his other hand he carried a sawed-off rifle with the barrel pressed to the back of her head. They moved as one body, their three heads so perilously close together there was no way our snipers could get a shot off.

I looked on and had to hand it to Leaf. The guy hadn't impressed me in any of our conversations as being particularly smart or scheming, and his background left nothing to suggest a man who planned things out to any great degree, but this business with the child astride his head on a shoulder ride was a masterstroke. That, or a piece of dumb luck that would save his neck for the next few heartbeats.

The three of them moved slowly as they crossed from the house to the small picket fence they had to get past in order to reach the chopper, and as they approached I thought, *Okay, he'll have to let go of the boy or the woman in order to clear it.* The fence wasn't much of an obstacle but for the three-headed way they had to move. If you can picture it, all three heads were essentially touching: the boy's resting atop his father's, and the woman's pressed up against the father's chin. I listened to the reports on the radio from our sniper team and heard nothing encouraging: "Sierra One, I don't have a shot."

"Sierra Two, I don't have a shot."

"Sierra Three, no shot."

Then: silence as the teams concentrated, each sniper peering down the scope of a high-powered bolt-action rifle made especially for him. Snipers who could put five rounds in a fifty-cent piece from hundreds of yards away. Fingers on a trigger that could soon mean the difference between life and death for three people, one of whom certainly wouldn't walk out of that field.

Leaf had the three of them moving in such tight formation, their bodies knitted and fitted in such a way that there was no clearance, no safe opening for our guys to take that critical shot without the risk of hitting the boy or his mother.

Somehow Leaf cleared that fence without breaking stride, without offering an open shot, and he continued to move toward the chopper. At this point Tom, our pilot, began to take off—which wasn't quite according to plan. I wanted Leaf to be at least halfway between the farmhouse and the chopper before it left the ground, him at some midpoint of no return, but here he was only about a third of the way across that field, too close to the house, I felt, for things to go suddenly awry. The pilot took off in a kind of cant, as we had discussed, in such a way that he threw off as much dust and wind and commotion in Leaf's direction as possible. There was grass and leaves and straw and weeds, all being kicked around in these great swirls, and I worried that Leaf would double back toward the farmhouse for safe haven. The noise from those blades, up close, must have been deafening, and I was quietly ticked that it wasn't closer still, as we had prearranged with the pilot. I wanted Leaf to have thought the situation through in his head to where nothing could go wrong for him—and then I wanted everything to go wrong, all at once.

I wanted him to panic—hell, I *needed* him to panic—but I needed him to panic and continue moving forward. There could be no turning back. Everything would fall from this right here and now. I silently prayed: *Lord, save this woman and her child*. And I knew full well that in so doing I was also praying for the death of Charles Leaf.

Mercifully, Leaf kept moving toward the helicopter, and as the pilot lifted off, also by prearrangement, our HRT assault team members set off a sequence of explosive diversionary devices—flash-bangs— behind Leaf and to his right. Our hope was that Leaf would turn at the sudden sound and that another flash-bang, immediately following the first, would set him reeling. And that's just what happened. With that first flash-bang he dropped to his knees, the boy still astride his head, the woman yanked to the ground out in front of him. It all happened in an instant, a gasp. Leaf jammed the rifle barrel into the back of Cheryl Hart's skull and whispered, "Good-bye, Kitten." It was a name he used to call her, a name she hated, a name so thick with menace and disdain she knew she was about to die. She worried how long it would take for the bullet to actually pass through her head, how long it would take for her to die, how much pain she would be in and how long it would take before she didn't feel the pain anymore.

Just then a second flash-bang pulled Leaf's attention momentarily away from Cheryl Hart. He turned his head just so slightly in the direction of the flash, and in that half beat one of our snipers found the opening we were desperately looking for. Where the three heads had been in alignment and in constant contact, there was now a thin sliver of daylight separating Leaf from his hostages. The little boy had been thrown back slightly as his father turned, and the mother had leaned away, and from a distance of about sixty yards Sierra One squeezed off a round that somehow found its mark in the split second between impulse and action, before Leaf could finish squeezing his own trigger. The heavy .308 round snapped Leaf's head back like he'd been spring-loaded, and he landed on the little boy as the woman took off screaming to the other end of the field.

It was almost dreamlike. The beautiful fall day. The whipping dust and wind. The roar of the chopper blades, tipped against the sheer power of those engines. The manicured field set against the lovely yellow farmhouse. The collection of agents and troopers sprinkled about the property. The gray armored vehicle that stood as our forward command post. Life, and death, and everything else besides, and when it all settled down Cheryl Hart was still running across that field, her hands in the air, screaming like Estelle Parsons in *Bonnie and Clyde*, and Charles Leaf lay motionless atop his son, his back to the boy's belly. It took a beat or two for it to register that the boy was also not moving, and I became so sickened by this realization I almost threw up. Goodness, it was so revolting to me to even have to think that this innocent child had been hurt—worse, to consider that, by my influence, I might have been responsible for whatever may have happened to him. I started moving toward the tangle of bodies and praying for the kid to move. It was probably just a few seconds after the shot had been fired, but it could have been hours. It could have been days. It could have been half my life, when you see a child in that situation. I tried to tell myself that he was okay. I reminded myself how good our snipers were. Really, I'd trust them with my life. I knew there was no way the little boy had been hit—not directly, anyway. There was always the chance that the bullet could have fragmented on impact; it could have splintered the bones in Leaf's skull and sent a chunk of skull out the back of his head and into the face of the little boy pressed close behind him. Hell, the torque from the whiplashing of Leaf's head could have seriously injured the boy, if the two heads collided.

Anything was possible, and the kid was not moving, and I thought, *Oh. God. Please.*

Again, this piece of the drama could have taken just an instant to unfold, but there was enough time for the mother to run clear across the field. There was enough time for every inconceivable outcome to alight in my racing imagination. There was enough time for me to think about my three kids back home and wonder what had gone on with them today at school. There was all the time in the world and no time at all, both, and as all these thoughts jockeyed for position in my brain I kept crossing the field toward that little boy. He was now my focus. I willed him to move: a toe, a finger, something. And as I reached the spot where the boy lay, I stepped onto tactical team territory. This wasn't such a good move, bureaucratically speaking, but I didn't care; I was too frazzled to even register what I was doing. Just as I never liked it when these guys tried to do my negotiating, they didn't like it when I got in their way, and it fell to them to deal with the aftermath of the shooting, whatever that aftermath happened to be. That was their job. They were all medically trained, and there was a full team from HRT, including an emergency medical technician, working furiously on Charles Leaf from pretty much the moment he hit the ground. As I moved toward the boy, I had time to think how absurdly ironic it was that a minute earlier we'd been devoting our entire on-site resources to killing this man, and here we were devoting our entire on-site resources to trying to save him. It was the strangest, most incongruous thing.

But Charles Leaf was dead, and there were no heroic measures or advances in medical rescue techniques that would ever bring him back. That .308 round through his head had seen to that. Our guys just had to go through these motions, just to be sure.

One HRT assaulter reached the boy a couple seconds ahead of me and hoisted him up into the air, and as he did so I could see the child's legs moving. I thought, *Thank God! Just Thank God.* And I did, I surely did. I might have dropped to my knees and cried but for what happened next. The tactical agent saw me approach and quickly spun on his heels and held the kid out to me like he was handing over a sack of mail. He was used to dealing with bad guys, I guess, and not frightened little kids. He was nice enough to the child, and comforting in what ways a man in black tactical clothing and a Kevlar helmet and weight-bearing vest could manage, but this was clearly not his area of expertise, and he must have figured the wimp social-worker hostage negotiator would be a little more suited to the task, a little more touchy-feely.

I grabbed the boy gladly—joyfully, even; only one squeeze and I could tell straightaway why the tactical agent had been so eager to pass the boy off on me. The little guy had soiled his pants, and I thought to myself that if there was ever a good reason to soil your pants it would be over what he'd just been through. Anyway, it was nothing. To the tactical agent it was a messy, big deal, but to a father of three kids it was nothing.

I carried the boy over to the tree line, about twenty-five steps away from where he had fallen, from where Charles Leaf lay dead. I set the child down on the grass. "Charlie," I said—his name was Charles Leaf II, and as I gave it voice I realized I hadn't thought of him as anything but "the boy," or "the child," or "the son," that's how detached and unemotional I'd been during the long hours of that standoff— "my name's Clint. Let's get you cleaned up."

All I had was a handkerchief that I pulled from my back pocket, and I couldn't do a very thorough job of it, but I managed to make him a little more comfortable, thinking to myself almost with a smile how it was that negotiators always landed the crappy jobs. That became my focus, making this innocent child a little more comfortable, wiping away some of his embarrassment, distracting him from the horrors he'd just experienced. I tried to talk to him, but I couldn't think of a single appropriate thing to say. What do you say to a four-year-old kid after his father's head has just been blown to bits between his own little legs? He pulled his pants back up and jumped back into my arms, just before his mother crossed to where we were at the edge of the field, and I was able to hand little Charlie over to Cheryl Hart. It was a nice thing to be able to do, this simple, natural act, placing a child in his mother's arms. They fell into a happy, tearful embrace, and I backed away, thinking that my work was done. Or, at least, that one piece of my work was done.

There were still some details to tie together, and the first of these for me was to seek out the sniper, Sierra One, who had shot Leaf and talk through the incident with him from all angles. Technically this wasn't part of my job, but it was something I had to do as a kind of courtesy. I mean, this guy was trained to be automatically professional in a situation like this, but no one's automatic all the time. He was most likely a husband and a father, and on some level he had to deal with the fact that he'd just taken a human life. He deserved to know why he had to pull that trigger, to balance out what he had done with why he had to do it, and I wanted to lay it out for him. Think about it: it's not like somebody stuck a gun in his face and he had to draw his own weapon to protect himself. No, he had lain some sixty yards away and looked down the barrel of his weapon through a six- or eight-power scope, put his crosshairs on the side of somebody's head— somebody he had never met—and punched a hole right through that head. Because we said it had to be done. It wasn't even a decision he'd been allowed to participate in. He was just part of a process, the end of the line to our endgame strategy. So I wanted to be sure he understood why things went down in just this way, why they had to have gone down in just this way.

I quickly found him. As it turned out, it was someone I knew rather well: a kind, mild-mannered, thoughtful, and intelligent professional I'd trained in hostage negotiation who had joined HRT to save lives. I laid it all out for him, and he listened, and when I was through he turned to me and said, "Clint, you're a good negotiator. I know you guys did everything you could. I know there was no other way. I don't look at it that I took one life. I feel that I saved two."

I was incredibly relieved that this man was so cool, so professional, to be able to process everything in such a logical, forthright, do-what-you've-got-to-do manner. He trusted us to do our jobs, just as we had trusted him to do his, and we managed to save two innocent lives. That was the heart of it.

Eventually I made my way back to the command post at the firehouse, and the SAC took me aside and inquired how things had gone with the sniper who took the shot. Then he asked if I would sit down and talk with Cheryl Hart and her son. Here again, it wasn't part of my job but I looked on these exchanges as part of the package, and to tell the truth I always welcomed the chance to talk to the victims at the other end of these ordeals. At the very least, it meant that we'd been successful, because they were still alive for me to talk to. I wanted to impress upon this woman how hard we had tried to talk Leaf down from his position, how carefully we had looked at all options, and how she'd done everything right during the standoff. Really, I was scared to death that she'd in some way feel responsible, and I wanted her to have our assurance that none of this had been her fault. Nothing that had happened before the abduction, nothing that had happened in the days since, and nothing that had happened on this day in particular.

I found her sitting with little Charlie in a big, empty hall off to the side of the firehouse. There was a table and two chairs sitting opposite, and I sat myself down on a folding chair to face her. Before we even got to talking, she asked me if I'd like to hold little Charlie, and I thought that was such a tremendous gesture. I was overwhelmed. You'd think, after what she'd just been through, she'd never let that child out of her clutches again, and here she was, just a half hour later, handing him over to me. She'd cleaned him up some and managed to get him into fresh clothes, but it wouldn't have mattered either way, not to me.

I sat with little Charlie on my lap and carefully walked Cheryl Hart through the events of the past hours, making sure to point out our reasoning behind each and every decision we'd made along the way. She let me say what I had to say, without interruption, and when I was through she said, "I understand." That's all: "I understand." Then she said, "The only thing that had me worried, after you'd shot him, when all the men in black came running out and started working on him, trying to save him, that they'd bring him back to life and he'd do this to us all over again."

As we talked, little Charlie sat in my lap, softly pounding his right fist into his left palm, over and over and over. There was a kind of soothing rhythm to it, as if he were lost in the motion. He didn't say a word. He didn't cry. He didn't fuss. He just sat very quietly and otherwise still on my lap, continuing to tap his little fist into his little hand, over and over and over, and I looked on and couldn't help thinking what this horrific experience must have looked like from his perspective. At such a young age, with such limited verbal skills and such a limited worldview, he couldn't have had any real idea what had just taken place. He couldn't really know that a spinning bullet had just passed through his father's head, while his own little legs had been wrapped around that same head. He couldn't really know that he would never see this man again. He couldn't really know how close he and his mother had been to their own deaths. He couldn't really know what death was. I don't care how many homicides he'd maybe seen on how many television shows, how many video games he'd possibly play where the goal was to blow off some guy's head—he couldn't really know. There was nothing, really, for this little boy to put into words— nothing to do beyond this soft, rhythmic pounding of his fist against his palm—and it was into this simple, repetitive act that he placed his fear, his anger, his frustration, his confusion . . . every little emotion he was experiencing and working to understand just traveled through his little body and out his little fist.

It was probably the most heart-wrenching moment of my entire career, to have to consider what this child had just been through, to have to look past his steady, rhythmic tapping to see the faces of my own children, Jeff, Jenna, and Jon. They'd been asleep when I ducked out of the house the night before, and they'd be asleep when I got back later that night, but they were there with me in spirit, with me and little Charlie, struggling to make sense out of a senseless act that would surely mark this child for the rest of his life. In one way or another, whether he could articulate it or not, now or in the future, he would be forever changed.

My eyes welled up, and I couldn't stop the tears from coming, and Cheryl Hart nodded that she understood.

After we made our good-byes, I drove my tired old Honda to the nearest pay phone and called home, and caught my wife, Dianne, cleaning up after dinner. "I haven't heard from you," she said. "Everything all right?"

No, everything was not all right, but I couldn't come right out and say so. Everything had turned out okay in the end, considering, but everything was not all right. I wanted to tell Dianne about the boy, about little Charlie. I wanted to tell her about the professionalism of our sniper, about the SAC and the other negotiators and tactical team members. I wanted to tell her about the way this woman had slept with a knife under her mattress, to protect her from her child's father. I wanted to share it all, but I was all choked up, and there wasn't time, and so I simply said, "We had to kill a man to save a mother and her child."

That was what it all came down to.

"Did *you* kill him?" she wanted to know.

I thought about it before answering. In the most literal sense, no, I did not pull the trigger, but our snipers had been prepared to fire, and the SAC had given the order to do so based on my opinion and my initiative. I made the case for it, and the HRT sniper carried it out. The SAC made the final decision to move forward with our plan, based on my recommendation. And so, if you want to talk about ultimate responsibility, I was all over this one, and as I thought about this I thought, too, about how rare it is for people to claim responsibility for their actions. In this case, there was no way to duck it—not that I would, anyway. Charles Leaf, if he'd gotten the chance to plead his case before some judge, would have probably blamed some other person, or some other thing, for what went down in that farmhouse and out in that field. It's one of the great problems of our society, and it drives me nuts. Everybody wants to lay this or that off on someone else. There's a built-in excuse for everything.

Oh, I wasn't breast-fed.

The Devil made me do it.

My parents beat the crap out of me when I was a child.

I was poor.

I was rich.

People used to hook car batteries up to my earlobes.

And on and on. I listen to all of these excuses and cringe. If you want to know who's responsible, look in the mirror. Don't look left.

Don't look right. Don't blame society. Don't blame the school system. Don't blame your mother. After all these years dealing with serial killers and rapists and bad guys like Charles Leaf, I don't buy any of that. I can't. I can't shake thinking that every time someone wraps his hands around some woman's neck and squeezes the life out of her, every time someone holds a gun to somebody's head or takes a child off into the woods and molests him . . . every time, they have a choice. And the choice is: *I can turn around and go home or I can do this terrible thing.*

I don't know why, but that's where Dianne's question took me, at just that moment. *Did you kill him?* "No," I said. "I didn't pull the trigger, but, you know . . ." My voice trailed off, and I didn't finish my thought. I didn't need to. I had a long drive ahead of me, and there would be time to explain it all later—or not—and as I pulled away I wondered once again how it was that the stuff of my days kept obscuring the stuff of my life. I mean, I'd been working this standoff for about eighteen hours, from the moment I'd picked up the phone the night before, and in that whole time I had barely permitted my thoughts to drift back to my family. Oh, every now and then I'd get a picture in my head of what was going on back home, or the idea of what this father was doing to this kid would bump right up against my idea of how things were with my wife and our three children, and I'd wonder where the reality lay. There's a constant tug and pull, when you work on the front lines of law enforcement, to separate what you do for a living from how you live, and it's an endless struggle. It truly is. When you get to the edge of the abyss and you peer over and see the depths of inhumanity, the bottom of that bottomless pit, you've got to be careful you don't fall over that edge. You've got to be able to check in and think to yourself, *That's not reality.* The bottom of that pit, that's not reality. Reality is my wife, Dianne. Reality is our three kids. Reality is a broken vacuum cleaner. Reality is having to change the oil in your car, or trying to figure out how to get three kids to three different soccer fields for three different games, with two adults and two cars to get them there.

And for Cheryl Hart, a woman who would send me Christmas cards for the next several years, thanking me for whatever part I'd played in saving her and her little Charlie, reality is having to make sense out of a harrowing ordeal that made no sense at all.

One more chapter in the book entitled *Man's Inhumanity to Man*, and the pages continue to fill. . . .

"TURN AND WALK AWAY"

The most emotionally and physically draining standoff of my career had its roots in a concurrent set of prison riots in November 1987, which in turn had their roots in the crosscurrents of the 1980 Mariel Boatlift, which of course flowed from the oppressive living conditions in Fidel Castro's Cuba—in all, an international chain reaction that washed upon our shores and sent us reeling.

Just to refresh our collective memory, the Mariel Boatlift was the large-scale exodus of more than 125,000 Cubans to American shores, played out for the media as if it might have been staged and set to music. At first blush it was a heart-wrenching scene. I can still remember looking on at the dramatic footage from that boatlift, night after night on the network news, wondering about the hopelessness and despair that had led these apparently good people to such extreme circumstances, never once thinking that these images would come back to haunt me on the job—or that there was perhaps more to those images than I knew at first to consider.

You know, it was always remarkable to me throughout my time in the FBI the way front-burner world issues would inevitably become the stuff of my days, and the stuff of these particular days was perhaps the most remarkable of all. Here's what happened: immediately following the boatlift, an Immigration and Naturalization Service (INS) review of each individual detainee revealed that approximately 20 percent of the Cubans seeking exile in the United States had a history of criminal activity or mental illness; subsequently, thousands of Cuban detainees were assigned to federal prison facilities around the country, including more than 1,400 to the United States Penitentiary in Atlanta, Georgia, and an additional 1,000 or so to the Federal Detention Center in Oakdale, Louisiana.

Flash forward to November 1987 and a U.S. State Department report calling for the repatriation of up to 2,500 Cuban nationals, and you had the makings of a brewing protest among the hundreds of Cuban inmates still incarcerated in those federal facilities. As we'd learn all too well and all too soon, it was a real powder keg of emotions and ideologies—and there was nothing for that powder keg to do but burst. Within days of the State Department announcement, hundreds of Cuban inmates began to riot, first in Oakdale and then in Atlanta, resulting in separate sieges at both facilities and the taking of hundreds of hostages, including prison employees and disinterested prisoners, and setting off a firestorm of controversy that would capture national attention for the next while.

Okay, so that was the front-burner world issue. The stuff of my days came when I was deployed to Oakdale with the FBI's Hostage Rescue team as negotiations coordinator and team leader for our hostage rescue effort, beginning a round-the-clock run of talks with Cuban leaders that ultimately resulted in a negotiated surrender, and following which I was immediately flown to Atlanta to offer support in the ongoing negotiations there. Naturally, with this second standoff already in its middle stages, I was in much more of an advisory role at the Federal Penitentiary in Atlanta than I had been at the Federal Detention Center in Oakdale, but I ended up drafting the surrender documents in each case and knew full well what our federal government had been made to give up in the interest of a peaceful solution. I also knew how close we came to having that peaceful solution turn to absolute shit.

There had been 28 hostages taken in Oakdale and 119 in Atlanta—and all were eventually released unharmed, despite several near misses and close calls and particularly heinous threats. The Oakdale riots lasted nine days. The Atlanta riots lasted eleven days. And in many respects the fallout from these two high-profile insurgences would be felt for years to come, in the world at large but also in the world of law enforcement. At the FBI Academy in Quantico and at law enforcement agencies around the world, our successful response in each case became a kind of template for how to effectively counter a prison riot, and as far as I know case histories of both sieges continue to be taught and studied.

I must admit, I'd never thought all that much about the plight of the Cuban people up until these two sieges beyond those first stirring images from the boatlift, but for a time in there, coming out of those tense negotiations, it was all I could think about. In Oakdale and Atlanta, I had just stared down the scourge of the earth, the very baseline of the human condition, and at the other end I couldn't shake thinking our government was in a can't-win situation we couldn't afford to lose. These inmates had been ruthless, but at the same time I was made to wonder at the source of that ruthlessness. On the one hand, you had Fidel Castro's harsh, totalitarian regime in Cuba, which resulted in the 1980 exodus that severely tested our immigration policies and our national patience in the first place. Back then, at least in some circles, it was widely thought that the U.S. was merely offering safe haven to thousands of decent, hardworking, God-fearing Cubans fleeing their homeland in desperate search for a better life, but over time it became apparent that Castro—at least in some cases—had merely emptied his prisons and his mental institutions and the underbelly of his society and made his problems the problem of the American people. Granted, some of these refugees were determined to improve their lot, but a great many were lost causes. I know, because I had to deal with them, up close and impersonal, on a nearly constant basis for a stretch of interminable days. I looked at some of the ways they treated each other, the ways they treated their hostages, the ways they treated other inmates, and couldn't believe they walked on two legs. Some of these prisoners were animals passing as human beings.

But I never played at social work or politics, and I tried not to pass judgment or value one cause over another. I reminded myself that I didn't create this problem and that I was a long way from understanding it, and yet it had fallen to me to try to deal with it. And it would fall to me again, four years later, after dozens of those same Cuban detainees—"graduates" of the Oakdale and Atlanta riots—had been transferred to the Federal Correctional Institution in Talladega, Alabama, for final processing prior to deportation back to Cuba. It might have been routine but for an attempted escape from the prison's Alpha Unit, a secure dormitorylike structure where thirty-two of those detainees were being held. At approximately nine o'clock on the morning of August 21, 1991, the day they were scheduled for deportation by the INS, a small group of Cuban inmates began a failed break that nevertheless succeeded in inciting tempers and galvanizing the other inmates. Upon their return to the unit following their aborted escape, the original group was able to organize 121 Cuban inmates and later that day took captive eight Federal Bureau of Prison (BOP) staff, three INS staff, and eighteen American prisoners who were also housed in the same unit, beginning a ten-day siege.

This was about where I checked in. I received an alert on my pager—here again, in the days before cellular telephones were such a widespread necessity—and called in to find out there was another full-scale hostage situation developing in one of our federal prisons. I hadn't learned any of the details just yet, except that I was to report to a secure FBI airport in northern Virginia, where I would be deployed by Bureau Learjet to the scene, so I hastily packed a small suitcase and said good-bye to Dianne and the kids, hoping I wouldn't be gone too long but knowing that I could be facing a difficult stretch. Joining me on the advance team for the FBI's HRT was the unit's commander and deputy commander as well as several logistical people—and the reason I was chosen, I was told, was because of my previous experiences in Oakdale and Atlanta. That's just what I needed, I thought sardonically, to be perceived as the FBI's resident negotiating expert on federal prison riots, which I guessed was like being assigned to the bomb squad at Pearl Harbor.

As I sat down on the plane and we prepared for takeoff, I was thinking back to the frantic scene of those two earlier riots. The knives to throats. The multiple confrontations. The constant screaming. The tightrope of negotiations. The never-ending threats to life. The never feeling we had a good handle on either situation, despite the positive outcomes. I knew full well that most of the inmates I'd be dealing with at Talladega had very likely been involved in one of those earlier standoffs and that they would be looking ahead with similar resolve toward a very different resolution. *Oh, no. Here we go again.*

A state trooper picked us up at the airport and drove us out to the prison, and by the time we arrived on the scene one of the hostages had already been released—a female INS staffer—bringing to ten the number of non-inmate hostages we had to try to save. We took the position that every little bit helped, and that on a percentage basis we were now significantly closer to our goal of getting every one out unharmed, so for the moment at least things were looking up. Of course, we also had to consider the 18 American prisoners holed up in Alpha Unit with the 121 Cuban prisoners, but there was no way to tell to what extent these prisoners had been co-opted by their fellow prisoners or which side of the standoff they were actually on, so at the outset the staff hostages were our clear priority.

As we were being briefed on the situation, I understood that these prisoners had already seen my bag of tricks at Oakdale and Atlanta. Of course, I knew this much on the flight down, but it took seeing the layout of the facility, and the choke hold the Cubans had on the Alpha Unit, and the growing swarm of news media and camera crews just outside the prison compound, to fully realize what I was up against. It figured to be an enormous challenge. You have to realize, the detainees-turned-prisoners reassigned to Talladega and awaiting deportation back to Cuba were the very dregs of the system, and here they were, four years later, still in prison, still facing imminent deportation, and nothing had changed since the last time we'd met except for the slow realization that the FBI and the U.S. Government had possibly sold them a line and a false bill of goods that first time around—because, after all, we were about to go through the same motions yet again.

Truth be told, I found myself dreading how things might go.

I was also astonished at the way we could walk into an up-and-running negotiation being handled by an inexperienced negotiator and wonder how we ever managed to resolve these standoffs. Really, before the formal study of the art and science of negotiation, we FBI agents occasionally managed to broker a peaceful resolution every now and then despite ourselves, and that's basically the approach that had been adopted here. There was no real structure to the negotiating effort upon our arrival. There was no systematic approach. There was a capable-enough female negotiator on the scene, doing what she could in an impossible situation, but I was careful not to step too forcefully on her toes, not wanting to be seen as a "pro from Dover" type who strong-arms his way into each new situation. I never liked to big-foot my way into an existing chain of command, and preferred instead to establish my experience in this particular area and attempt to earn the respect of the others involved. In any case, I believed this woman was at an extreme disadvantage, genderwise, going up against these Cuban sociopaths who had no real tolerance or regard for women in the first place, so I was quickly able to convince her that we would all be better off if she handed the reins over to me while continuing to work in an advisory capacity.

By the end of that first day there was an entire team of FBI and BOP negotiators on the scene, and a companion team of FBI and BOP psychologists, although at the beginning I got the distinct impression from the BOP professionals that they would have much preferred to handle the entire standoff by themselves—a position I couldn't begin to understand, especially since our team eclipsed theirs in terms of training (and experience with these very hostage-takers!) and considering that we might have been thrilled to have them on our side to round out our focus. I thought, *It just goes to show you how even in a time of profound, overwhelming crisis a silly misperception of a nonexistent turf war can cloud a sound professional opinion.* But I also thought, *Hey, that's human nature for you*—and went about my business just the same.

We all had the early impression that we would be dug in for the next while, and as I silently kicked myself for not packing a couple extra sets of clothes I worked out a time-sharing arrangement with a colleague in the SOARS unit named Gary Noesner, determining that even though he'd never been through a similar riot we would each work opposite twelve-hour shifts. I was the overall team leader of the FBI negotiating effort, so I took the 8:00 a.m. to 8:00 p.m. shift, knowing that most of the heavy lifting on this impasse would probably occur during daylight hours—although in actual practice we were each on the scene for fourteen, sixteen, and on at least one occasion twenty-four hours a day. That's how it goes sometimes, in a protracted negotiation. Typically, I'd arrive on the scene at 7:00 each morning and linger past midnight—not least because Talladega was essentially in the middle of nowhere. The closest hotel room was in Oxford,

Alabama, about thirty minutes away, so I found myself driving eighty, ninety, sometimes one hundred miles per hour, back and forth on the interstate, in a constant hurry to get to the prison each morning or to get back to my hotel room each night to maximize my precious few hours of sleep, knowing I'd have to get up the next morning and make the trip all over again. Sometimes it made more sense to forgo sleep and stick around, to be closer to the action, than to be shuttling back and forth to my hotel.

A number of times I'd get to the hotel and lie in bed unable to sleep, caught thinking through the events of the day or ahead to the next day, trying to anticipate what the Cubans might do and beginning to formulate a response. There was always some new horrifying turn to occupy my full attention to where I had to almost separate myself from each day in order to adequately prepare for the next. I learned to stand in the shower at night and imagine all of the hectic events of the previous day as scales on my body. The steam and hot water would wash over me for thirty minutes or so, with the scales/challenges of the day slowly peeling off and floating down the drain. It was just a mind game I played with myself, but it seemed to work. Anyway, it was the only way I could sleep, and sleep was essential, because I had to arrive fresh, alert, and positive the next morning to the negotiator's room and announce, "Okay, today's the day we get them out." And I had to believe it, too, because if my conviction didn't come across, I worried I'd lose the hope and enthusiasm of the other negotiators.

Talladega wasn't like Oakdale—or even Atlanta, for that matter. True, there were many of the same players, on both sides of the standoff, but the mood was different. At Oakdale our shift of negotiators would go off duty and wind up in some honky-tonk bar, usually in the company of the local FBI ASAC, Mike Kahoe. We'd sit and drink and unwind, laughing at what some folks call gallows humor. Why? Well, we'd looked the hangman in the face all day long, day after day after day, and this was one way to cope. Also, we couldn't afford to cry. We needed the release. We needed to decompress, to be able to not take ourselves or our situation too seriously, because if you're too serious you can get too tight.

But it wasn't in us to laugh at Talladega. It wasn't in us to unwind—at least not as a group. We all went through our separate motions, lost in our private thoughts, hoping against hope that we might find the strength and the great good fortune to see things through.

Our first essential task at Talladega was to prepare a list of ways to begin a dialogue with the Cubans without setting them off. In any negotiation, as in a chess match, your opening moves are among the most strategic and the most consequential, so our initial approach was all-important. Remember that great *Seinfeld* episode in which George and Jerry talk about the concept of *hand*—as in *maintaining an upper hand in any given situation*? Well, that was sort of what we were after here, because as any experienced negotiator will tell you, the advantage in most negotiations tends to tilt in the direction of the party being pursued, especially at the outset. If we kept making overtures to the Cuban prisoners and kept getting rebuffed, we'd lose some considerable edge; and so, in the language of *Seinfeld,* we looked to maintain as much hand as realistically possible. The idea was to get the Cubans to reach out to us without a precipitating incident that might lead to violence, and our list of possible approaches ran from least-intrusive measures to most-intrusive measures. I was in favor of initiating one of these least-intrusive approaches first, before ratcheting things up a notch if it proved necessary, and prevailed upon my colleagues that this was the way to go—not unlike climbing the rungs of a ladder, one rung at a time.

As it happened, we reached first for one of the oldest tricks in my bag—and one I certainly hadn't had in reserve during the Oakdale or Atlanta riots. I decided to smoke these guys out, only not in a cowboys-and-Indians sort of way, or even in a more high-tech tear gas sort of way. No, I looked to smoke them out in more of a suggestive way: with the aid of an enormous portable barbecue pit that happened to be on-site at the prison. It would never have occurred to me in a million years to do just this, were it not for the sight of the giant barbecue drum laying low against one of the buildings, but there it was. Let me set the scene to illustrate the impact of such a move. The prison was laid out like a college campus: a sprawling fenced compound with several large buildings positioned like dormitories around a semicircle. One of these buildings housed the Alpha Unit, where the Cubans were holding forth, and directly outside that building we positioned a ring of BOP Special Operations Response Team (SORT) members dressed in heavy tactical clothing—noting, of course, that they didn't carry any weapons, unlike our HRT and SWAT teams. Understand, the inmates were not heavily armed in any kind of traditional sense, but they had successfully managed to contain themselves in a fortified area, under lock and key, and they had at their disposal a vast assortment of shivs and knives and spears and various other handmade, prison-workshop–type weapons. Their arsenal included an interesting assortment of Hawaiian-type slings, which they used to shoot arrows and rocks and bricks—to menacing effect, as will be made clear. Their weapons and their strength in numbers were enough to thwart their comparably few hostages, but they were no match against our show of force, which is why I thought it was essential to display our presence outside their windows.

I was reminded here of a line from our SWAT team leader in Atlanta, FBI SA Leon Blakeney, who remarked, "Only a fool brings a knife to a gunfight." We could certainly overpower the rioting inmates, but none of us were certain we could get to all the hostages before they were murdered.

I should mention here that our decision to show our force wasn't any kind of slam dunk or sure thing. In fact, this being a federal facility and a standoff of international consequence, there were all kinds of agencies and figureheads represented at the command post we'd established in one of the buildings across from Alpha Unit. The powers that be were all over this one, reaching up and through the Attorney General and all the way to the White House, and at any given moment they included the warden at Talladega, the regional director from the Bureau of Prisons, multiple FBI SACs and ASACs, various other BOP officials, wardens brought in from other federal prisons, and representatives from the INS and the U.S. Marshals, and each one seemed to want to weigh in on almost every move we negotiators looked to make. Unlike the seat-of-the-pants, make-it-up-as-I-go-along mode I was able to enter into during some of my lower-profile hostage-barricade situations, even my hunches and best guesses at Talladega had to be vetted by a group of about twenty people, none of whom were used to seeing eye-to-eye on anything—although, to be fair, they were generally good about seeing things my way when I could make a good case for them. This show of force was a prime example. It should have been a no-brainer to parade our might and our resolve in front of the Cubans, just short of rubbing their noses in it, but even a no-brainer-by-committee has its detractors. Or, at least, it needs to be justified. Ultimately, I was able to prevail upon these well-meaning folks that such a display was an appropriate first move, so we put our BOP SORT officers into position, shoulder-to-shoulder, with their bullet- and shiv-resistant vests, helmets, pads, and nightsticks on full display. They looked like an NFL team carrying baseball bats, and as soon as they were in place the Cubans began demanding that we remove or diminish our armed presence outside their building, which of course we were not prepared to do.

This was one of the less intrusive measures we deployed early on, to try to get a dialogue going with the inmates, and in the response we were able to learn that the Cubans had no clearly defined, elected single leader (that we knew of) among their ranks. This was both a good thing and a bad thing. We heard from several inmates, with no unified voice, which I took as a sign of weakness on the part of the inmates and at the same time a sign of trouble from our perspective. After all, how could we expect to negotiate effectively if there was no one to speak for the other side? A couple of inmates eventually took on more of a leadership role, but none took to it naturally—or convincingly. All we kept hearing were a bunch of loose demands being showered down on us from the Alpha Unit windows like a slapped-together wish list. The Cuban inmates wanted to be declared U.S. citizens. They wanted the United Nations to pass new laws on their behalf. They wanted sanctions against Cuba. They wanted money. They wanted a whole litany of unacceptable, not-gonna-happen–type things, delivered from a place of nothing-to-lose, which left me thinking we'd have a tough time breaking through the vitriol and the language barrier and the desperation and the ignorance and the clear lack of leadership and focus to broker a workable solution.

As I had feared all along, this was turning out to be a tremendous challenge.

In any case, the theatrical show of force had clearly put the inmates on edge, and as we stood outside the Alpha Unit building I noticed a large barbecue pit off by one of the other buildings. It was one of those big, hollowed-out drums, about the size of a couple of VW vans, and built on a set of rollers so that prison officials could wheel it to different parts of the campus for barbecues. The grill was a bit rusted and weather-beaten, but it was clearly in good working order. I knew the inmates were running low on food by this point, probably to the point of mixing packets of ketchup with water to make tomato soup, and that it would be a good long time before we reached the phase in our negotiations where we would start sending in food, but I thought we could establish and maintain some of that all-important *hand* if we rolled the barbecue pit near the Alpha Unit windows and had ourselves a cookout, within easy eyesight and nose range of the Cubans. It sounds a little petty in the retelling—or, at least, a benignly cruel and unusual form of punishment—but that's just what we did. As theatrical shows of early force went, I liked this move for its subtle power and for the way it reinforced that we were clearly in charge. I ran it by the powers-that-be first, and made an effective argument for it that reached a little bit beyond the fact that I was just plain hungry, but before long we were cooking up a serious mess of burgers and hot dogs and steaks, treating our tactical team to a feast—and in the bargain torturing those poor inmates with the sights and sounds and smells of all that good food, a kind of nonviolent "tactical assault" on their senses.

Next thing we knew, the Cubans were ranting and raging through the windows, threatening to kill one of the hostages if we didn't move the barbecue. I'd expected to get a reaction out of these inmates— clearly, that was the whole point—but nothing like this. A few of these clowns actually mistook the giant grill for some kind of Trojan horse, thinking we were using it to stage an assault of some kind—one even thought it was a missile launcher!—and the leaders got so riled up about the grill they even put one of their female hostages on the phone to argue for its removal. This poor woman was apoplectic, screaming and begging for her life and pleading with us to remove the grill. "They're going to kill us if you don't," she implored. "Please."

I had to take this call in front of all of the agency heads during an otherwise routine negotiations strategy meeting, and it was more than a little disconcerting to have all my well-meaning, colleagues weigh in with their takes on how to deal with this frightened and frantic hostage. (Did you ever have twenty-five people listening in on your urgent conversation, making "helpful" suggestions along the way?) Anyway, it was a tense situation, made more so by the eavesdropping nature of the call, but I managed to respond calmly to the woman that she needed to explain to her captors that there was no need to feel threatened by the grill, that we had simply discovered it on the premises and figured it would be the easiest way for us to feed these hungry BOP officers. Still, she kept at it. The Cubans were insistent, she said.

They didn't want the grill going outside their windows. "You're the FBI," she said at one point. "What are you doing having a barbecue?"

To this, I had no easy answer, but before I could even blurt out a reply, one of the Cubans pulled the telephone from the woman's ear and started fuming about how he and his fellow inmates were going to kill all the hostages, one by one, if we didn't remove the barbecue grill. That was his one and only demand at just that moment. Forget the U.N. Forget citizenship and sanctions and clemency and whatever else these guys had been seeking. Right now, they just wanted us to stop cooking outside their windows. This one Cuban kept spewing line after line of absolute evil, all over this suspicious-looking mobile barbecue. It was not at all the reaction I was expecting, but it was a reaction just the same, and I had to respond to it.

I ran it by our various agency leaders, who were turning out to be surprisingly supportive of what I was trying to do, and they agreed with my recommendation to stand firm on the all-important barbecue negotiating point, although I did get the distinct impression that quite a few of my colleagues thought I was nuts for coming up with the notion in the first place. Again, it seems like a small thing now, all these years later, but at the time it loomed about as large as the crisis itself. To the great credit of my many superiors, I never got the feeling from any of these folks that they resented my being there or anything like that. I never heard a single one of them say, "You better be right about this, Van Zandt," or anything equally inappropriate. They trusted me to make good, thoughtful, experience-based decisions, and here my experience told me that if we essentially ignored the Cubans on this essentially nonissue, we would come out ahead. I wasn't too worried that they would kill one of the hostages over something like this. It would have made no sense, and I had no choice but to assume these people would base their actions on something that at least resembled logic. I mean, if we had brought in an armored personnel carrier and parked the thing right outside their window in a show of force, it would have been reasonable for them to perceive it as threatening. But a giant barbecue grill? Come on, I thought, how threatening was that?

Eventually, the Cubans backed down on the barbecue, and the threat level was reduced. In fact, there was a change in "leadership" among the hostage-takers over this one incident, and when the new guy took charge he was smart enough to simply ask nicely that we move the grill a few feet away from the unit's open windows. That's all it took. He didn't demand that we move the grill, and he didn't issue any threats: he just put it in the form of a reasonable request, so I thought it appropriate that we honor it to reinforce our willingness to cooperate, within reason. We rolled the grill several feet from the building, and we continued to feed our people, and in the back-and-forth it was confirmed for me that there would be no one effective leader to emerge from this group of inmates. If one leader faltered or lost the respect of his fellow inmates, he would be swiftly replaced. This new one seemed the most levelheaded of any we'd seen so far, but I was afraid he wouldn't last; sooner or later there would be some issue or other to trip him up as well. Already I'd spoken to several different individuals, and even to a representative group, but nobody seemed willing to take on the responsibility of being the spokesperson—and if there was anyone claiming to be the brains of this particular outfit, he had yet to make himself known.

Another key to this early round of negotiations was my refusal to count the eighteen American inmates among the hostages, which would have increased the hostage count from ten to twenty-eight. For one thing, I didn't want that higher number to take hold in the hostage-takers' minds or have them thinking the stakes were any greater than they actually were. For another, I didn't want to encourage a situation where we'd start negotiating for the release of American citizens and have them send out one of these prisoners instead of one of the prison workers, and took the position that the so-called inmate hostages were of no interest to us. They were prisoners, and as far as we were concerned they were where they rightly belonged: in prison. In truth, we of course wanted to see the American prisoners safely out of Alpha Unit, but I didn't think it was necessary to let the Cubans know this just yet. If they chose to release the American inmates, one by one or all at once, that was up to them, but we were not about to barter for their release or acknowledge them as hostages until the ten civilian prison workers were safe. Here again, we took another strong position on what might have seemed a small point, but I was able to hold fast to it against a many-headed team of Cuban negotiators and thereby win another early round.

One of the most difficult moments of these negotiations concerned the hostage-takers' attempt to win public support for their cause. With each passing hour, it was becoming more and more clear that this may have indeed been a slipshod prison riot, hatched on the fly and nurtured on the run, but the one constant to the Cubans' effort was their zealous desire to call public attention to what they believed was their wrongful treatment by the U.S. government. We anticipated as much, from our experiences in Oakdale and Atlanta, and here in Talladega the inmates ran true to form. Early on, they made three specific demands regarding media attention. They wanted camera crews from CNN to be permitted to enter the compound, along with a Hispanic CNN reporter who might be sympathetic to their story. They wanted a female reporter from a Spanish-language Miami newspaper, who happened to be on-site as part of the press corps covering the crisis, to be brought inside Alpha Unit for an interview. And they wanted an attorney who had worked with them since the Mariel Boatlift and represented their positions at Oakdale and Atlanta to be permitted on the scene to act as a kind of spokesperson.

Now, it is one thing to make such demands, and quite another to grant them, but we were at a point in our negotiations when I felt I needed to throw the Cubans some sort of bone. Not a big bone, mind you, but something to chew on. The old axiom that you've got to give in order to get holds especially true in situations like this, so we looked carefully at these three requests to see which might be the least intrusive. To my thinking, the print journalist from Miami seemed our most reasonable option, especially considering that she was already there covering the story, and I prevailed upon my many bosses to grant her access. That done, I went to work on the Cubans, attempting to broker a concession of some kind in exchange for allowing a half-hour interview with the reporter. Clearly, we couldn't just deliver this female reporter without expecting the inmates to give back something in return, and I determined to win the release of at least one hostage in the exchange—preferably one of the female hostages.

I conducted my discussions in English after making a few failed attempts in Spanish, over the phone and face-to-face, but also after determining that I might have an advantage if I kept to English. That's always a central dilemma when you're dealing with a bilingual group, whether to pursue negotiations in your native language or theirs. Here, after attempting to negotiate in Spanish through a translator, I noticed that the Cubans were inclined toward tremendous emotional spikes when they spoke naturally among themselves. They were an excitable bunch, and they'd get all pumped and whipped into a frenzy about whatever point they were making, and their energy levels were generally through the roof. I was blessed that my good friend and fellow negotiator, FBI SA Fernando (Fred) Rivera from Miami, was with me for our third go-round on the prison riot front, not least because he spoke fluent Spanish and related very well with the inmates. Even so, when the inmates were made to negotiate in English, a language with which they were all familiar though not exactly fluent, there was more of a flatline response as they struggled to translate what I was saying or waited on a translator to do it for them. It forced them to sit on their hands a little bit, emotionally speaking. They got what I was saying, for the most part, but they had to first hear it in English and then process it in Spanish, and by that time there was nothing to do but make sense of it, so I started sticking to English wherever possible, to keep these guys on more of an even keel.

In English, then, I managed to convince the Cubans to release one of the female prison officers in exchange for the visit with the Miami print reporter. At the time, I counted the concession as a small but significant victory. The Cubans kept coming back to CNN and the attorney and insisted that they be allowed on the unit, but I kept shooting them down on these fronts and focusing them back on the print reporter, maintaining that they had misstated their demands to me, which could not have been my fault, and that I had honored my end of the bargain. I continued in this way until it appeared we had reached an accord, and after the deal was finally cut we went to great lengths to find the reporter and to get her to agree to spend thirty minutes with these guys to get their side of the story—not too hard of a sell to a reporter about to get an exclusive. She was briefed by BOP and FBI media representatives, and then I spent about an hour with her, going over basic negotiating concepts, emphasizing how hard we were all working to resolve this standoff nonviolently, and encouraging her to trust her journalistic instincts while at the same time keeping a careful eye on the bigger picture.

At the last moment, as I was preparing to escort the reporter and her still photographer to the unit, the Cubans took a sudden about-face and started calling for the CNN video cameras and for their attorney. They claimed that they had negotiated in good faith, and that this had been part of the deal all along, but apparently they didn't know the meaning of *good faith* because I had been quite clear on this one point. That, or there was a whole lot lost in translation. I'm guessing it was wishful thinking on their part, more than anything else, but they were quite adamant about it. No matter how hard Fred Rivera and I tried to talk them down from this notion, in English and in Spanish, they kept insisting that the deal was for CNN *and* their attorney *and* the Spanish-language print reporter.

We went back and forth on this for a too-long while, until once again it appeared we had reached an understanding, and as we walked over to begin the interview and collect the female hostage, I reminded the reporter once again what was at stake. "Do your job," I told her. "Let them tell you their story. But if they start ranting and raging and making demands, we're out of here. Take your cue from me."

The Alpha Unit was set up in such a way that what happened next was like a perp walk out of a bad movie, the way we had to pass this gauntlet of prison-barred doors just to get to the Cuban leaders. The prisoners were reaching their arms through the locked bars and rattling their shop-made weapons and snarling like caged animals, shouting every piece of imaginable and unimaginable invective our way. I was thankful that my limited Spanish wasn't good enough to pick up what they were saying—and a little embarrassed for the reporter, who could of course understand and appeared to wince at every word— but we pressed on. Behind us, on the outer perimeter, there were dozens of BOP officers and federal officials anxiously awaiting the release of the promised hostage, a female Caucasian in her early thirties. And yet, the deeper we advanced into the Cubans' territory, the more hostile and venomous their remarks became—to the point where I no longer felt I could trust these individuals. I knew enough Spanish to get that they were gutless and sleazy and low, and apparently they knew enough English to let it be known that the terms of our deal were no longer valid. All of a sudden they were again insisting that CNN be let in on the scene and demanding to see their lawyer. I thought, *What is up with these people?* We had a negotiated agreement—twice!—and I could not have been more clear on my intention to limit the outside visit to this one print journalist, but nevertheless we were right back where we'd started.

Regrettably, this poor female hostage was left dangling. Almost literally. A few of the inmates dragged her over and jammed her head up against the bars and pressed a knife to her throat. It truly was like they were dangling her out in front of us, almost the way you'd wave a carrot in front of a donkey to get him to move in a particular direction, a metaphor I choose deliberately because their actions suggested they were out to make an ass out of every one of us on the side of the law.

At the same time another group of Cubans started grilling the journalist on her allegiances, asking her whose side she was on, the government's or theirs, and they started to threaten her as well; and as the first group began to close ranks around the female hostage, I knew things had taken a turn for the absolute worst. We were all up against it, the poor hostage most of all. She was fairly terrorized, to be pinned against the bars in just this way, a knife still lodged against her throat, while her captors threatened to kill her if they didn't get their way. All she had to do was close her eyes and she could picture her own death.

I looked on and thought, *Okay, this is something new.* I don't mean to sound cold or heartless about it in the retelling, but at the time I remember thinking this was something so completely out of my experience, and so completely beyond my expectations to be positioned just a few feet from a hostage when her captors vowed to kill her immediately unless I did what they asked of me, also immediately. I gazed into this poor woman's eyes and saw abject fear. (Who knows what she saw when she gazed into mine? Utter bewilderment, probably.) Then I looked at the Cuban who held the knife to her throat, who happened to also be the leader of their group at this time, but I got back nothing. His eyes were blank, his face without expression, and I wondered what he was thinking, if he was thinking anything at all. It was like looking into the eyes of Steven Spielberg's mechanical great white: hollow, empty and without a sign of emotion.

The woman didn't say a word, but she knew she was about to die. Her eyes were pleading: *This son of a bitch is going to kill me. . . . Do something about it . . . please!* But there was nothing I could do. As tears welled up in her eyes, she again imparted the word *Please!*

So what did I do when there was nothing I could do? I turned to the female reporter and said, "Turn around and walk away right now."

She looked at me like I was the devil incarnate. "I can't just walk away," she said. "They're going to kill this woman."

"Just turn around and walk away," I said again.

And we did. Hardest thing I ever had to do in my career, to walk away from that female hostage, her head jammed up against those bars and that knife pressed to her throat, but my gut told me there was no other move. I was close enough to reach out to her, to hold her hand, or to lunge at her captors, but that would have gotten us nowhere except deeper into trouble. To her great and everlasting credit, that poor, frightened hostage was stoic but ashen-faced. She couldn't believe we would just leave her there like that. She didn't say anything, but it was clear she couldn't believe it. The reporter, too, was fairly incredulous.

"What the hell are you doing?" she said at one point as we ran that reverse gauntlet, past the cussing and yelling and baiting.

"I'm taking away their audience," I said.

I said the same thing a short time later to the bosses at the command post. They knew what had gone down, but they were struggling to understand it. "Why would you walk away like that?" they wanted to know.

"Because there was nothing else for me to do," I explained. "The Cubans weren't going to listen to me. If I stood there any longer, I was afraid they would kill this woman just to spite me, just so I would get the full impact of her death and have it weigh on my conscience. That's how these people think, and I'm not going to give them that. I thought she'd be safer if I turned and walked away, if I took away their audience."

"How can you be sure?" one of the supervisors wanted to know.

"I can never be sure," I said. This was true enough—and one of the miserable facts of my professional life. I could spend my entire career studying human behavior and still never be sure how a person is going to react to this or that situation. I can make an educated guess. I can follow a hunch. I can go by past experience. But I can never be sure. All I can do is what I think is right, what I think is best. That had been the nut of my professional life: if I'm right, I'm right; if I'm wrong, she's dead. I don't mean to minimize the value of a human life, or come across as flippant or cavalier, but that's the simple truth of it. As a hostage negotiator, you are frequently out on the edge, drawing on your experience, your knowledge of human behavior, your instincts, and your power of prayer to calculate each next move. You can never be sure that you are certain about any one thing; there are no behavioral absolutes, and anyone who suggests otherwise has probably been smoking those funny cigarettes without labels. You do the best you can, and hope for the best, and live the rest of your life with the results.

Mercifully, in this one instance at least, I turned out to be right. We walked away and the guy didn't kill the female hostage. In fact, the other inmates were so unimpressed with the way this guy handled the showdown that they immediately replaced him as their chief negotiator. He was too much of a hothead, even for this bunch of hotheads, but more than that, he had lost face. There I'd been, worrying about *"hand"* and maintaining a psychological advantage in our talks, but to these Cubans nothing was more important than *face,* and here I guess it appeared that the only way to save theirs was to switch gears.

We later learned there was a great deal of infighting among the Cubans immediately following this incident, and yet, within just a couple hours they contacted us to reopen talks and indicated that they were willing to go through with our original deal: the release of the female hostage in exchange for a thirty-minute interview with the female reporter. For a third time we cut that deal, allowing the new inmate leadership a certain amount of face while we preserved a certain amount of "hand," and as I stood outside Alpha Unit, awaiting the release of the hostage, I half expected her to be furious at me for the way I had left her hanging. She was strong when she came out, but as soon as she reached the arms of a BOP official she broke down, and as I stood off to the side and watched her I worried she might be the only hostage we would see safely through these negotiations. I knew the Cubans would stonewall us again. I knew this had been a major concession for them, and I feared their shifting group consensus would cost us in the days ahead.

As it played out, this would be the only negotiated hostage release of the standoff, not counting the earlier release of the INS staffer that took place before FBI negotiators had arrived on the scene.

Among the remaining hostages, we were most concerned about one of the BOP officers, who in the interest of privacy I will refer to here as Smith. An extremely large, muscular man, Smith had reportedly been abusive to the inmates on a number of occasions prior to the siege. He had allegedly tied them up and beaten them and generally made a career out of mistreating them, and now that the tables had been turned and he had become the prisoners' prisoner, we feared for his safety. We worried about his health too. He suffered from diabetes, and we were given instructions to negotiate particularly aggressively for his release, to where every conversation about the hostages eventually came around to his condition. Given his history with the Cubans, Smith was probably the last hostage they were inclined to release, but we kept pressing the issue, especially after we had won the release of the female prison staffer, who reported that the hostages had been made to surrender their prison ID badges, which were then placed into a bag and drawn in a morbid lottery, to see who would die first—a terrifying scene, made more so by the fact that the hostages were made to watch it. Predictably, Smith's was the first badge drawn.

Other than this one and only hostage to be released on our watch, we were unable to confirm the well-being of the remaining nine prison employees or the American prisoners, beyond the anecdotal confirmation we received in the released hostages' debriefing. However, at some midpoint of the siege we were presented with an opportunity to negotiate medical attention for the hostages, as well as for the American prisoners and Cuban inmates, in exchange for something to eat. Food is often a powerful motivator in hostage-barricade situations, and this deep into the standoff the Cubans had grown mighty hungry. There had been some food on hand, early on, but not nearly enough to feed such a large group over such a long period of time, so their defenses were down on this point. Also, several of the inmates had suffered various injuries during various mini-conflicts along the way and were in need of medical attention, so it was an obvious move to attempt to bundle these basic needs together on our terms. The deliberate bonus here was that prison doctors would be able to observe the prison workers and bring back an accurate head count and a report on their condition.

These were some of the most distressing days and nights of my career—and certainly the longest. You look at the coping skills you need to have, the stresses that continue to mount as each day unfolds, the vulnerability you can't help but feel being away from hearth and home in the midst of such wild, violent uncertainty. In my case, at times like these, I looked to my faith for support. Each night I counted myself blessed for my strong Christian beliefs. Each night I thought of Dianne and our children and the shared values that sustained us all. Each night, as I tossed and turned in my hotel bed, I found myself praying that I'd be able to drift off for a few peaceful hours, so that I could awake refreshed and recharged and ready for more of the same. On some nights I might have even cried—at the suffering and uncertainty of the hostages, and at the immoral acts of the Cuban inmates, who in their own uncertain way were suffering, too. And in the morning, driving back to Talladega at breakneck speeds, I never once reached for the radio. You know, it's interesting, but now that I think about it, I don't think I even read a newspaper during the entire standoff. I didn't have any idea how these events were being reported in the media, and I didn't want to know. The radio in my compact rental car held absolutely no appeal. Instead, I'd use that half-hour drive to decompress, to take time to consider the day, and to pray strongly for a peaceful resolution.

Understand, I realized that negotiations are sometimes necessary to facilitate the tactical process, and that a peaceful resolution might not find us on this pass, despite my prayers and best efforts. I realized, too, that in some situations my role was to merely buy time for various leaders in law enforcement to make their variously difficult decisions, to stall while tactical forces are put in place, to allow an assault plan to take shape, to gather intelligence from the scene. I knew this was all part of the process and that a good chance remained that my prayers for a peaceful resolution would go unanswered, at least in the way I wanted them to be answered. A part of me knew that the most likely outcome at Talladega would be a tactical resolution of some kind. It was always possible that a peaceful surrender would emerge as a by-product of our protracted negotiations, but I had to be prepared for a tactical intervention.

Still, I hoped and prayed. I asked for a sense of knowledge, and strength, and wisdom, so that I could be used as an instrument of God's peace. I tried to marshal all of my resources as a card-carrying Christian, and to draw on whatever other resources I could find: my family, my colleagues, my belief that we were all headed down the right road, for the right reasons. And I vowed to keep a positive out-look, no matter how drained or weary or frustrated I might have been. In fact, one of my colleagues asked me one early morning as I arrived at the prison how I was doing, and I was able to honestly answer that I was doing great. He asked how I was handling the horribly long hours, and I was able to say that they were no trouble at all. And I meant it—or, at least, I knew I had to mean it. I knew I had to show that our negotiations were going well, not only to the Cubans on the other side of those negotiations, but to the friends and colleagues on my side of the barricade. The moment I exhibited any physical or psychological weakness myself, I knew, was the moment we were done.

On a lighter note that will hopefully prove enlightening, I started to worry that I would run out of clothes before we ran out of options. I should have learned my lesson at Oakdale and Atlanta and packed for the long haul, but I had been too hurried and harried to take along anything more than a couple pairs of jeans, a couple casual shirts and a set of tactical clothes. Like I said, I might have known, and I am reminded here of some protracted diplomatic negotiations that took place with the Soviets during the Reagan administration, in Iceland, where the story goes that the Americans had taken hotel rooms for a month while the Russians had taken rooms for a year. On the twenty-ninth day, which side was going to be feeling the most pressure to resolve their differences? Well, that same concept applies to a protracted hostage negotiation and the amount of underwear you thought to pack. Pretty soon, you get to where you've turned your briefs inside out—twice!—and you know you can't wear them anymore, and there's no time to use a Laundromat, and every Wal-Mart and Kmart in town has been cleaned out by other agents who also neglected to pack enough clothes, and it's not hard to see how your resolve might weaken or how yesterday's deal breaker might suddenly appear like it wasn't such a bad idea after all.

My clothing actually got me into a tough spot, after meeting with the powers that be and determining that we needed to shake things up with the inmate negotiators, in order to move things in a positive direction. I had the not-necessarily-bright idea of staging some type of commotion during one of our formal negotiating sessions. We'd regularly meet with four inmates' representatives and our four-person government team, which came to include a BOP psychologist and a BOP psychiatrist. We met in a small prison office, but these meetings were increasingly unproductive, so I suggested that I might lose my cool in front of the inmate negotiators over some issue or other to see if that might move things forward. The plan was for me to get dramatically upset, and pound my fist on the table, and storm out of the room, which would hopefully signal the Cubans that we were growing impatient and that they should quickly cut their best possible deal before they lost all. The only problem with this plan was that I ran out of civilian clothes before we could put it into place, and I showed up at the prison that day in tactical gear. Cargo pants, a military sweater, boots—the whole deal. So when I blew my top in the negotiating session, I didn't come across as a civilian or an FBI agent or some professional suit brought in to mediate a conflict: as far as the inmates were concerned, I was a representative of the U.S. military. I had only meant to get the inmates thinking they were running out of time, and here I had them thinking the military was about to come flying in on choppers, gassing and firing at the inmates as other troops stormed the doors and seized the facility, reminding me of a valuable lesson I should have already known: it's not so much what you say or how you say it as it is what you're wearing when you say it, and how you present yourself. You are what you wear, at least in the minds of rioting Cubans.

Generally speaking, though, it was a sound strategy to set the hostage-takers on some kind of edge. Wherever possible, we looked to make the living conditions as untenable as we could for the Cubans, without actually letting on that this was our goal. In a standoff such as this one, there are a number of strategic things you can do as a negotiator to make the bad guys uncomfortable. On the third day of the standoff, for example, we shut down television service to Alpha Unit, setting the inmates on edge and causing further friction among their leadership group. We also flooded the area with external lighting, reinforcing the Cubans' impression that they were under close and constant watch, and during the first few days we increased the lit area at regular intervals. And at various times during the ten-day siege, we cut off water service to the unit. One of the most significant of these strategies was to line the hallway leading to the negotiations room with big sheets of black plastic. We were constantly shuttling Cuban leaders in and out of rooms and cell areas for formal and informal negotiation sessions, and I didn't want them to be able to look around and see what we were doing. This was a calculated move designed to create a sense of sensory deprivation, even paranoia, but at the same time I realized it wouldn't do us any good to have these inmates eye-balling FBI agents or BOP officers sitting around drinking coffee or shooting the breeze on the phones.

Now, about those handmade Hawaiian slingshots. On the third day of the siege, the Cubans made their way to the roof of their building. It turned out the rooftop was the only perch available to them to display signs and messages that would in turn be picked up by the news cameras positioned across the street from the compound, so I suppose it was inevitable that they would make their way there. In Oakdale and Atlanta the inmates had no access to the roof, but here the roof emerged as part of the captors' fortified area. It also presented a grave danger to the hostages, because as soon as the Cubans claimed the roof it became part of their threat package, as they fell into the unpleasant habit of threatening to throw one of the hostages off the roof if their demands weren't met. They even looked to secure the roof from us by shooting rocks and bricks down at the BOP officers with their sling-shots. As handmade tools went, these suckers were pretty effective, and it took a couple beats for us to mount an appropriate counter-attack, which we did with a pepper ball assault. A pepper ball looks like a tiny baseball with a hand-grenade pin on it, and when it lands against a hard surface it "detonates" by shooting off hot rocks the size of ground pepper in every conceivable direction. It's used by police to disperse and control crowds, and here it proved fairly effective in thwarting the slingshot attack—so effective, in fact, that we were able to "take back" the roof from the Cubans.

This was a big victory for us—or, more accurately, a big setback for the Cubans, because a more effective leader might have been able to secure the roof with a greater show of resolve and a stronger sense of strategy. As it played out, though, we were able to regain control of the roof and use it as a bargaining chip in future negotiating sessions, allowing the Cubans access to display their messages but prohibiting them from bringing any of the hostages there.

As the stalemate dragged on, it became apparent to every one of us on the negotiation team that there would be no peaceful solution or surrender. There was just no way we were going to talk these guys out; they never wavered in their demands, which the U.S. government was not going to meet, which put us at a stalemate. The mood among our group shifted to where it was no longer a question of *if* we were going to assault but *when*. I made the case to the on-scene commander that we could either do it on our time or on the prisoners' time. "Give me a chance to create a window of opportunity for us," I argued. "I can create some ambivalence on their part. I can create some denial on their part. I can create a false sense of security. And then we can find our opening and we can go in and do what we have to do."

And so I set about it. We held a series of face-to-face meetings with five representatives from the inmates and five representatives from our side, which now included Dee Rosario, a Puerto Rican–born FBI agent negotiator who along with agent Pedro Toledo served as the government's lead negotiators at the Atlanta riot. The second sit-down was actually the more unusual of the two, because it was due to occur in a driving rain, which would have placed the Cubans on one side of the bars in a covered cell alcove and left us on the outside in the open courtyard, open to the elements in the middle of a ridiculous downpour. I realized we were at the stage in our stalemate where I needed to give the Cubans some reason to think they were winning their fight, but it would have offered them too great a psychological advantage to conduct this session with that kind of edge, with them bone-dry and us dripping wet. We put the meeting off, hoping for the rain to subside, but as the rain continued to beat down hard on the area, I asked some of the BOP officers to construct a makeshift shelter, with some plywood and a tarp, to cover our chairs like a mini–picnic shelter, and we were able to hold the session on relatively equal and somewhat dry footing. There's an old saying: a good FBI agent never goes hungry and never gets wet—something that I had evidently failed to fully grasp over the years.

During the first of these sessions, incidentally, we all wore bullet-proof vests to protect against the steel shafts and arrows these guys still had in their cache, but by the second session I no longer saw the need, believing that it suggested we were afraid of them, something we could not afford to project. Interestingly, Gary, the other FBI negotiations leader, suggested to the FBI on-scene commander, without running it by us first, that both Fred Rivera and I were needlessly risking our lives by not wearing vests; I heard this and reminded myself that some people just don't get it. Anyway, at each of these sessions, the Cubans kept hammering home their demands, which now included the establishment of a committee, to include representatives from the United Nations, the Red Cross, a federal judge, a congressman and others, to formally negotiate on the prisoners' behalf. Again, completely ridiculous, not-gonna-happen type things, but at this late stage we went through the motions of taking them seriously, all the while looking for an opening to make some kind of tactical move as the threats to the lives of the hostages continued.

On the day before we ended the standoff, a decision was made to move on the prisoners—or, in agency parlance, to "go tactical." I was told that the decision came from the very highest levels of government, which I took to mean the Attorney General, with guidance from the director of the FBI. I also took it to mean that I couldn't question the decision. That was no longer my role. Plus, you have to realize, the decision wasn't announced in any kind of formal way, at least not to agents on my level. We weren't part of the discussion, even though I could read all the signals and see where we were headed. So, without ever being expressly told, I realized my role had changed. I realized that I had worked as part of a team to keep negotiations moving forward, toward a hoped-for peaceful resolution, but that now we were looking to disarm the Cubans by force and that it fell to me to help facilitate that process. And so, from that moment on, every move I made was with this in mind. I let the Cubans continue to hammer us psychologically in our few remaining negotiating sessions. We allowed them to beat us on the release of the BOP officer Smith, but not to where we would stop pressing for it. After all, we had asked so frequently and so forcefully about Smith—"the officer with the high blood pressure," as the Cubans kept calling him—that if we all of a sudden stopped asking it might have appeared suspicious. Remember, no surprises until the last surprise.

On the night before we were hoping to make our move, we also cut a deal to deliver a small amount of food to every prisoner and hostage on Alpha Unit, once again in exchange for a medical inspection by a prison doctor that would allow us to determine the condition of the hostages one final time. This time around, the deal was struck in such a way that the Cubans were able to convince themselves they had rustled food from us, and to feel good about that, while we were able to accomplish our goals at the same time. As I've indicated, this was typical of most of our negotiations at this late stage. I started surrendering more and more to the prisoners' demands, acquiescing in both my actions and my demeanor, basically letting them beat the tar out of me with their words without lashing back. Instead of standing my ground, the way we had done in the early rounds, I was now retreating and shrinking from the barrage of psychological punches I was allowing myself to take. And the Cubans were pleased with themselves for dishing out such a beating. Understand, we hadn't bent to their demands so much as let it be known that we had no choice but to consider them, which was enough to get them relaxed and complacent and feeling like they were making progress.

We spent a good deal of time, by committee, figuring what *exactly* we would feed all these people, and after all kinds of deliberation with INS, BOP, and FBI officials and prison psychologists and even a full-blown nutritionist, we decided to give each individual a foam cup of rice and beans and meat, along with a slice of bread. We even deliberated how much to fill each cup, before settling on a little more than halfway, which we all agreed would be just enough to meet the immediate physiological needs of the hostages—who as far as we knew hadn't eaten in several days—but not so much that the Cubans could keep some of their portions in reserve and make it last for several days. We also wanted to give the prisoners enough to eat so they might feel a little sleepy, so there was a whole mess of calculating and measuring and head scratching going on around that particular conference table—all of which left me thinking it was a good thing caterers didn't plan their menus by committee, because they'd never get anywhere and the multitudes would go unfed.

We also served coffee, knowing of course that the Cubans were big coffee drinkers. Someone rolled in a giant urn filled with a hundred or so gallons of coffee, and just as we started to roll it toward the Alpha Unit to serve it to the inmates, I thought to ask a much-too-obvious question: "Wait a minute guys," I said. "That's decaf, isn't it?"

The prison officers who had been assigned to this food and beverage detail looked at me like I was some sort of Martian. Of course, the coffee wasn't decaffeinated, so I started doing some ranting and raging of my own. We wanted to help these people drift off to sleep, not to keep them awake, so I insisted they drag the caffeinated coffee back to the kitchen and dump it out and brew another great pot. They were also great sugar fiends, the Cubans, so I was careful to cut their sugar supply by about three-quarters, because here again I didn't want them lacing their coffee with so much sugar that they were zipping around their cells all night long. I wanted them to hear lullabies, not reveille.

The deal was that each hostage had to come up to the bars outlining the cell area to receive their foam cup of food, so that we could ostensibly ensure they were getting a full portion. If we had any kind of opportunity in the exchange, we would also attempt to tip the hostages to a possible assault later that night or early the next morning, so they would know to steer clear of all doorways and windows, but we eventually thought better of this; we didn't want to encounter the Stockholm Syndrome, named after a hostage-bank robbery situation in Sweden in which one or more hostages famously cooperated with their captors initially because they had become psychologically aligned at some point during the ordeal. Next, the hostages would be allowed to remain at a table that was visible to us through the bars until they had finished their meager meal. Then they would be returned to the interior portion of the cell area, in such a way that we would hopefully get some idea where they were being held, relative to the structure of the building—information that would prove invaluable to us as we staged our tactical assault to take back the prison.

The inmates, for their part, were thrilled with themselves for negotiating such a fine and satisfying meal—albeit one served in a foam cup—and started blowing smoke about demanding three meals a day from here on in and throwing hostages from the roof if we didn't deliver them in a timely fashion. They were all heady and pumped, and it was fascinating to me the way it took just these few measures to get the prisoners thinking they were now in control, to feeling confident that the stalemate had finally turned their way, to get them looking ahead to their imminent release. It was such a classic, textbook response. Where there had once been frustration and hopelessness, there was now a tremendous expectation of success—which we hoped would leave them with their guard down. That, on top of the food and coffee, would be enough to send them off to a sound sleep and sweet dreams of approaching freedom.

At about 2:00 on the morning of August 30, we made our move. Hundreds of tactical agents—FBI, mostly, but there were also some folks from INS, BOP, and the U.S. Marshals in on the rescue, all of them decked out in black tactical clothing—moved stealthily about the campuslike compound into position. We had been able to insert hidden microphones in the cell block and listened in while the inmate lookouts began to get that something was up.

"Hey," one sleepy lookout called out to his partner. "There's people out there."

"No," responded the next lookout. "There's no one out there."

"There's a truck out there," insisted the first guy.

"No," said the second, "there's no truck out there."

"Holy shit!" said the first guy. "They're here!"

Then, as if on cue, the HRT-led assault team stormed the Alpha Unit using detonating cord, or "det cord," a flexible fabric tube containing a high explosive designed to transmit the detonation wave to blast the door off the cell block, basically blowing the crap out of the place. I was across the way in the command post area, but even from that distance it was a devastating, deafening series of blasts. A few of the hostages had been previously instructed to keep away from all doors, and we figured they had spread the word, so our assault guys were able to set off those booms without too much worry. By the time the Cubans figured out what was going on, they had been stormed by surprise. They looked up and saw all these FBI agents pouring into Alpha Unit in full combat gear, wearing helmets and wielding submachine guns, and I'm guessing it must have scared the crap out of them; God knows, it would have scared the hell out of me.

The one great glitch to the assault was that one of the charges at the main cell-block doors refused to go off, and we had our guys working it with no success as the assault team stacked up on the wrong side of the door. We had yet to locate any of the hostages at this point, and worried that they might be situated in the area closest to this one door, which meant the Cubans now had all kinds of time to get to them. Gary Noesner, my negotiations counterpart, was standing next to me. "They can't get in," he shouted. "It's going to be a bloodbath."

My heart just sank. Really, I was wound tight as a clock and fairly exhausted to begin with, and now the prospect that all these tense hours might have been for naught or that all those innocent people might be killed in a swift show of foolish revenge was too much to consider. I didn't want to hear it. I refused to hear it. I told myself that if I didn't think it, it wouldn't happen, so I wrapped my mind around something else. Anything else. It was like someone had put a bullet in my heel and the blood was just running out. I was in denial, I guess, but I was in the good kind of denial. That's the difference between me and the bad guys: They were in bad denial, thinking they had won the day and that they had negotiated effectively for their release. I was in good denial, hoping for the best and refusing to acknowledge the worst.

Finally, there was a massive explosion by the main doorway to the cell block. It couldn't have been more than a minute since our guys had burst onto the scene and made their presence known, but it seemed like forever, and now FBI SWAT and HRT agents were literally picked up and blown aside by the blast. There was an outburst of metal and stone and brick, followed by another too-long minute or so while we awaited word on the fate of the hostages.

The inmates were fairly crazed and frantic once our guys stormed in, so our tactical guys had to subdue them with a series of disorienting flash-bang explosions, the same devices we'd used to divert Charles Leaf's attention as he crossed the field on that farm in Sperryville, Virginia. It's a nifty little device that looks somewhat like a Coke can, with an explosive charge that generates a deafening sound and a blinding light, temporarily disorienting anyone close to it. The

Cubans were trying to locate their spears and their knives, but every time one of them made a move for a weapon, one of our guys would throw a flash-bang at the inmate's feet. The idea was to intimidate the prisoners without firing a shot at them, so instead we just flash-banged them into submission until we had located all of the hostages and spirited them out of the cell block to safety.

As dramatic rescues go, this one was right up there. It was a flat-out success: from a tactical perspective, from a negotiating perspective, and all around. And as the hostages began filing into an open area in the courtyard outside of the command post, there was a great deal of emotion and hugging and backslapping and cheering from virtually every corner, until at one point I checked myself and realized that I wasn't doing any of that hugging or backslapping or cheering. A part of me wanted to join in, but I didn't have the first idea how. I was emotional, to be sure, but I couldn't identify which specific emotion I might have been feeling. I was numb, and worn down by the ordeal to where I couldn't think or feel a thing.

I didn't want to talk to anybody. I didn't want to be around anybody. I couldn't even stand the sight of the Cuban prisoners being searched and cuffed and stripped and laid out in the dirt like tuna just hauled off the boat. This deep into my career, I knew enough about myself to recognize this as part of my post-ordeal routine, but it still took me by surprise each and every time. I never saw it coming, and here I just wanted to get away from everybody and everything. Next thing I knew, I had stumbled into a small, dark office somewhere in the bowels of the prison. From the decorations and doodads dotting the poster board above the desk, I guessed it was some secretary's office, and I went inside and closed the door and helped myself to her chair and sat down and allowed my emotions to flow. At one point I looked up from my sobbing and realized I was shaking—literally shaking!—that's how bent out of shape I was. I must have sat there for twenty minutes, trying to compose myself, until I finally had to talk myself down. I reminded myself that I was a trained counselor in post-traumatic stress disorder, so I went to work. *Counsel thyself,* I thought. *Get a grip. Don't just sit here and be this wimpy little guy.* And this tough-love, self-counseling approach was getting around to working, the shakes and tears were abating, when a decorative plaque caught my eye on the wall above the desk. It was a quote from the Bible, Philippians 4:13: "I can do all things through Him who will strengthen me." It was—literally, figuratively, spiritually—an ominous sign. I stared and stared at that plaque for the longest time. It was a line of Scripture I had committed to heart as a small boy, and here it was, right in front of me, reminding me what I had known all along—and it struck me just then as about the most calming thought I could have.

Just then one of the negotiators came into the small room. "What are you doing here?" he wanted to know. "The hostages want to meet with the negotiators. You're the team leader. You've got to get on out there and represent us."

And so I did. I got myself together and went back outside and met with all of the hostages, and here again the mood about the place was shot through with jubilation and relief, but I remained somewhat numb to it. I didn't know what to say to these good people—and, frankly, I didn't have the presence of mind to listen fully to what they were saying to me. I simply accepted the handshakes and hugs that happened to come my way and moved through the crowd, back outside to where the Cuban prisoners had been corralled and laid out in the dirt. Under the bright floodlights they appeared far less menacing than they did a short hour earlier. They were stripped to their shorts, hands behind their backs in plastic handcuffs, their faces in the dirt, and the sight of them there—desperate and beaten and pissed—was such a stirring signal of the human condition. FBI agents and BOP officers were still digging them out of the rubble, all this time later, and soon enough there were more than one hundred of them, all alive and well and lined up in dirty little rows, and I took in the scene and felt everything and nothing for these Cuban prisoners. They had been absolutely diabolical, the way they considered the lives of their hostages to be such throwaway commodities; and yet, in their own way they were doing what they could to bring about change, and I tried to understand the one impulse against the other.

I walked up and down those lines of bound and nearly naked prisoners and wanted desperately to feel something. For their misguided actions. For their plight. For the relentless agony they had caused the hostages and their families. *Something.* But I couldn't feel hatred. I couldn't feel sadness, or remorse. I couldn't feel a blessed thing—not even a sense of relief that the ordeal was finally over and that no one had been seriously hurt.

The day after the siege came to an end, the thirty-two inmates awaiting deportation were sent packing back to Cuba, and I caught the bulletin on the radio and thought, *So that's that, huh? All these man-hours. All this anguish and pain and suffering. All this energy spent on a reckless mission that hadn't amounted to much more than a half-filled foam cup of rice and beans.* And I thought again of the plaque above that secretary's desk and wondered how in the name of God I could draw strength from such as this.

But that's the way it is in life, I reminded myself. You learn from every encounter, good and bad; that's the only way you know for sure that you're still alive.

"BRING HIM BACK ALIVE"

Over time, as the threat of U.S. citizens being kidnapped around the world became more and more prevalent, we created a core group of experienced FBI hostage negotiators fluent in more than one foreign language and provided them with advanced hostage negotiations and crisis management training to deal with such situations. The idea was to safeguard Americans and American interests abroad with the same diligence that we brought to the task at home. We also put together a standard cocktail of shots and inoculations that would allow us to travel the globe on a moment's notice, and identified several international crisis management companies that supported insurance companies across the world in kidnap and ransom matters, commonly known as "K&R" insurance. For the most part, these companies were well known only to multinational corporations that might sometimes find their top executives working in remote, third-world–type areas where conflicting business and political interests might leave them vulnerable.

Indeed, this was the scenario facing Michael L. Barnes, a 41-year-old oil company executive from Los Angeles, just a couple years after the Bureau had stepped up its preparedness in this area. Barnes, a principal of the California-based Unocal Corporation, and vice president and general manager of its Philippine Geothermal, Inc., subsidiary, was kidnapped at gunpoint en route to his office in Manila on January 17, 1992, setting in motion a sequence of events that put our new international rescue program to every kind of test. Unfortunately, the kidnapping became public knowledge within just a few hours, including news of a reported $20 million ransom, which of course greatly complicated investigators' ability to "quietly" identify the group holding Barnes and to negotiate for his safe return.

Let me offer a bit of background on the region before addressing the details in this one case. Although kidnappings were far from rare in the Philippines, this was the first publicly acknowledged kidnapping of an American in Manila. Prior to the Barnes case, the last-known high-dollar kidnapping took place in 1986, when Mitsui general manager Noboyuki Wakaoji was kidnapped while driving his car just south of the Philippine capital. Wakaoji was taken by individuals believed to be members of the Communist New People's Army (NPA), a known Muslim separatist group that was constantly fighting with the Philippine army and police. Wakaoji was released months later after payment of a multimillion-dollar ransom, although the identity of his kidnappers was never conclusively revealed. Many suspected a joint NPA–Japanese Red Army (JRA) operation, which I guess would be like Osama bin Laden throwing in with a U.S.-based hate group to launch another attack on America, but NPA's believed affiliation with the JRA was never fully proved.

The Alex Boncayao Brigade (ABB) was just one of several NPA factions and splinter groups and was believed responsible for over two hundred murders, mainly police officers. After the murders ABB killers would hang lists around the necks of their victims, listing their alleged transgressions. The ABB was also believed responsible for the 1989 murder of U.S. Army colonel James Rowe, a local military adviser on counterinsurgency operations in the Philippines. Col. Rowe was tough and savvy and always carried a .45 automatic in the small of his back, physically and mentally prepared to defend himself at all times, and yet the NPA–backed ABB still managed to kill him on a busy daytime street. Other splinter groups were believed to emerge from the NPA, including the soon-to-be-identified Red Scorpion group, which would soon enough command our front-burner attention.

Now, on to the main story. In August 1991, Barnes's company, PGI, received three letters from an individual identified only as Ka Hector, demanding "revolutionary taxes" to ensure the continued safety of PGI's Makba facility. The letter demanded an initial payment of $200,000, threatening that if such monies were not paid, then PGI personnel would be kidnapped and its Makba plant destroyed. A similar letter arrived the day before Barnes was kidnapped, five months after he and his colleagues were put on alert.

On the face of it, this was simple extortion of the kind that occurs daily in such remote corners of the world: part of the cost of doing business in these regions. Even in the United States, such payments are sometimes routine in some industries, widely considered as "protection" that allows businesses to continue to operate. "You pay, you play," the mantra goes, but once executives bend to these types of demands, they begin to realize they can never cease bending and that they have placed themselves, their families, their employees, and their facilities in ongoing jeopardy.

Barnes, like other expatriates living in and around Manila, had received regular security briefings from the U.S. embassy's regional security officer, or RSO. The RSO's job was to handle all security matters related to the embassy and to other U.S. interests in the area. I had trained many RSOs in hostage negotiation techniques, teaching them to conduct initial negotiations in the event that someone from the embassy got grabbed by kidnappers or terrorists, and in this one case at least the local RSO had warned Barnes and other ex-pats to watch out for surveillances being conducted around their homes and offices by unknown individuals. Barnes in particular had been cautioned to vary his daily routines, including the route he drove to work, the time he drive to work, and the vehicle he drove to work. Regrettably, Barnes took only some of the advice to heart. He was accustomed to keeping a routine, he told us later, and didn't see the need to vary that routine even under such a transparent threat, and you can make the argument that it was his refusal to take these easy precautions that made him a marked man.

Understand, kidnap gangs normally look at a number of potential victims at the same time, trying to identify which prospective victim would be the easiest target, and if you suspect you're being watched, there are some simple strategies you can adopt to cover your butt. If you think you're under surveillance, you can drive down a dead-end street and immediately do a 180-degree turn, heading back at anyone who might be following you; or you can take four quick right-hand turns to see who follows you in a 360-degree circle back to your original location. In these ways, and in others, a moving surveillance is fairly easy to detect, but a "static" or nonmoving surveillance is much harder to identify. In a static surveillance, the kidnap gang may have various operatives positioned on the sidewalk along a route you may be known to frequent, or standing on the street, riding a bike, sleeping in a doorway, watching from a rooftop, leaning against a doorpost or phone booth, looking out an apartment window, and on and on. Over time, they compile a record of your schedule, and your schedule then becomes theirs, and you might as well slap a bull's-eye on your back because you're about to become their next kidnap-for-ransom victim.

We later learned that Mike Barnes had been under surveillance for three months in late 1991, dating back to those original threat letters, and during that time the kidnappers were waiting for the best moment to strike. Finally, at about 6:30 a.m. on January 17, 1992, Barnes left his residence by chauffeur-driven Mercedes, the same vehicle he always took, at the same time he usually left for work each morning, along the same route he usually traveled. As he approached his office, in front of the Metrobank building in downtown Manila, he noticed a dark-colored van enter the road in front of his car. The van slowed to a crawl but stayed in the lane directly in front of Barnes's Mercedes. The closer Barnes got to his office, the slower the van in front appeared to go, effectively boxing in Barnes and his driver in the lane behind them. Then, just as the Mercedes attempted to enter the parking lot of Barnes's building, a Mitsubishi Pajero—an off-road, SUV-type vehicle—cut the car off. Barnes's driver slammed on his brakes but there was nowhere to turn. One man jumped from the Pajero's front passenger door, and two others emerged from the left and right rear doors; only the driver of the Pajero remained in the vehicle, with the engine running. Barnes knew immediately he was in a bad spot, and figured his best hope was that this was a simple robbery attempt—failing to realize, of course, that just a week earlier an employee of the Asian Development Bank had been robbed and eventually killed after a similar approach.

The three men approached the Mercedes brandishing automatic weapons. Barnes, remembering the advice of the RSO not to fight in such a situation, quickly made up his mind to cooperate. He was ordered at gunpoint to exit his vehicle; the driver of the Mercedes was left alone, and he made no move to help Barnes, who slipped out of his seat belt and did as he was told. Barnes was handcuffed and blindfolded and shoved to the rear floor of the Pajero, with two kidnappers taking the seats on either side of him.

Despite the blindfold, Barnes knew the area well enough to guess at the route the Pajero took from the scene: left on Paseo de Roxas, right on Buendia, right onto EDSA, and then south for thirty minutes or so on the superhighway. At some point, the kidnappers turned into an area with speed bumps and considerably less traffic noise, which Barnes took to be a small residential community. The car finally stopped and Barnes stepped into what he assumed was a private home.

The kidnappers were all Filipinos, but Barnes did not know this at the time. He had only seen the face of one of his captors before he was blindfolded. He was led to a small bedroom and recuffed to a length of chain attached to the bedpost on a single bed frame. The rules explained to Barnes were simple: Don't take off the blindfold, don't try to identify anyone in the house, don't cause any trouble— and, above, all, don't try to escape. The words of the RSO finally echoed in Barnes's mind as the reality of his situation sunk in, and he knew that his only chance to emerge from this ordeal alive was to follow these instructions to the letter.

He would remain in this same room, under these same conditions, for the next sixty-one days.

Barnes's kidnappers later gave him new clothes, including three pairs of underwear, three pairs of shorts, and three shirts. He was also given a comb and a new toothbrush—a care package not unlike the one a new inmate might receive upon entering prison. One of his captors led Barnes to a shower stall on a daily basis, attaching the length of chain to which he was handcuffed to the rail of the shower curtain.

Soon a man came to Barnes's room and introduced himself as "the Major." He announced that Barnes had been taken by mistake; the intended target had been another American who had been involved in a notorious drug bust the year before. But this did not mean that Barnes wasn't valuable to his kidnappers. The Major asked Barnes to speculate how much money his company might pay in ransom to gain his release, and Barnes allowed that he did not know. The money was important, the Major said, because the kidnappers were part of the

Young Officers Union, an insurgent group looking to finance a coup against the Filipino national government. The Major said his group would put a $20 million ransom on Barnes.

Barnes wasn't too worried about the number. He knew his company carried K&R insurance on him and other top executives. He knew PGI had the resources to cover that kind of tab. He also knew that there was established precedent for American companies to meet the demands of terrorists and kidnappers on behalf of their employees. What he couldn't be sure of, however, was whether or not his colleagues would be allowed to pay the ransom, because even from his perspective, blindfolded and chained to a bedpost, he knew that to bend to such extortion once was to bend to it again and again and again.

Other than the Major, who visited from time to time, Barnes rarely spoke to his captors. When the kidnappers played the radio or the television in the house, they were always tuned to local stations, and the only language that Barnes heard was the native Tagalog; among themselves, the kidnappers only spoke in Tagalog. Occasionally, Barnes would recognize a Western song on the radio such as "Please Release Me," "Born Free," or "The Green, Green Grass of Home," and came to the conclusion that his captors had a mischievous sense of humor. Behind his blindfold, he determined that there were usually four or more kidnappers in the house at any one time, and that additional members of the group seemed to come and go at all hours of the day and night, again suggesting that he was being held in a private residence or safe house of some kind.

After several days of captivity Barnes was led to a room and told to sit down. He understood from the Major that he was to participate in a press conference, but no one ever asked him a question and he was not given an opportunity to speak. He heard a great many new voices around the room and assumed a large group had gathered. He could also hear the sound of metal to metal, leading him to believe that weapons were being passed about, and the blare of music in the background. Nothing was said to him in the room, and none of the kidnappers made any kind of formal statement that Barnes could make out, but it turned out the group had assembled to tape a video to document Barnes's current condition. Behind the table where he sat hung a large flag identifying the Red Scorpion Group as his captors, and their show of force indicated that they were indeed heavily armed. Local police were later able to identify a link between the Red Scorpions and the NPA, and it was at this point that the U.S. State Department requested FBI assistance.

This is where I came in, through my work in the Bureau's SOARS unit and its Hostage Negotiations program. Typically agents were dispatched on international cases on a short-straw basis, which essentially meant that if you drew the short straw you had been "volunteered," but in this one instance I actually did volunteer to fly to Manila to attempt to bring about Barnes's safe release. I thought I had something unique to offer—the right mix of experience and insight, perhaps—and so I stepped up. Almost as soon as I had my hand in the air, I had been given my shots and my malaria pills and my marching orders: "Bring him back alive." Everything else was left to me.

A pessimist would not have liked my chances as I flew off into a hotbed of terrorist activities conducted by local guerrillas with a track record of murdering law enforcement officers. And not a single one of them could have cared less that I was an American FBI agent on a mission. To them I was just another fly in their ointment—and to make matters worse, this fly couldn't even carry a gun. Owing to a rather archaic policy having to do with national sovereignty, we were restricted from carrying our weapons into foreign territory. It was a concept I understood and respected, but I thought Uncle Sam might grant me an exception on this one, given the Wild West aspects of Manila at the time, with heavily armed gangs holding up the local banks on a regular basis, and shotgun-toting private security guards stationed outside the local convenience stores to deter robbers. It was like sending me off on a scuba diving mission without an oxygen tank, but I had to play by the rules, which I of course took to simply mean that I couldn't bring my weapon from the United States to the Philippines. If I happened to find a handgun once I breezed into town, it was another matter, and from here on in I moved about knowing that if I had to shoot somebody I would not be in a position to wait around for the police afterward.

I knew enough about countersurveillance techniques to score fairly high on the professional paranoia scale, and as I familiarized myself with the dark, uncertain streets of Manila I caught myself looking endlessly over my shoulder, awaiting a sneak attack at every turn. After a year in Vietnam and countless years on the job in the States, I'd be damned if I was going to let some seedy third world operative take me without a fight. Mike Barnes had done what was right in his situation, and I would do what was right in mine, and as I thought back to the sad fate of Col. Jim Rowe and the terrorist and guerrilla forces that limned this strange city, it never once occurred to me that a far smaller but far more deadly assailant would soon threaten my life on this venture into the unknown.

Bad custard, best I could figure. That's what nearly did me in, as I wrote earlier in the prologue to these pages. A couple weeks in to my time in Manila, I stepped into a reasonable-enough-looking restaurant with some of my colleagues on the Barnes case, and against my better judgment I sampled one of the desserts on display—a mistake that would cost me dearly. Over the next few days I suffered such an acute and agonizing case of diarrhea that I must have dropped twenty pounds and lost more fluid than I could possibly replenish, all of which left me on the brink of collapse that afternoon in the U.S. ambassador's office—and sent me back to Virginia for a week or so to recoup, refuel, and otherwise recharge my batteries.

For the most part, though, the dangers of Manila were a bit more out in the open than bacteria. Like many other third-world cities, the place was completely up for grabs. Women? Boys? Girls? Drugs? Whatever you wanted, it was there for the taking. Neon signs on the local bars all but commanded you to enter and take up with some young girl for the night, for the week, or longer. Cheap beer. Watered-down booze. Lives for rent or sale. That was the Manila I discovered in February 1992. Drugs could be had on every corner, along with fake Rolex watches and spiced monkey meat (or maybe it was cat or dog) cooked over a filthy fire. Up and down the streets, I'd come across women and children—sad and desperate and hopeless—lying on the sidewalks, barely able to raise one hand to beg the money that might prolong their lives for one more day. It was a killing, heartbreaking scene, and there was no end to it.

Even the local pastimes were depressing. There was a popular Australian bar that was a hangout for cops, crooks, and ex-pats of every type; the real draw for this rowdy crowd was "midget tossing," an activity that seemed fueled in large part by massive quantities of Foster's. One wall of the bar was covered in Velcro, and the owners of the place hired a group of local midgets—or, perhaps, really small Filipinos—to suit up in Velcro body suits and submit to a strange humiliation. They looked like little space cadets awaiting a flight to the moon, and the mostly drunk, mostly Australian patrons would pay the local equivalent of five or ten dollars for the chance to toss one of them against the padded, Velcro-covered wall. Done properly, the Velcro suit would stick to the wall and everyone would have a good hoot and holler at the odd ways the poor midgets would be positioned on each impact, and I looked on and thought, *Sodom has a twin sister, and her name is Manila.*

I had a great room in a large downtown hotel, just a few blocks from the American embassy. I didn't talk on the room phones because I thought they might be bugged, and I never left my laptop computer in the hotel room, even though it would have taken the National Security Agency to hack into it anyway. During the day it was locked away in the embassy and at night I worked on it in my room. My personal protection antennas were always up in such environments, and my conscience was functioning in its default Southern Baptist mode, which basically meant that that there wasn't much for a guy like me to do in Manila but work and sleep—this on the theory that if you believe in truth and justice, you need live it also.

You know, it occurred to me at some point during the weeks-long negotiations for Barnes's release that this right here is the difference between folks on the right side of the law and folks on the wrong side of the law. There is a small but statistically significant percentage of the population, probably around 3 or 4 percent, that are not burdened with a conscience. They have no social, no moral, and no ethical constraints. They do whatever they want, to whomever they want, for no reason at all. They rob, rape, kidnap, and murder without a thought to the human toll that they leave in their wake, believing that those of us with consciences are limited and weak, leaving us easy pickings and logical targets. Psychologists and lawmakers may call these guiltless, guileless, and heartless individuals sociopaths, psychopaths, or antisocial personalities. To cops and crooks, they're guerrillas, terrorists, and killers. By any name, this was how the sides stacked up in the Barnes kidnapping, and on the not-even-close-to-level playing fields of Manila there were just enough players seated on the sidelines (crooked cops, crooked reporters, crooked politicians) to make this far more of a challenge than any such kidnapping would have been in a more controlled environment like the United States.

We did the best we could. I worked the case with the local FBI legal attaché, an agent of matching rank who was assigned to the U.S. embassy in Manila and represented the Bureau in criminal investigative matters in that area of the world; the RSO; a U.S. military adviser and other members of the ambassador's staff; and, from time to time, the ambassador himself. There was also a representative of an international crisis management company that had been retained by Barnes's employers in Los Angeles as part of their K&R insurance coverage. There wasn't anyone in our group fluent in Tagalog, so we had to identify a representative of Philippine Geothermal and make him a trusted agent, which of course led inevitably to complications: Something is always lost in translation through these third-party negotiators, no matter how competent or diligent they are in their job. The frustration here is that these sensitive discussions are too often played out like a childhood game of "telephone," and by the time the translation reaches those of us at the end of the line, its original intent may be lost.

We would meet at various locations around Manila, depending on who was needed at the meeting and who was available. Sometimes we would meet in the ambassador's office, the site of my near downfall by food poisoning; other times we'd meet in hotel rooms, at the police department, on a military base, or in a local bar—preferably one without the distraction of midget tossing. Contact with the kidnappers was frequently on their terms, even as we tried to get them to reach out to us on a daily basis. As in all of these protracted negotiations, a schedule was key. From our perspective we wanted to keep the kidnappers on a strict schedule, calling at appointed times, even if nothing of substance was discussed or accomplished during those phone calls. Sometimes they'd meet the schedule and sometimes they wouldn't, and in each case it was a tactic or a posturing of some kind. They wanted to call the shots, and we wanted to let them believe they were calling the shots, and somewhere in the middle each side attempted to wear the other down.

The kidnappers were initially upset to learn that the FBI was involved in the case. They were used to running roughshod over local police. Indeed, many of their ranks might have been former or current cops, and certainly several maintained close ties with the local police department, so the idea of having to deal with an American FBI agent was anathema to them. We were an unknown. Plus, our involvement was a clear sign that the stakes had been ratcheted up in this one case. Whatever folks might think of us back home, it seems those three letters—FBI—carry a powerful message around the world, something akin to the Bat Signal Police Commissioner Gordon would shine above Gotham City. I don't know that we struck fear in the hearts of these Red Scorpions, but if given the choice they would have preferred us to steer clear.

Throughout my stay in the Philippines, my "Batmobile" was a run-down rental, and it was always an adventure driving the streets of Manila at night because the locals turned off their headlights, thinking it would save gas. Some of our group took cabs around the city to save themselves the anguish, but I wasn't about to cast my fate to some local driver who might or might not have had his own ties to the kidnappers. (A word of advice, for those who find themselves in need of a taxi and believe they're being followed: Never take the first cab that pulls up in front of you. Take the second or third cab and be safe.)

We were led to believe that Barnes was being moved about the region and held in a different location each night, and with each contact we attempted to corroborate the victim's well-being. In Bureau-speak, this is known as "proof of life," and since we couldn't talk to Barnes directly, we always had a list of questions at the ready—the name of his childhood pet, where he had attended grade school, his mother's maiden name—to determine whether or not he was still alive. If he was already dead, of course, the kidnappers could never come up with the answers to these questions.

Occasionally the kidnappers would orchestrate one of those photo-op propaganda moments as described earlier, sending along video of Barnes sitting in front of one of their Red Scorpion banners, flanked by kidnappers wearing masks and carrying AK-47s, usually with a newspaper held up in the background indicating the date the footage was recorded.

We made no real progress, other than the fact that Barnes remained alive and that there were ongoing negotiations, but soon enough a picture emerged. The Red Scorpions were united against the Filipino government. What was unclear, at first and throughout, was whether they were a true nationalist group, trying to present their own candidates in a viable attempt to overthrow the current regime, or whether they were just in it for the money. Twenty million dollars was an awful lot of money, and one of my first tasks was to try to cut that number down to size. Philippine Geothermal might have been willing to pay the initial ransom, but I felt strongly that if we could reduce the amount of the demand we'd be in a better position to negotiate for Barnes's release—and to forestall such kidnappings in the future. We couldn't have these groups thinking these American executives were easy prey—$20 million here, $20 million there—because there'd be no end to it.

We set up a command post in one of our hotel rooms, where we'd brief the Philippine Geothermal representatives on our progress. Telephone line tracing was still in the dark ages in Manila, and even the technical representative that I brought in from the FBI Lab in Washington was unable to get the local telephone service to successfully trace the kidnappers' calls back to their point of origin, so we were flying blind in this one respect. The language barrier was also getting in the way of our talks, with every statement having to be filtered through a translator. In any language, though, the stakes remained clear: $20 million or Barnes would be dead. No compromise. No other deal. The kidnappers were dug in, and we were up against it.

Three weeks into the kidnapping, Barnes was forced to make a tape-recorded statement for his wife and for Philippine Geothermal to review; he was also made to write a letter to his employers and to his spouse, and as I read over their shoulders I was reminded that these are tough situations for the families and colleagues and friends of the kidnap victim. They want to help—they *need* to help—but their concern puts increased pressure on the negotiators acting on the victim's behalf. Still, they remain involved because they're family, and their emotional ties are often a life force for their loved one in captivity. In Barnes's case, he later told us that he spent his days—sixty-one in all— praying, meditating, and daydreaming about driving his Corvette along the California coast, something that symbolized freedom to him. He also built his dream home—brick by brick, piece by piece— working the details in his mind until he got it just right. He did as much physical exercise as he could manage while attached to a six-foot length of chain, including knee bends and lying on his back and running his legs in an "air bicycle" motion. To exercise his mind, he tore through a book of crossword puzzles in the first weeks of his confinement, but his captors failed to supply him with additional books as they had originally promised.

When I returned to Manila following my brief convalescence back home, I didn't like that we hadn't moved all that much from where we'd been before I took ill. We were still at $20 million, still talking, and still no closer to seeing Barnes to safety. After so much time— nearly five weeks, at this point—we should have made more progress, so I brought in other FBI negotiators, including Special Agent Max Howard, perhaps the toughest negotiator under fire on our team, to help balance our approach. The idea of meeting that $20 million price tag was anathema to those of us charged with safeguarding the bigger picture. It would be open season on every U.S. ex-pat in the Philippines. Some years earlier Exxon had paid approximately $18 million to secure the release of one of its employees, touching off a spate of multimillion-dollar ransoms across Central and South Americas as well as in parts of Asia. Soon the Exxon ransom payment paled alongside the $60 million ransom that some believe was paid by the president of an Argentine firm for the release of his two kidnapped sons in 1974.

Early on I had explained to a Unocal corporate security official, a man who prided himself on having been a lieutenant in the peacetime Army and therefore well schooled in combating guerrillas, that we needed to prepare for one of at least four different scenarios in this case: Barnes would be released without a payment of ransom (possibility: slim to none); Barnes would be murdered with or without the payment of a ransom (possibility: as likely as not, but there was also the chance that a subsequent ransom would be demanded after the first one was paid); Barnes would be released upon the ransom payment (possibility: iffy at best, especially if the full amount had been negotiated down); Barnes would be rescued after a deliberate assault by a police or a military tactical team (possibility: likely, but there would be great human cost, and it was unclear whether Barnes would survive the attack). Admittedly, none of these potential outcomes was particularly encouraging, but I advised that we had to prepare for all of them.

"A tactical rescue," the corporate security guy scoffed, "that'll never happen." I later learned that this guy went back to the U.S. to meet with his Unocal team and the assistant director of the FBI's Los Angeles field office and reported that I was "an FBI cowboy," a term I didn't much mind but was nevertheless offered as a negative. Of course, the Barnes kidnapping had made all kinds of headlines in California, and it was such a big, ongoing story that it placed the entire Unocal operation under a great deal of public pressure.

"Get this guy the hell out of there," the security guy railed, insisting that someone else from our office be put on the case.

With this, the assistant director got on the phone to Manila and wanted to hear from me what was going on. He wasn't about to sell out one of his own agents, but he wanted to get the lay of the land—straight from the cowboy's mouth. I explained what I saw the options to be, and why, and the assistant director agreed with me on every point, promising to handle the Unocal people on his end and leaving me responsible for my end, which would ultimately—and hopefully—include the release of Michael L. Barnes.

I reminded myself yet again of the many roles the hostage negotiator takes on in a protracted standoff. Depending on the situation, I am a talker, a father confessor, a trusted ally of the kidnapper, an escape and rescue facilitator, and an advocate of the tactical assault rescue option. I'm a fisherman of sorts, and I have a great many psychological lures up my sleeve, one of which is what the British Special Air Service (SAS), their equivalent to our U.S. Army Delta Force, calls "the final option": surgical firepower and highly trained manpower in the form of an established hostage rescue team to carry the day and rescue the victim. It sounded great in theory, and on our home soil it often sounds great in actual practice, but here in Manila we were a little short on resources. All we needed were a well-trained and well-armed rescue team, a lead on Barnes's exact location, and a little luck—not too much to ask, I thought.

The Manila police had recently developed a SWAT capability, but it was a far cry from our full-time SWAT and hostage rescue teams back home. Still, it was a place to start, so I asked the U.S. Ambassador to bring in ST-6, the U.S. Navy SEAL team from Virginia, with the best counterterrorism and hostage rescue capability in the Navy. These guys could work miracles, and I felt strongly that if we could add their insight and expertise to our arsenal we could surely mount a successful rescue.

Unfortunately, the ambassador didn't quite see it the same way. "I understand why you want them brought in," he said, "but the Philippine government would never approve of us undertaking such a high-profile mission on their soil."

This struck me as yet another example of diplomacy at its best and bureaucracy at its worst, and I went back to the drawing board for another strategy. If there was to be a hostage rescue mission, it would have to be conducted by the local police—and, despite their newly minted SWAT capabilities, they simply were not capable of carrying out such a mission with any reasonable chance of success.

Meanwhile, negotiations with the kidnappers were now lasting only a few minutes, and there were frequently large gaps between negotiations. Most troubling of all, though, was the tone and tenor of these discussions, which had grown more tense and difficult with each passing week. Even in Tagalog, before having it filtered through a translator, I could sense the mounting rage and frustration on the part of the kidnappers, who clearly felt they had not been taken seriously enough that we would meet their demands. Their threats to kill Barnes and put an end to this standoff were mounting, and it was time to get the locals on board with a credible threat of our own. To supplement the local effort, I called FBI Headquarters and requested a couple of guys from our Hostage Rescue Team, preferably former Navy SEALs or guys with a military special-ops background who could come in and teach close-quarter battle techniques to the local police. I also needed ammunition and flash-bangs, which the State Department wasn't about to send our way, out of diplomatic concerns, but my longtime colleague and onetime coconspirator in the Covenant, the Sword and the Arm of the Lord siege in Arkansas, Danny Coulson, the first commander of the HRT and now an FBI deputy assistant director, was able to slice through the red tape and get it done. Like the best FBI agents who had vaulted into the Bureau's upper ranks, Coulson knew how to skip some of the fine print and focus on the bigger picture.

Training went quickly with the Filipino PD SWAT team: the local police were fast learners and relished the opportunity to be trained by the best of the best in law enforcement. The police department had an English-language capability, so we were able to communicate effectively, and if they needed to translate further down the chain of command, they were able to do so efficiently. We got our points across fairly well. We gave them ammunition. We gave them flash-bangs and taught them how to use them. Over a period of a week or two we did extensive training at a nearby naval base, where we were joined by some Filipino Navy SEALs, and eventually built this ragtag police SWAT team into a respectable hostage rescue unit—that is, until the State Department got wind of it and shut the effort down. By this point, though, the local police were good to go, and able to carry out an effective rescue, should negotiations continue along at a standstill pace. I don't want to overstate their capabilities here, but they went from carrying, say, 99-to-1 odds against being able to pull off a successful mission to about 50-50.

As negotiations continued, we began to develop a contingency plan of attack. The local police SWAT team would have to quickly enter any building or home in which Barnes was suspected of being held, then move with even more speed through the rooms of the building to find and rescue Barnes before one of his kidnappers had the opportunity to kill him. No small feat. We knew from experience that at least one kidnapper would likely be designated to kill the hostage as the rescue team entered the building to save him; therefore, our operatives had to train the local team to effectively use the flash-bangs we had provided to get the kidnappers' attention, and to then by force and surgical shooting techniques neutralize any kidnapper who attempted to kill Barnes. Again, no small feat. Put yourself in the position of a tactical team member. If you take your time making entry into the residence, and then if you stop to advise every terrorist of his rights and handcuff him and pass him outside before you enter the next room looking for the hostage, Barnes would be dead five times over. Speed, surprise, and violence of attack were needed, and if not fully applied, the body count would include police officers and the hostage.

It was time to go and to go hard.

And yet, I never lost hope on the negotiations front. Always, I sought a peaceful talking cure to these situations, and I was the last of our group to give up the ghost on a brokered truce, but I had to be prepared. We still knew that our primary tactic would be to seek any type of negotiated solution that could bring about Mike Barnes's safe return. He was our main responsibility—along with that of the dozens of men and women who were now trying so desperately to find and rescue him. But if all else failed, we still had to have "the final option" at the ready; otherwise, Barnes was a dead man.

Throughout the standoff and our unsanctioned training operation, we worked with the highest levels of the local police department, even cutting out some senior officers that the national government had suggested that we keep out of the loop; they knew their people better than we could on such a short breeze through the region, and if our government sources suspected some high-ranking official of being on the wrong side of this standoff, we had no choice but to trust them.

At some point the police antiterrorism squad was able to identify several members of the Red Scorpion Group, and they moved quickly to develop potential informants within that group. The key to this effort turned out to be the girlfriend of one of the gang members, who pointed us to five different safe houses where Barnes was most likely being held. Surveillance was instituted on the five locations, but we still had to make an educated guess as to Barnes's location. All along we had been led to believe that Barnes was moved from safe house to safe house, perhaps even on a daily basis, but after monitoring these five locations for several days and seeing no movement, we came to the inescapable conclusion that Barnes had most likely been held in the same location for extended periods.

It was now sixty days since Barnes's initial capture, and we had not been provided proof of life for over a week. We didn't know if he was dead or alive, or if he was really holed up in the small house we had decided to target, but we had to put our chips on a number, and the number we chose was this one local residence. The game plan was to hit all five locations at the same moment, with the HRT-trained local police SWAT team taking the house we'd chosen as most likely to hold Barnes, one located in nearby Paranaque.

Day broke on March 18, 1992, Barnes's sixty-first day in captivity, much like it had for the previous two months. Barnes was still blindfolded, still chained to the same bed in the same small room, still daydreaming about driving his Corvette through the California hills. He counted time by the crow of the rooster, and the delivery of his meals, and the long, quiet hours of presumed nightfall. At around 1:00 p.m., he was lying on his bed and meditating while his guards watched television in the next room. Suddenly, Barnes heard an unfamiliar (and unexpected) commotion outside the house; one of the guards came running into Barnes's room, disconnected the length of chain that hooked Barnes to the bed, and wrapped the chain around Barnes's neck, forcing Barnes into a crouched position on the floor. Next the unidentified kidnapper jammed a pistol into the side of Barnes's head and told him to keep quiet. Barnes was aware that something was happening and could only hope that the authorities were trying to rescue him—or could he? If Barnes had listened to the briefings offered by the U.S. embassy's RSO, he would have known that the two most dangerous times for a hostage or kidnap victim are when they are first captured and when the authorities come to rescue them via a tactical assault. He'd survived the first such hurdle and was now apparently facing the second, and he must have known that, one way or another, his fate was about to be resolved.

With the chain now wrapped tightly around his neck, Barnes was dragged in a steel choke hold from his bedroom into the kitchen area of the house. Flash-bangs began going off throughout the house. Barnes's ears were ringing because the sounds were so loud, but he could only see the flashes of light through the multicolored cloth that served as his blindfold. His kidnapper was now dragging Barnes back and forth across the room by his neck like a rag doll, a semiautomatic pistol to his head. Gunshots were heard inside and outside of the house as Barnes's captor dragged him toward a door. And then, on our choreographed signal, a second door burst open and another round of flash-bangs was set off, punctuated by more gunshots.

It was in the middle of all of this orchestrated chaos and frenzy that Barnes's captor finally shouted, "I have the American and I am going to kill him," still pressing the barrel of his pistol deep into Barnes's temple, and as he did another flash-bang went off just to the side of Barnes.

It only took a split second, but it was a split second we had been counting on for the past sixty-one days. The Red Scorpion guard momentarily turned his attention toward the sound of the last exploding diversionary device, and as he did so he was hit by a hail of automatic-weapon fire, thereby meeting the same fate as all of his fellow gang members. The pistol dropped from his hand, and as the kidnapper fell to the floor he somehow retained hold of the chain around Barnes's neck, yanking on it one final time as in a dead man's clench.

The Filipino SWAT team stormed the room and rushed Barnes from the immediate kill zone, his bare feet hardly touching the ground as they fled the room with him. Still blindfolded and deafened by the flash-bangs, barefoot and chained around the neck with the smell of burned gunpowder filling his senses, Barnes was rushed to safety by his rescuers; and as they removed the blindfold that had been in place for over two months, Barnes finally realized that he had been saved. He didn't know exactly who had done the saving, but as his eyes adjusted to the scene it became clear. Thirteen bullet-riddled bodies lay strewn about the house: his captors. And there was a similar scene at the other four targeted houses in and around Manila, which were also hit at the same time, in much the same way.

Local police took Barnes to a nearby staging area, where his chains were removed and he was given something to drink. Then he was whisked away to police headquarters and away from the nightmare that had been his life for the previous two months. He would now get the chance to drive that Corvette down a twisting California highway, and he might even get to build that new house he had fantasized about. Life was indeed sweet.

One month later some of these same Filipino police officers killed six members of the Red Scorpion Group and recovered a list of victims marked for future kidnappings, including the names of several prominent Chinese-Filipino businessmen.

Later that same month local police hit yet another Red Scorpion Group safe house, shooting and killing Alfredo de Leon, the suspected leader of the group, ending the reign of the country's most notorious killer and extortionist.

But Alfredo de Leon's influence was felt even in death when, almost one year following Barnes's rescue, the Filipino government filed murder charges against twenty-nine police officers who were part of the group that raided the five Red Scorpion Group locations on March 18, 1992. The local government indicated its belief that two or more of the alleged kidnappers were shot in cold blood by the police raid teams.

I was back home in Virginia, with another year of more-of-the-same under my belt, when I caught this bulletin on the news and I counted myself extremely lucky: that I had gotten to work a good case with great FBI agents; that I had helped to put together a team that saved an American businessman from certain death and eliminated a group of murdering terrorists before they could kill more cops and more innocent citizens; and that I had gotten out of Manila alive. It would have been ironic, I thought, to survive a near-fatal bout of salmonella poisoning, a killing mess of red tape administered by my own State Department and some of my superiors back home at FBI Headquarters, and an agonizing stretch away from Dianne and the kids, just to have stuck around and been charged with murder by the very government I was risking all to serve and protect. And so I revised my thinking on this one case, amending my conclusion that life was indeed sweet to allow that it was also sometimes sour, and confusing, and shot through with so many mixed signals, it's a wonder we ever get anything accomplished.

And yet, we do.

DAVID KORESH, TIMOTHY McVEIGH, TED KACZYNSKI

"I GOTS TO KNOW"

I retired from the FBI in August 1995, thinking I'd about had my fill of front-line duty. It was about time. I'd been an FBI agent since 1970, and in that time I'd seen my family bounce from Rome, Georgia, to Rochester, New York, to Fredericksburg, Virginia. I'd seen my kids grow into adulthood. I'd seen a great deepening of my faith and focus as my career path rerouted me from a new agent at the FBI Academy, to a rookie agent in the field chasing bank robbers, to a veteran expert on negotiating strategies, and soon enough to an authority on profiling, international threats, and terrorism-related issues—a sea change that took me from theory to practice and all the way back to theory. Along that way, I'd seen every piece of human flotsam and jetsam, every scourge on society, every horror and nightmare and personal tragedy you'd care to imagine—and quite a few, frankly, that I cared to forget, although the ghosts sometimes return at night to relive such matters.

I was tired. I was only 50 years old, and I'd slogged through enough crap, logged enough miles, endured enough sleepless nights in lousy motel rooms and truck beds (and, on one occasion, in the middle of a flooded soccer field in St. Croix after Hurricane Hugo), and had suffered enough fools and heartaches and disappointments to last a thousand lifetimes.

In the back of my mind I'd always thought of pulling the plug on my career after twenty-five years and looking to make a go of things on my full pension while I was still young enough to light out on something new, but there were a couple assignments in there that reinforced my timetable and helped me to put an exclamation point on things. The first and most prominent of these was a drawn-out incident that would blot the reputation of the FBI for millions of Americans for years to come—to many, it's a blot the Bureau can never erase—and leave my colleagues facing a harangue of charges ranging from a misuse of power, to a miscarriage of justice, to a general and persistent mishandling of a sequence of unfortunate events. In the fallout, the fifty-one-day standoff outside of Waco, Texas, in the winter and spring of 1993, pitting FBI and ATF agents against an apocalyptic (and heavily armed) quasi-Christian sect known as the Branch Davidians, would become known as our Alamo, our Waterloo—and it was a wearying thing for me and my fellow agents to find ourselves the object of all that finger-pointing.

The Branch Davidians, an offshoot of the Seventh-day Adventists, were headed at the time by a would-be rock-'n'-roll guitarist turned charismatic leader named David Koresh, who became the public face of this drama. In many respects the emerging crisis leading up to the Waco siege unfolded pretty much like it did in Arkansas with the Covenant, the Sword and the Arm of the Lord. The confrontation began routinely enough on February 28, 1993, when ATF agents arrived at the Branch Davidian compound in Mount Carmel, Texas, and attempted to execute a warrant for Koresh as part of an ongoing investigation into charges of child abuse and possession of illegal weapons. It might have been a routine operation, with the right mix of speed, surprise, and firepower on the side of the law, but it was not to be. A tactical resolution was sought before any attempt at negotiations; the Davidians were not surprised at all; ATF agents were outmanned and outgunned; four ATF agents and six Branch Davidians were killed in a peremptory shoot-out, with an untold number injured. Before anyone could figure what went wrong, Koresh and his followers had holed up inside their community building, beginning one of the longest and most notorious sieges in contemporary American history and culminating in what is widely regarded as one of the largest-scale boondoggles in the annals of federal law enforcement.

The upshot: following an overwhelming tear-gas assault begun that cold, windy Texas morning, a raging fire destroyed the compound on April 19, 1993, consuming Koresh and seventy-four followers, including twenty-one children, and igniting a debate that continues to rage as to the source of that fire, the self-inflicted wounds on many Davidians, and the overall handling of the incident by government agencies.

I'll leave the details of the Waco tragedy to history, which to date has included formal investigations by the FBI and the Department of Justice, and a ten-month investigation led by former Republican senator John C. Danforth, at the appointment of then Attorney General Janet Reno. And I'll leave the bulk of my own personal notes and reflections to another volume, because over the course of the siege we FBI agents on the scene collected enough material to fill an entire shelf at the local library. Here, though, I want to shine a narrow cone of light on myself and share just a little bit of my relevant thinking on the case—at least regarding the aspects that had to do with my growing sense of closure on my FBI career. I also want to share a passage from the long discussions I had with Koresh, pages and pages of which have been transcribed in Treasury, ATF, and FBI records.

Realize, I was at the Mount Carmel compound for a big chunk of those fifty-one days, although curiously it was a good long while before I was sent to the scene because someone in the SOARS office got it in his head that my Christian faith might leave me susceptible to Koresh's evangelical teachings. (At least, that was his stated reasoning.) I actually had a couple conversations about this with a couple FBI supervisors—people who will remain nameless to protect their outright stupidity—who suggested that my judgment might be compromised by my personal religious beliefs.

"Any chance you'll go down there and identify with Koresh and his movement?" then–deputy assistant director Mike Kahoe asked, cutting right to it. Mike had been an ASAC at the Oakdale prison riot, when we negotiated the inmates into a nonviolent surrender, so we had a good history.

"No chance, Mike," I responded, trying my best not to appear offended. "Not gonna happen."

"Good," Mike said. "I know it wasn't an issue at Oakdale, and I assumed it wouldn't be the case here, but I had to ask. Hope you don't mind."

I shrugged like it was nothing at all, but of course I minded. How could I *not* have minded? After all the time and all the good work I'd done in my career—after the principled ways I'd tried to carry myself, in and out of the office—it set me off to have to answer to the suggestion that I'd be sucked in by a loose screw like David Koresh simply because of my belief in God and Christianity. It rankled. *What, I'm going to go down to Texas and bond with Dave, just because he reads the Bible? What kind of backward thinking is that?*

Still stewing, I went down to Texas the following day, in the second week of the standoff, and I wound up spending countless hours with Koresh, working diligently to pierce his veil of spirituality, trying to make sense of his wild ramblings while at the same time trying to talk some sense into him. It was, on reflection, an all-but-impossible task, although while I was in its middle there were moments when we suddenly seemed to make the kind of connection necessary to bring about a laying down of arms. And then, just as suddenly, those moments would pass and I would once again worry about the likelihood of ever talking Koresh out of that compound.

At one point, for one frustrating example, our circuitous conversation turned to my responsibilities as a Christian weighed against my responsibilities as an FBI agent, an apparent conflict of interests and beliefs to a guy like David Koresh that we very nearly set aside.

Quoting from the transcript:

CLINT: David, let me ask you this . . . What is the opinion of your flock of the authorities that are outside of your complex? What do they represent? Is there an opinion or a teaching provided that this represents Babylon?

DAVID: Well, Babylon is anything that's contrary to God's word. Would you not agree?

CLINT: As a Christian and as an FBI agent, I don't find myself and my responsibility contrary to God's word.

DAVID: Well, if you were an apostle, then you would not be working for the FBI. You'd be out ministering, like Paul the apostle.

CLINT: Well, I can do both, though. I can minister . . .

DAVID: Well, not really . . .

CLINT: . . . within the context of my responsibility and still carry out what I'm supposed to do as an FBI agent.

DAVID: Well, now Clint . . .

CLINT: . . . no, you got to understand, David, that I've spent years, you know, as an FBI agent, always saying if I'm supposed to do something else, if I'm supposed to give this up and go on a mission field, I want to do it. I would sell my house. I would give up my car. I would, you know. Those things mean nothing, and I would very quickly move out into that field if I was told to do that. But I'm in a field. I'm in a mission field right now.

DAVID: Right. Well, I agree with you as a . . .

CLINT: . . . but I've not been told to give up. Go away. Go out and do something else. I've been told, Stay where you are, and minister where you are.

DAVID: Well, then that's what you have to do.

CLINT: And you've got so many people out there outside of your complex. You know what, what bothers me, David, is I think sometimes there's a *we* against *us* type of mentality here where the Branch, where your flock is the we, and everybody outside of your flock may be them. And that's not correct. That's the diversity that you talk about that shouldn't take place. And I don't think it is taking place . . .

DAVID: Now, I . . .

CLINT: . . . but if I was in your position, David, if I was in your position, I would as a Christian, as a believer, I would want to bring the situation, number one, to the world's attention, so they could hear through me what took place, and number two . . .

DAVID: They're going to . . .

CLINT: . . . take it into man's court and resolve it into man's court, then.

DAVID: Clint, you're being very clever. But nonetheless . . .

CLINT: No, David. See, now, okay, that bothers me . . .

DAVID: Well . . .

CLINT: . . . when you hear honesty and you attribute it to cleverness.

DAVID: You're calling it honesty . . . but are we going back to the negotiation part or are we going back to the fear of God?

CLINT: Let's say, I'm sitting in my house on a Sunday afternoon, knowing this situation has gone on, and to get a call to come here with no reason for that to take place, unless some divine intervention is saying here, to come here, that you can do some good based upon your beliefs and your background, and to have you attribute that to a rank-and-file negotiator . . .

DAVID: Well . . . first of all, we're Christians. Yes or no? Then let's have respect to God. Let's come up hither. Now, up hither, there's no FBI agents except you, okay? And me, I'm a mechanic. I'm a carpenter, alright? I like to build houses. I'm a guitar player. According to the flesh.

CLINT: Well . . .

DAVID: I mean, that's just the things we do in the world.

CLINT: Okay, and I've built cabinets, too. And I've built furniture before. So . . .

DAVID: Praise the Lord, so?

CLINT: . . . so, you know, we can say, you know . . . as far as I'm concerned, I'm the most important carpenter, and what better lifestyle or employment could I model my life after?

DAVID: Exactly. So now we come up hither, and we see God on the throne. And the father hands the book to the lamb. Okay? Now that's what we were interested in.

CLINT: You know, I have understood you from the beginning, David. I've understood that your mission and the responsibility of you and your flock you feel differs from what the authorities outside of your complex have . . . And yet I draw a very strong analogy between the missions of both, because there are many Christians out here who want to resolve this positively and who want to see the Lord's hand on this situation and bring it . . .

DAVID: But you also know that there are many who are not Christians out there. And because . . .

CLINT: Well, I mean, let's talk about the world, okay? There are many out there who are not Christians. I mean, you know, if you want to take a head count and say, Okay, how many FBI agents are Christian? Raise your hands. Does that do any good? What does that accomplish? But they're here. And they care. And they want to see this resolved non-violently. But we have two different plateaus. And I understand that . . . and you're saying we're working with a spiritual clock, and we have spiritual direction . . . and the authorities out there are working on man's clock, and don't ask us to punch in on your clock . . .

In another exchange, one of over 850 that our group conducted with individual Davidians, Koresh indicated that he could never come out because he knew what "Bubba" would do to him in jail. *Bubba* was his term to describe the average Texas jail inmate, and he was expressing his fear that as a suspected child molester the other inmates would have their way with him in jail. "Brother Clint," he said, addressing me by what would become a familiar nickname in our talks, "I couldn't face that."

I promised Koresh a private cell, to ease his worries on this one matter at least, but he wouldn't go for it, leading me to believe that he knew all along how this showdown would end.

We went on and on in this way, for hours and hours—Koresh the puppeteer and the FBI the puppet—over the phone and face-to-face, until it became more and more apparent to me and my supervisors that the folks on the tactical side saw us nowhere in no kind of hurry. We didn't necessarily agree with that assessment, but there were two distinct sides to the FBI effort, as there almost always are in an open-ended siege, and to my tactically minded colleagues we were buying time and nothing more. In truth, our negotiating position wasn't hopeless, and there were some reasonable directions we could have still taken this thing that might have brought about a peaceful resolution, but progress was admittedly slow and uncertain. We would take a great step forward every now and then, but soon enough it would be countered by a couple of great steps back as our mounting tactical presence and physical show of force began to appear more than a little contrary to the spirit of these discussions.

As I've indicated, I don't want to get into a blow-by-blow account of the Waco incident; that's not for this book. And I certainly don't mean to suggest that my negotiator colleagues and I could have ultimately succeeded in our goal, or resolved the situation nonviolently, or anything of that nature. Again, let's save all of that for history. For now, in these pages, I merely wish to point out the aggravation I felt on such a public stage, and the profound sorrow I felt at what I will probably always regard as an avoidable loss of human life. Also, and significantly, I want to reflect on the emotional toll of this drawn-out ordeal, especially when set against what had already been an emotional roller coaster of a career, because I must admit I was just one fuse short of burning out by the time this siege went down.

I don't think there's any denying that there were those of us on the negotiating side who were made to sit on our hands a bit as the tactical team took over and the idea of an orchestrated assault on the compound began to take shape, and I looked on and couldn't shake thinking that we were ratcheting up the stakes a little too hastily. I'll offer that much. And yet, I'd been around enough to know how things go in these types of situations. I knew that in order to resolve a situation tactically you have to be the tiger that jumps on the zebra and rips its heart out straightaway. That's how it works. Once you get to that stage, you can't let the zebra get up and kick you, because if that's the case you should never have gone after the zebra in the first place. Let the zebra alone, or stop the zebra in its tracks.

I watched the Branch Davidian compound burn to the ground, silently praying that the misguided children and adults would come streaming from the inferno like Shadrach, Meshach, and Abed-nego at the command of Nebuchadnezzar in Daniel 3:26, but I did not have the power to call them out; our bullhorn pleas were ignored, and as I stared forlornly into the flames and saw too many faces of too many innocents, I felt as if I had been asked to spend all this time beating my head against a wall we had every intention of crumbling, and I began to feel for the first time that perhaps I had been at this game a little too long. The sense of loss was too palpable, too much, too great—and, to my thinking at least, too easily avoided.

The second, less obvious white flag on my FBI career was waved in South America of all places, on the border between Ecuador and Colombia, where I had gone to negotiate for the release of an American hostage. The background to this backstory was the same as it was in the 1992 Mike Barnes kidnapping in Manila: in the mid-1980s I started a program for FBI hostage negotiators to facilitate the release of United States citizens and foreign nationals kidnapped abroad, and here I was called in when an American gold miner was snatched in the Amazon by terrorists and dragged off into some godforsaken triple-canopied jungle in Colombia. I don't mean to diminish the incident, but it was one of those dime-a-dozen, under-the-radar crises that frequently went unreported by the American media and yet happened all the time. Colombia, after all, was the kidnap capital of the world; most of the world just didn't know it.

Long before the September 11, 2001, attacks on the World Trade Center and the Pentagon, Americans were easy targets for folks looking to make a statement on the world stage—and, as often as not, those targets would lead eventually to someone like me. In these types of situations, in isolated, undeveloped areas, I operated pretty much as a lone wolf, reaching out to local contacts, calling my own shots, developing CIA and other intelligence sources, doing whatever I could think to do to get the job done. One of the most confounding aspects of these assignments was the fact that in certain countries I needed special permission to carry a weapon, which always struck me as a whole bunch of unnecessary red tape and an unfair disadvantage. It was Manila all over again. I mean, there I was, in some remote corner of the world. No one was watching my back. There was no way I could *not* have a gun. And so, also as often as not, I invariably found a way to secure a weapon, on the rogue idea that if I got involved in a shooting, the thing to do would be to move on—this, on the recommendation of local authorities. Don't wait for the cops to get there. This time out, I managed to get a gun through a CIA agent in Ecuador, who also set me up with a number of key contacts as I attempted to broker for the American's release.

A couple days into this particular adventure, I found myself traveling with an Ecuadorian army major to a back-jungle border town in the north of the country. I was off in search of a CIA source, a native chieftain who lived way out in the thick of the jungle, thinking he might have information that might in turn lead me to where the American was being held by Colombian guerrillas. The border town was a thrown-together collection of run-down wood-plank buildings linked by dirt streets, and it was so close to the border that during the day it was occupied by the Ecuadorian military and by night it was taken over by the Colombian guerrillas. There was this strange, tacit time-sharing agreement between the two camps, but we were traveling in broad daylight so the Colombians were at bay. It was nearing lunchtime when the army major turned and asked if I wanted something to eat, which I always heard as a loaded question in such a remote area. Did I want something to eat? Absolutely. I was starved. Did I want to actually eat something in this primitive place? Probably not. Throughout my third-world travels, I'd picked up diarrhea, dysentery, and pretty much every other food-based disease on the books. That one time in the Philippines I became totally dehydrated and about died, winding up face-first on the floor of the U.S. ambassador's office in Manila and then in a local hospital with IV tubes coming out of my arms and legs and delirious thoughts bouncing around my brain, so I guess you could say I had my share of close calls.

Back to lunch . . . Despite my probably valid concerns, I was hungry enough to keep an open mind, and we stumbled into an establishment that purported to be a restaurant. It was a crude, ramshackle building with unfinished wooden floors and no apparent source of electricity. The place was dark and dank and the only lighting was by oil lamp. Certainly there was no refrigeration, which made the idea of lunch all but out of the question. There was a chalkboard off to one side, on which were scrawled the various items available for purchase. My army-major guide translated for me, but when he saw I still couldn't get what he was talking about he said, "Come with me."

We walked outside to the back of this multiacre compound, toward a nasty, filthy area littered with nasty, filthy animals in nasty, filthy cages. There was a meandering swamp limned with green slime. The army major walked purposefully about, inspecting the animals, and every couple steps something would lunge out at us, or pop its oily head from the swamp, or otherwise make its presence startlingly known. Snakes, chickens, a weird-looking gator . . . a nasty, filthy menagerie. The idea was, you were supposed to walk around this compound and pick out what it was you wanted to eat, after which the folks who ran the place would kill it for you and cook it up and put it on a plate and call it the daily special.

At some point as we were going over the "menu," I noticed what appeared to be giant rat, about the size of a small dog, begin to approach from about twenty-five yards away. The thing was huge and disgusting, and it looked like it was staring right through me. For an unnerving moment or two I wondered which one of us was on the menu. Then the rat started to move toward me, slowly at first but then the damn thing seemed to pick up speed, and as I began to backpedal away, back toward the building, I reached instinctively for the "borrowed" 9mm pistol in the small of my back. I thought, *If this thing bites me, God knows what I'll contract.*

Finally, as I reached for my gun to "defend myself" against this giant rodent, my Ecuadorian army major intervened.

"Don't shoot," he said. "You shoot it, you got to eat it." Then he picked up a rock and tossed it at the huge, hairy rat and the creature ran off.

All of a sudden I wasn't all that hungry. "I think I'll pass," I said. "I'll get something to eat later."

I don't mean to sound frivolous by comparing the monumental catastrophe and aggravation of Waco to the relatively benign disgust and distaste I might have felt in the jungles of Ecuador and Colombia, but there was very definitely a connection. The two incidents were emblematic of my frustration, and each in its own way signaled the end of a long, difficult road. Each, in its own way, was a kind of tipping point, and when I thought back to either one of them I found myself also thinking it might be time to pack it in and move on.

(Note: we were eventually able to secure the release of the kidnapped American gold miner—another win for the good guys.)

There was a personal footnote to the Waco tragedy, which—*not* incidentally—found me on the second anniversary of the burning of the compound and the death of David Koresh and his Branch Davidian followers, and I mention it here because of the way it illustrates the kind of work I was doing toward the end of my FBI career. It also stands neatly as a transitional episode, bridging the fieldwork I used to do exclusively to some of the more theoretical approaches and assignments I had begun to take on over time. On the second anniversary of Waco, on April 23, 1995, I sat in my office as a cable television network ran its live feed from the federal building in Oklahoma City, where a bomb or series of bombs had gone off, causing massive and unthinkable destruction. In those first moments following the devastating bombing, none of us in law enforcement had any real leads on a suspect or a possible motive, and as I watched the building burn I took a call from the Criminal Investigative Division at FBIHQ, seeking someone with a background in profiling. I happened to catch the call. The fire at the federal building was still raging, debris was still cascading to the ground, and there were no firm reports on casualties.

The FBIHQ supervisor introduced himself and said, "What's your initial take on this?"

I introduced myself right back and said, "Well, I can tell you one thing: it was a Waco man."

The phone went silent for a couple beats, not least because the knee-jerk thinking, following the first World Trade Center bombing in 1993 and the general uncertainty in the world around, was that this Oklahoma City bombing was probably orchestrated by some Middle Eastern terrorist or third-world radical out to call attention to his cause or his faith or his country. That was the mood of the room—and it was very much the opening line of investigation throughout the Bureau. And yet, there I was, stating rather conclusively that this bombing was perpetrated by a Waco man.

My colleague on the other end of the phone said, "What?"

"You heard me," I said. "Someone who identified with Waco in some way."

"Why Waco?" I got back.

"Check the calendar," I said. "It's the second anniversary."

"So?" he said. "Couldn't be a coincidence?"

"Could be a coincidence," I allowed, "but I don't believe in coincidences. Plus, you have to understand, anniversary dates are very important to people."

This much was certainly true. I mean, what man hasn't taken it in the shorts for missing an anniversary or a birthday? On a more serious note, I knew guys in Vietnam who can still tell you the day *and* the hour they got shot. I got hit by a grenade fragment in Nam, but I don't remember the day it happened; I don't want to. Me, I was never cut that way, at least not about my time in Vietnam. I knew a lot of folks who died over there—good guys who died before their time, more than 65,000 of them—but I can't go to the Vietnam Memorial and cry for them every time around. I can't. That's just not me. But it is like a lot of people. In fact, most folks who operate on the kind of fringe that allows them to bomb a federal office building in a busy downtown area probably have their calendars marked by all kinds of anniversaries, and it's not hard to make the leap to seeing how this Waco date could loom mighty large.

I continued: "Bottom line, this is not a fluke, this coming two years to the day after Waco."

"Go on," the guy at headquarters said.

"You're probably dealing with a white male," I surmised. "Probably acting alone or with one other person. Probably single, in his mid-twenties. Probably prior U.S. military. Probably a member at one time or another of some splinter survivalist or paramilitary group."

"And his motive?" came the question.

"The motive," I said, "is because after Waco he was so upset with the ATF and the FBI that it's been seething inside of him these past two years. That's why the anniversary date is so important: to show how pissed he was at his own government. And that's why he struck at a federal building."

Of course, I was just thinking out loud, making this stuff up as I went along, but that was a lot of what we did as profilers. There's a science to it, yes, but there's also a *feel*—something more akin to broad-brushed art than the study of, say, fingerprints or DNA. We had to put together pieces of the puzzle until something made sense—realizing, of course, that we usually didn't get to play with all the pieces in our game—and the more I spoke the more these pieces seemed to fit. That is, until the other agent let on that the Bureau was already chasing a suspected Egyptian terrorist who had just boarded a plane in Oklahoma City headed back to the Middle East. The early thinking was that this explosion had its footprint somewhere in Beirut, of all places. "This has international terrorism written all over it," he said.

"Maybe so," I said, "but you asked me for my take and this is my take."

With that, my colleague thanked me for my time and that was the last I ever heard from him on this matter, and as I turned my attention back to the television and to those disturbing images I thought to myself, *Okay, I'm not a soothsayer. I can't* really *tell why a certain type of person might be driven toward a certain type of aberrant behavior. All I can do is offer up my best guess, and if that best guess falls short I can dig deeper and come up with another. And another.*

In the end, once Timothy McVeigh was identified as the Oklahoma City bomber and I could see a great many of these best guesses turn out to be accurate, I was reminded all over again of the futility I'd begun to feel as I moved further and further from the true criminal cases that had drawn me to the FBI in the first place. It didn't matter that I had been proven right. And it wouldn't matter that McVeigh would later tell a reporter about this guy Van Zandt, an FBI negotiator from Waco, who watched the fire burn and said that this was what wars are started for. No, what mattered to me was that I had been right and that it *still* didn't matter, a learned truth that found me alongside a gnawing realization that I had become just another piece of an elaborate, bureaucratic puzzle.

And so I retired. Then–FBI director Louie Freeh gave me my 25-year key, called me a pioneer in my area, and allowed that the FBI needed experienced agents like me, but I put it all behind me and looked ahead to what I might do next. I looked longest and hardest at a familiar career path trod by pretty much every other retired FBI agent in my acquaintance: private security consultant. I had a number of associates who had gone this route upon their retirements, and things had worked out pretty well for them, so I figured things would work out pretty well for me too. Anyway, that was the plan. Besides, it was what I knew. It was who I was. And it was something I could do from my living room, in my running shorts, with my eyes closed.

Three months into my new career, in November 1995, I took a call from a female attorney/private investigator in the Washington, D.C., area with a curious proposition. She represented an anonymous client who possibly held a link to the infamous "Unabomber" mail-bombing case that had just recently taken its own compelling turn with the publication that September of a 35,000-word manifesto in the *Washington Post* and the *New York Times*. She knew who I was, the attorney said. She knew my reputation. And she was wondering if I had any experience in the areas of behavioral, compositional, and linguistic analysis.

Now, one of the first rules of independent consultancy, no matter what the field, is that you don't say no to anything—not at first, anyway, and probably not on second thought, either. This is especially so when you're just starting out. Whatever the proposed assignment, whatever the request, and whatever your qualifications to deliver on same, the thing to do was grab at it and make like you're the only person for the job, even if it wasn't exactly in your wheelhouse.

"Would you be able to analyze a series of documents and help us determine common authorship?" she asked.

"Well," I said, repeating the rallying cry of independent consultants everywhere, "I have a team."

In all fairness and humility, I *did* work with a team of academics, behaviorists, and forensic specialists who were indeed world-class experts in this field, although at just this moment they were probably in their own living rooms, probably also in their running shorts, and probably also with their eyes closed. Nevertheless, I filled the attorney in on some of the cases we had worked, both with the FBI and off on our own, collectively and as individuals. "We do this sort of thing all the time," I said, which might have been a stretch but was close enough to the truth.

"Fine," she said. "I want to hire you on behalf of my client, but I'm unable to tell you who that individual is or what his or her agenda might be in this case."

I thought, *Hmmm. This could be interesting.*

The attorney wanted to send over two typed copies of handwritten letters provided by her client—one of them was written one to two years earlier, the other five to seven years earlier—which we would then compare to another document to determine the possibility of common authorship.

"What's the other document?" I wanted to know.

"The Unabomber's manifesto," she said, dropping her own little bomb on what had up until this moment appeared to be a routine assignment.

I thought, *Hmmm. This could be* really *interesting, but what were the chances . . . ?*

Realize, the Unabomber case had stymied law enforcement agencies across the country for almost eighteen years, dating back to a May 1978 package bombing at Northwestern University, after which the perpetrator was initially known at the FBI Crime Lab as "The Junkyard Bomber" because the bomb appeared to have been made from ordinary household items such as plumbing pipes and sink traps. There followed an almost annual sequence of bombings—on university campuses and at airports and related locations, including a Boeing plant and the home of an airline industry executive. There was no denying a link among these package bombings, and yet, beyond the similarities in each case, there were no clues that might have led to a possible suspect. The bomber did not lick the stamps affixed to his packages, left no fingerprints, and offered no motive. As the case dragged on and the bombings continued, it became the longest, most extensive, and most expensive manhunt in contemporary law enforcement, while authorities scratched their heads and stretched their resources in pursuit of a serial killer who had claimed responsibility for killing at least three people, injuring twenty-three others, disrupting our transportation system, and setting an entire nation on edge. And still nobody had any idea who this guy was or what he might be seeking or where he might be hiding. All we had was a too-familiar police sketch of some featureless white male in a hooded sweatshirt and sunglasses, a shaky eyewitness identification we all knew could be off the mark.

I knew a great many agents who spent years working on this investigation, only to retire in their own despair, no closer to solving the case than when they had started out; in fact, the open investigation ran longer than a great many FBI careers. Just two months earlier, while I was still on the job, there was an internal shoot-out in our Behavioral Science Unit at the FBI Academy over whether to endorse the publication of the Unabomber's so-called manifesto—a meandering, self-serving diatribe entitled "Industrial Society and the Future"—or not to give in to this type of extortion. (The Unabomber offered to end his killing rampage if the *Times,* the *Post,* or *Penthouse* magazine agreed to publish his treatise in its entirety.) On the one hand, we feared, you'd have every ragtag terrorist in the world wanting to issue his or her own public statement in the mainstream press on the back of this precedent-setting move we were considering. On the other hand, we hoped it would put an end to the bombings, and the bonus was that somebody could read this thing and recognize who this guy was, because of course you can't write a 35,000-word document and not sign your name to it a couple hundred times.

Now, I had just retired from the Bureau and was finally working for billable hours, and I was once again presented with an opportunity to work the case—this time from the outside. What were the chances of that? And yet, there I was, at a desk in my living room, taking down information and preparing to work on the biggest ongoing criminal investigation in the country. Clearly the attorney knew who wrote the two letters she was planning to send over. Clearly she represented a client who had reason to believe the letter writer and the Unabomber could be one and the same. And clearly she and her client weren't about to give up the identity of the letter writer—especially not to a recently retired FBI agent—until they were made absolutely certain that he or she had also written the manifesto. In many respects it was like a gift-wrapped case in that my client already had a good idea what the outcome of my investigation was going to be; he or she merely wanted to corroborate a hunch before acting on it.

We worked backward at the outset. We looked to rule things out. We studied the long-winded manifesto and looked for ways to eliminate the writer of that document as the writer of the two known letters, and on first and second analysis there proved no obvious way to eliminate the possibility that the same individual had written all three documents. There were too many similarities in tone, syntax, phrasing . . . and on and on. We went at it again and again, and each time out we could not determine conclusively that the authors were *not* in fact the same, which left us instead determined to prove that they *were* in fact the same. To do so, we developed separate profiles of each writer, and on each side of the ledger we came up with an individual who was most likely white, most likely educated, probably on a Ph.D. level, most likely in his early fifties. The writer of the two letters and the writer of the manifesto each expressed a transparent mistrust of society, and technology, to where he was probably living at some remove from society and technology, probably in a very rural environment with limited to no contact with family or neighbors or anyone else in the outlying community: a hermit, most likely, with a little too much time on his hands for someone with so much misplaced anger and misguided education.

The two psychological profiles seemed to fit pretty well, so we moved on to a linguistic analysis, and here again things matched up, so we started thinking the writer had been the same in each case. Of course, we allowed for the possibility that there can always be a parallel universe: There can always be two or more individuals from a similar background who subscribe to the same set of beliefs. There can always be multiple disaffected 50-year-old white male Ph.D. types living out in cabins in the woods, cut off from society and thinking that the whole world has gone south. I mean, there were times when I might have been able to sign on to the same worldview, and this could have easily described the lifestyle and perspective of a whole lot of people. After all, that's how movements and hate groups and paramilitary organizations get started, right? And yet, the documents were shot through with enough similar thoughts, ideas, and phraseologies to suggest the strong likelihood of a link. The two experts who were working with me—a psychiatrist and a psycholinguist—were much stronger in their assessments that the writers were one and the same. They checked in at about an 80 to 85 percent likelihood, but I backed off on that figure in my final report to the attorney—because no one has a lock on the truth in a case like this. Who can say with absolute certainty that there was only one individual out there who fit this same profile, at just this moment in time, in just this way?

In my report and in my follow-up conversation with the attorney, I stressed the need for her to get in touch with the FBI immediately, to let the authorities know she had a possible lead on the Unabomber's identity. She assured me that she would, after conferring with her client, and I felt I had no choice but to leave it at that. And yet, I couldn't leave it alone. I was like that guy in the *Dirty Harry* movie, the one Clint Eastwood is about to drop the hammer on after a shoot-out. Remember that scene? It's one of the all-time great movie moments, particularly from a law enforcement perspective, because the bad guy has clearly been counting bullets, trying to determine if Clint Eastwood has another round left in the chamber before laying down his own weapon. And before the poor mope can figure his next move, Clint Eastwood reminds him that he's staring down the barrel of a .44 Magnum, the most powerful handgun in the world, capable of blowing his head clean off his shoulders, and then he asks him if he wants to take that kind of chance.

Are you gonna take that chance, sucker?

Finally, the bad guy puts his gun down and Clint Eastwood makes to walk away, but the bad guy calls him back. "I gots to know," the bad guy says. "I gots to know." And with this, Clint Eastwood points the gun and pulls the trigger and there's nothing but a click—empty as the day it was issued.

Are you gonna take that chance, sucker?

I gots to know.

That's how it always is, out there in the field. You're always counting shots. Consciously, subconsciously . . . it becomes routine. You have to know when to reload, or when the other guy needs to reload, and every FBI agent and cop I ever talked to about this movie always loved this scene for the way it reinforced the point that you need to pay attention, to keep count in life or die trying.

Well, here I found myself thinking, *I gots to know.* It wasn't enough to weigh in with the likely probability that the Unabomber had written those two letters and that my attorney and her client could possibly lead authorities to the identity of one of the most wanted criminals in American law enforcement history. I needed to know for certain—that we had identified the guy and that he had in turn been identified to the FBI, both. And so, on my own dime and on my own authority, I reached out to another team of experts, and we went at the process all over again. Working backward. Ruling things out. Developing separate psychological profiles. Doing a comparative analysis. And bringing the fresh and unique perspective of these new experts to the same task. After a couple weeks we came back with an even stronger finding, this time determining that there was a better than 85 percent likelihood that the Unabomber was our guy, so I fired off a second report to the attorney, at no additional charge.

I followed it up with a phone call. "Look," I said, "I just had to go at this thing again. This is somebody who has threatened to blow an airplane full of people out of the sky. This is somebody we've been chasing for eighteen years. I gots to know, you know. Here's a second analysis, much stronger than the first."

"That's great," she said. "Thanks. I'll take it to my client."

"You need to take it to the FBI," I pressed. "You've got to get whoever your client is to take it to the FBI."

"I'll take care of it," she said. "I know what I've got to do."

And I knew what I had to do as well. I couldn't wait for this attorney. I couldn't wait for her client to sign off on any kind of disclosure. As far as I knew, the attorney had yet to reach out to the FBI following the first report, so there was nothing to ensure that she would make the call following the second. So what did I do? I went to the FBI myself. As a consultant, I wasn't bound by the same attorney-client privilege that may or may not have been keeping this woman from doing the same. Yes, I had a professional responsibility to my client, but I believed I also had a moral obligation that superseded that professional responsibility. And as far as my moral obligation was concerned, I believed it fell on the side of right and in the best interests of both public safety and national security. Plus, I was a former FBI agent, and there were professional responsibilities that came along with that as well. So I made the call.

I reached out to a friend in the Behavioral Science Unit, in a back-channel approach to an agent in particular who I knew was working the case. And I laid it out for him. Told him we'd done two separate analyses within the past couple weeks, both of which suggested a strong probability that my client could identify and possibly even locate the Unabomber. Told him I didn't know for sure who my ultimate client was, but that I was working through a third party. "The client's attorney says she's going to go to the Bureau and share what she has, but I don't know if she has or if she will," I said. "Can you tell me if you've heard from her?"

Now, the FBI is a funny organization. When you leave, you leave. The Bureau doesn't want to know from you. You can come into the office the very next day and it's like you never existed. You can call in looking for some information or a friendly assist from a former colleague, and it's like you're running into a brick wall. The mentality is, either you're an FBI agent or you're not, and here I was most decidedly *not*. There is no honeymoon or grace period after you retire. You're gone. I'd get retired agents calling me when I was still on duty, asking me for this or that piece of information or evidence, and I'd have to tell them I just couldn't help them out. So I understood the tough spot I was putting this one agent into. I even acknowledged as much.

"Look," I finally said after an awkward silence, "I'm not asking you to tell me what's going on in the case. All I'm asking is, if something doesn't come up in the next couple days, if someone doesn't call in with a potentially significant lead on the identity of the Unabomber, just get back to me and let me know. And I will either get my client to come to you or I will tell you who my client is."

And that's how we left it. I didn't know what more I could do at that point. All I knew was that I couldn't leave room for the prospect that the Unabomber might put a bomb on a plane and blow up three or four hundred people while I was sitting there in Fredericksburg, Virginia, at my desk in my living room, knowing in some way, shape, or form who this guy was, and not doing anything about it.

To my client's great credit, she convinced her client, David Kaczynski, to come forward. Kaczynski was the brother of Theodore John Kaczynski, a Harvard University graduate with a doctoral degree in mathematics from the University of Michigan who in 1967 suddenly quit his prestigious teaching position at the University of California—Berkeley without explanation, setting in motion a series of bizarre and unfortunate events that led to an isolated life of hermitlike seclusion in a cabin built on a remote tract of family-owned land in Lincoln, Montana. David Kaczynski, who had been estranged from his brother for a number of years, began to believe that his brother Ted might be the Unabomber after reading the published manifesto and recognizing some disturbing similarities.

Armed with our two reports, I later learned, David Kaczynski contacted the FBI through yet another attorney and brokered a deal on his brother's behalf. This was in February 1996, approximately two months after he made initial contact with me through his first attorney. The deal was David Kaczynski would come forward with information linking his brother to the package bombings and the published manifesto and lead investigators to the cabin where Ted Kaczynski, the Unabomber, was possibly residing in exchange for a promise that the federal government would not seek the death penalty in this case. David Kaczynski supplied investigators with copies of my two reports and the two letters as well as additional letters and materials.

The FBI was all over it, assigning every available linguistic and profiling and Behavioral Science expert, and comparing and analyzing every piece of available evidence, to where finally the various agents working the case were able to push back their chairs from their desks and stand up and shout, "Case closed, this is the Unabomber!"

On April 3, 1996, Ted Kaczynski was arrested at his cabin in Montana, and once again I caught myself looking at pictures on CNN—pictures of the same 50ish white male I had described in my report, looking about as disaffected as you'd have to be to send all those explosives through the U.S. mail. Kaczynski was indicted in Sacramento for the murders of a computer store owner and a timber industry lobbyist, and for the attacks on a geneticist and a Yale University computer expert, and in New Jersey for the murder of an advertising executive. There were other charges as well, and despite the protracted and far-reaching nature of the case—or perhaps because of it—his capture was met with great fanfare within the Bureau. Really, by all accounts, it was a red-letter day for the hundreds of agents who had spent hundreds of thousands of man-hours on the case, which now seemed ready to be put to bed.

It was in this context that I received a phone call that would signal a dramatic new beginning for me in my new career. One of David Kaczynski's attorneys reached me on the phone the night before a press conference to announce the details surrounding Ted Kaczynski's arrest and his brother's involvement. He said, "I know you did the analysis, and when reporters ask me who made the connection and identified the Unabomber, I'm going to mention you."

I was dumbstruck, and more than a little embarrassed. I'd just spent the first twenty-five years of my professional career working in a *we* organization. What's that old cliché?—there's no *I* in *team*? Well, it rings especially true at the Bureau. It wasn't like us FBI agents to take credit for anything. What counted was getting the job done and putting bad guys away, not any glory or personal recognition that might come our way as a result. It was a professional mind-set that was consistent with my own personal philosophy. I heard this and thought, *No, sir, this is not the way I do business.* And I said as much. I said, "You really don't have to do that. In fact, I'd prefer you don't. You got the right guy, that's all that matters."

"No, Clint," the attorney said. "If the question comes up, and you know the question is going to come up, I'm going to mention your involvement, because frankly if you hadn't put those pieces together for us, I don't think my client would have come forward."

I tried again to talk him down from his plan, but about the best I could get out of him before he raced off the phone was a not-too-promising "We'll see how it goes."

Sure enough, the next morning Dianne and I were glued once again to the television, this time with our youngest son, Jon, this time to watch the press conference as the attorney who called the night before took the podium and made an opening statement. The press conference was called for 9:00 a.m., and by 9:02 he had "outed" me to the entire world. He didn't even wait for the question to be asked, just came right out and said that former FBI profiler Clint Van Zandt, who currently lives in Fredericksburg, Virginia, where he works as a security consultant, was the person who did the original analysis that lead to the identification of Ted Kaczynski as the Unabomber. He even referred to my consultancy firm by name: Van Zandt Associates.

Basically, he did everything short of holding up a banner with my address and phone number, and I sat there in my living room knowing full well what would happen next.

I turned to Dianne and said, "How long's it gonna take?"

She said, "How long is what going to take?"

I looked at the phone and said, "For that to ring."

As soon as I said it, the first call came—and the calls kept coming. From long-lost friends and family. From the media. From other law enforcement agencies. From potential clients. Over the next two weeks, I did over one hundred interviews with news organizations from all over the world. I know it was over one hundred, because that's where I stopped counting. There were satellite trucks parked in our front yard day after day. At one point, in what may or may not have been a first (at least, for an FBI agent), I appeared on all three network morning shows simultaneously: ABC's *Good Morning America,* NBC's *Today* show, and CBS's *The Early Show.* I taped one interview the night before, pre-taped another the next morning, and appeared live on the third, and as it happened, all three segments aired at once. Dianne even took a picture from the Green Room at the studio where I was doing the live interview, with my mug on three separate monitors, representing the live feeds from the three major networks, which I count among my most unusual keepsakes.

At first I looked on all this attention as a great, good thing, giving me a chance to speak positively about law enforcement in general and the FBI in particular. In the weeks and months leading up to Kaczynski's arrest, journalists and pundits had been ragging on the FBI for taking eighteen years to catch this guy, and now the talk was that it took his brother to come forward before the Bureau could do anything about it. So I took the opportunity to talk about all the good work the FBI had done over the years, and all the good work it had done in this particular case. Whenever a journalist asked me to reflect on who the true heroes were in this investigation, I pointed first and foremost at David Kaczynski for having the guts to turn in his own brother and for recognizing that his responsibility to society was greater than blood.

In a compelling aside, a Kaczynski family attorney reached out to me sometime later, asking if I would testify in the death-penalty phase of the case. Apparently the government was reneging on its promise to David Kaczynski not to seek the death penalty against his brother Ted, and the family wanted me to help. I thought about it long and hard. On the one hand, Ted Kaczynski was a mass murderer who deserved the worst our criminal justice system had to offer. And yet, on the other hand, as a former FBI agent, I knew what it takes to ask a mother to turn in her son, a wife to turn in her husband, or a brother to turn in his brother. I knew that if David Kaczynski was left with his brother's blood on his hands, that if his willingness to place his civic responsibility over family was rewarded with his brother's execution, then every FBI agent and every police officer would hear about it for years to come, every time they needed to ask another relative to turn in a family member. The repercussions could hamper criminal investigations for generations. And so I agreed to testify on Ted Kaczynski's behalf—not to spare him a fate he undoubtedly deserved, but to spare his brother. Fortunately, federal prosecutors came to their senses, Ted Kaczynski was sentenced to life in prison, and David Kaczynski was saved from the self-doubt that would have been his cross to carry for life. Justice, in its own way, had been served.

David Kaczynski was a true hero. His actions were a big, brave deal. It was also big and brave the way ATF agents and bomb squad technicians pored over Ted Kaczynski's cabin, digging in the dirt for hidden explosives, never knowing what they might find. Those were the real heroes here. Me, I sat a desk and performed an analytical procedure and coordinated a team of experts who sat at their own desks doing pretty much the same thing. There was no heavy lifting there. It was fortuitous that we could put two and two together in such a way that it added up to an arrest, but the hard work fell to the cops and the ATF and FBI agents and postal inspectors who were burning shoe leather for eighteen years looking for this bastard.

But still the media calls kept coming. Ted Koppel. The *New York Times.* My sons were catching calls for me left and right, trying to coordinate my suddenly ridiculous appearance schedule, and from time to time it appeared that every satellite truck on the East Coast was parked on our street, and we just had to laugh about it. I didn't ask for all that attention, and I didn't think I deserved it, but there it was. At one point, in the spirit of surprise and good cheer that seemed to flow from Ted Kaczynski's arrest, I turned to my kids and said, "Let me know when Larry King calls. That's when you know you're hot stuff—when Larry King calls."

Eventually, of course, Larry King got around to calling, but even then I refused to see myself or my accomplishments as any kind of big deal. I was doing my job was all it was, and circumstances fell in such a way that the FBI was able to solve one of the biggest cases in recent memory. That was the beginning and the end of it right there, as far as I was concerned. And yet, here was Larry King, wanting to know if I could come on his show the next night. As it happened, I had already committed to Ted Koppel's *Nightline* program that evening, so I found myself in the unlikely position of having to turn down Larry King.

How's that for hot stuff?

"How about tonight?" Larry King asked.

Last I'd checked, I didn't have any interviews booked for that evening that couldn't be rescheduled. "Tonight could work," I said.

"I'll tell you what," he said. "I've got Ted Kennedy on tonight, but if you can come on, I'll bump him."

And that's just what happened, allowing me my best personal claim to fifteen minutes of fame—that I bumped Ted Kennedy off *Larry King*—and at the same time to reflect on how what I now did for a living put me in the strange crosshairs of public attention.

The appearance itself was surreal. Larry King asked me what to do if you thought you'd received a bomb through the mail, and I was dumbstruck. "Look for wires sticking out of the package," I said, fumbling, "or a return address you don't know, or excessive postage."

(Note: mail bombers tend not to want their bombs returned to sender for insufficient postage.)

"No," King demanded, "what should you do if you think you have a bomb?"

My two sons, Jeff and Jon, had traveled with me to the studio, and they were sitting just off camera, trying not to laugh at their old man, who now appeared boxed into a corner. I looked at them and blurted, "Well, you could have one of your kids open the package first."

Larry King coughed all over me, I guess to cover up my flippant remark, and as soon as I said those words I knew I'd blown it on live television, before millions of viewers. For weeks folks would stop me on the street, asking me if I'd really let my children open a package if I suspected a bomb was inside. It was meant as a joke, but I realized as soon as I gave it voice that people aren't inclined to joke over such as this.

In any case, the viewing public seemed to forgive me my unfortunate choice of words this first time around the media maze, because in the years since I've gone from being an anonymous FBI agent, working my butt off in pursuit of truth, justice, and the American way, to a sought-after talking head and media pundit—all in the time it took to answer my phone and see a relatively small case to completion.

And I thought yet again, *Hmmm, this could be interesting.*

SURVIVAL STRATEGIES 101

"As time drags by I have far too much time to think. . . . The thing that keeps going over and over in my mind is that I'm a pawn on a chessboard and I only know enough about chess to know not many pawns make it the whole game."

—FROM A KIDNAP VICTIM'S DIARY

When I travel the country—lecturing, consulting with clients, giving interviews—I'm struck by the number of people who want to know what they can do to protect themselves and their families in these uncertain times. It's the front-burning issue of our day, wouldn't you agree? This was very much the case when I first retired, and it remains especially so in the wake of the September 11, 2001, attacks on the United States, after which all anybody seemed to want to talk about were security issues. Anyway, it's all anybody seemed to want to talk about to *me*.

It is an uneasy subject, to say the least—and, I suppose, the obvious—and yet, whenever possible, I try to set folks at ease in what ways I can with some of what I've learned in all my years of experience. Still, the truth is there's nothing in my experience that can reasonably be expected to set anyone totally at ease. Indeed, most people want me to sugarcoat the message and tell them there are measures they can take to absolutely, positively, and completely safeguard their loved ones in the face of unimaginable terrorism, sadism, antagonism, and any other kind of antisocial ism you'd care to comprehend—and some you'd just as soon not. Unfortunately, that's just not the case, as we all know too well. There are, however, some basic strategies and concepts I helped to develop over the years with various colleagues at the FBI and other agencies and organizations that, taken together, offer a useful blueprint to understanding the mind-sets of hostage-takers and kidnappers in all kinds of scenarios—and, in turn, the resulting mind-sets of hostages and kidnap victims—and I offer them here.

To begin, let's be clear on the distinction between a *hostage* and a *kidnap victim*. According to a definition I wrote for the FBI's Critical Incident Response Group, which trains FBI and police negotiators to deal with hostage, barricade, suicide, and kidnap situations at the FBI Academy in Quantico, Virginia, a hostage is "a person held and threatened by a subject or subjects to force the fulfillment of substantive demands made on a third party." A kidnap victim is "a person seized and detained or carried away by unlawful force or fraud, often with a demand for ransom." A kidnapping implies that a person has been taken against his or her will, by individuals possibly *unknown* to the authorities—and, more importantly, held at a location unknown to the authorities. Negotiations may be conducted between individuals representing the victim's family, business, or government, including law enforcement authorities and someone representing the kidnappers. In a hostage situation a person is usually held against his or her will at a location *known* to the authorities. Typically the authorities would have surrounded the location where the victim is being held, and a trained crisis team would conduct negotiations to secure the safe release of the hostage—and, hopefully, the hostage-taker.

These might appear as subtle distinctions, but the differences are key and certainly worth highlighting. The principal difference, of course, is that the location of the hostage victim is always known, while the location of the kidnapping victim is only sometimes known. Another significant difference is in the types of demands set forth by the subjects, and the wiggle room a negotiator like myself might have in seeking the "talking cure" to which I devoted most of my career. Realize, a negotiator will normally have greater psychological leverage with the hostage-taker because of the implied physical threat of the surrounding law enforcement officers responding to the scene. Conversely, a kidnapping does not usually present the benefit of such an implied threat, which means that skilled verbal diplomacy is needed to bring about the safe release of the kidnap victim, usually in exchange for something more than the promised safety of the kidnapper.

We tend to think that the world used to be a kinder, gentler, and *safer* place, but criminal abductions have been with us since the beginning of recorded history. Just look at the Bible: When Abraham's nephew Lot was taken captive by the armies of four kings, as chronicled in the Book of Genesis, Abraham assembled a 318-man hostage rescue force and successfully rescued his nephew. Jump ahead to the Roman Empire and note that Julius Caesar was captured by the terrorists of his day—pirates—in the year 75 B.C.; in the end, Caesar ably negotiated a ransom for his own release and subsequently had his kidnappers killed. And in our early history, 115 American sailors were kidnapped by pirates in North Africa. To resolve this situation, the fledgling U.S. government was forced to pay a $1 million ransom, one-quarter of our national budget at the time, to gain the sailors' release. This last stands in direct contrast to recent U.S. policy not to negotiate with terrorists for the release of kidnapped U.S. citizens, although it's important to note that our government does indeed engage in discussions with terrorists when such situations arise; in fact, we'll do (most) everything in our power to negotiate for the release of U.S. citizens held by kidnappers, but the government itself will not pay a ransom or submit to any demands in order to effect such release. (This, readers may recall, was casually redefined by the Reagan administration during the Iran-Contra affair.) Again, a subtle distinction, but all the difference in the world when you're in the middle of such a standoff.

In a kidnapping scenario, negotiators might anticipate demands for money, the release of prisoners, political concessions, or other types of considerations. Negotiators responding to a kidnapping must also be concerned with the kidnappers' ability to operate safely and confidently in their surroundings. Do the kidnappers know the national, political, religious, and geographic environment where they kidnapped the victim, as well as where they are holding the victim? Do they have the ability to speak and understand the local language? Do they have a logistical and a financial base that can support them during extended negotiations for the release of the victim?

There's a lot to consider in every criminal abduction, but negotiators are frequently able to find patterns of behavior among hostage-takers and kidnappers that help them to at least hit the ground running—this on the theory that if it's ground they've covered before, they might as well leave a trail. That said, we have been able to identify four distinct categories or characteristics among hostage-takers: the trapped criminal, the prison inmate, the terrorist, and the mentally disturbed individual. *The trapped criminal* rarely plans on taking hostages; he does so in an attempt to assure his own safety and possibly aid in his escape when confronted during the course of a crime. *The prison inmate* may take a hostage to shield himself from the authorities during an escape attempt or to gain attention while protesting prison or social conditions. *Terrorists* take hostages to gain the attention of both the government and the media—and, hopefully, international recognition of their cause. And *the mentally disturbed hostage-taker* is in turn identified as one of four distinct personality types: the psychopathic/antisocial individual or professional criminal who takes hostages to further his escape after the commission of a crime; the paranoid schizophrenic, who takes a hostage to somehow right a perceived wrong; the depressed individual who might take a hostage, possibly a relative, while he attempts to sort out the difficulties in his life and possibly consider suicide; and the inadequate individual who takes hostages because of his fear of the authorities after an aborted criminal attempt on his part. Like shades of gray, there are also variations of the above that negotiators must consider, distinctions that may only come out during the course of a prolonged negotiation.

Conveniently, kidnappers can also be placed into four categories: the opportunist or novice criminal, the religious or politically motivated individual (now and forever known as a terrorist), the mentally deranged individual, and the professional criminal. *The opportunist* may be constrained by poor planning and lack of true criminal expertise; *the religious or politically motivated individual* may be willing to die or to kill his victim to promote his cause, which might include a concept of a hereafter, entry into which the individual may or may not be entitled as a result; *the mentally deranged individual* may kidnap or kill for the thrill, owing to confusion or psychosis; and *the professional criminal's* motivation for kidnapping will usually center on financial gain, with extensive planning to ensure his escape and ability to spend his illegally obtained goods.

It is within the confines of these distinctions that we negotiators make quick judgments and shift-on-the-fly decisions regarding the safety and well-being of the victims. Yes, we've been down these roads before—too many times, if you ask me—but to a hostage or a kidnap victim, it's almost always a first, and a victim's initial response to his or her circumstance can play a vital role in events going forward. Consider: when an individual is criminally abducted, it is almost always sudden and dramatic and alarming and terrifying. Chances are the abduction will also involve a struggle of some kind, even a violent struggle. The hostage or kidnap victim is taken to a totally alien and perhaps even harsh environment and held prisoner for a period of time that could stretch to days or weeks or months.

What I've learned over the years is that the victim who is mentally prepared for such an ordeal is better equipped to survive such an ordeal. But how do you prepare for something like this? How do you imagine the unimaginable? For certain top-level executives, high-profile individuals, and international political figures, these unthinkable circumstances are thought through and assessed on a constant basis. Security consultants like myself are brought in to consider various scenarios and to train would-be targets and potential victims on how to alter their routines to avoid easy capture and how to instruct friends, family and business associates to respond to kidnappers in what often seems the inevitable event of that capture. But what about the rest of us? What about the ordinary individual trapped in such extraordinary circumstances as these? How should we react at the moment of capture? Well, at the outset, our choices are to resist, run, or submit—but do we really have a choice? Until and unless we can determine a sure path to safety, our best move—our *only* move, really—is to submit.

Like the military and like trained law enforcement authorities, kidnappers and hostage-takers count on speed, surprise, and violence of attack in order to accomplish their objectives. If you truly believe yourself trapped, without any reasonable chance of escape, do not precipitate or exacerbate your injury by resisting. Do what you are told. Studies reveal that the vast majority of kidnap victims who are injured are injured early on, either in the actual act of kidnapping or in a premature show of resistance. For the most part, kidnappers and hostage-takers want to keep their victims alive—and, to the extent possible, unharmed—and victims will do well to keep this in mind.

As in any new circumstance or unfamiliar situation, there's usually a period of adjustment experienced by the victim, during which he or she will experience feelings of shock and disbelief, uncertainty and fear, panic and doubt, guilt and anger. I've seen and heard it all, over the years—from victims going into blind rages, to victims rendered momentarily speechless or immobile, to victims being unable to control their bodily functions. I suppose we can't know how we might react in such dire circumstances until we find ourselves in the middle of them, but it's always a good idea to take a deep breath, to take a rational view, and to remember that the odds of surviving remain overwhelmingly in your favor as long as you continue to play the game. Break the rules of the game—that is, refuse to follow orders or fail to show an appropriate level of calculated fear or respect toward your captors—and you tilt those odds against you.

Indeed, most hostages and kidnap victims are not mistreated or abused unless they bring it on themselves. With this in mind, victims should focus on what it is they *can* do, as opposed to what it is they *can't* do:

Eat what you are given, when you are given it.

Sleep when you can and as much as you can. (Did you know that many victims sleep as much as eighteen hours per day?)

Take every opportunity to exercise, even if it's just isometrics from a sitting or prone position.

Record a mental picture of your surroundings and commit everything you can to memory—from a physical description of your captors, to the sights and sounds that might be coming in from an open window—without letting on that you are taking note.

Find the correct balance between proactive and submissive behavior, keeping in mind that you don't want to become what we sometimes called a "proctologic personality"—meaning "a real pain in the butt."

Keep a positive outlook. One great way to do this is to take a bath or a shower, if given an opportunity, as well as shaving and changing clothes. It's essential to maintain your dignity without flaunting it to your captors, and keeping up with your basic hygiene goes a long way toward presenting a strong front.

Thank your guards if they show you even the smallest kindness, and try not to demonstrate disdain or disapproval at their harsh treatment.

If you find yourself engaged in conversation with one of your captors, keep it light and on the surface; any discussion of political views or religious ideals or desperate circumstances can only lead to agitation. Some hostages have survived by letting their captors know about their family members, humanizing themselves in the minds of their kidnappers. But proceed with caution here: such personal information can also be used by the kidnappers as additional leverage in various extortion schemes.

If you're being held with other individuals, learn to rely on each other for support. A lot of times we learned of situations where multiple victims were able to communicate with each other through a series of improvised hand signals (such as: one finger for *I'm okay* and two fingers for *I need out, by any means*), in much the same way military prisoners might communicate with a sequence of tap codes.

Remain calm.

Pay close attention to and follow all instructions given.

If you've been moved from one location to another, try to estimate the time, distance, and direction that you traveled to your current location. While you're at it, memorize useful information about your abductors and your environment—but again, don't get caught doing it (in other words, don't write anything down).

Do not struggle or make sudden moves. Do not shout unless you believe that doing so will bring immediate assistance. And if it comes up, try not to worry about any drugs or medications that might be administered to you against your will: they seldom have lasting effects, and kicking or screaming or resisting in any way might do you more harm than the drugs themselves.

And take heart in knowing that more than 90 percent of kidnap victims survive their ordeals.

A relatively new development in hostage situations has emerged in recent violence-in-the-workplace incidents. Here's the increasingly common scenario: a current or former employee; a husband or boyfriend of an employee; a vendor; a disenchanted stockholder; or some other person with a gripe against a company (or one or more of its employees) bursts into the workplace waving a gun and threatening to kill everyone. Employees run for the doors, diving under their desks or locking their office doors from the inside—all logical responses to such a dramatic change in their routines. If you remain inside of your place of employment and can safely dial 911, do so. If you are the lone hostage and no one else is aware of your plight, there are a number of possible safety valves available to you. Some companies, for example, have developed an internal set of communication codes for just this eventuality, such as reversing the now universally known *911* digits— an easy-to-remember distress code we urge in our "Violence in the Workplace" corporate training seminars. For example, if you are in a threatening situation and unable to leave your office, place a call to an assistant, or an operator, or a security officer and announce that you need "a copy of form 119," thereby alerting others of the threat against you.

Naturally, surviving any hostage or kidnapping ordeal sometimes means escape, and you'll need to count the cost before attempting any type of move. Frequently, survival means a negotiated surrender of some kind, but just as often it can mean a successful rescue, and here you'll want to be prepared for every eventuality. Police, military, and hostage rescue teams sometimes use gas or flash-bangs to bring about the release of hostages and kidnap victims, and it's important to keep a cool head during such an effort. The best thing to do in any rescue attempt is to stay as low as you can, on the floor at the side of a room if possible, with your hands on your head. Do not move when author-ities enter the room. In fact, it's probably a good idea not to do any-thing until you are specifically instructed to do so. Also, anticipate that you will be initially treated like a criminal until authorities can sort the good guys from the bad guys; you might even be tied or handcuffed: do not resist; let the rescue team do its job.

I'm well aware that a lot of these precautions and guidelines fall into the easier-said-than-done category. Just to reinforce the point, we can never know how we might react in such extreme situations until we find ourselves in such extreme situations. Most of us will be able to live our lives with no personal connection to any criminal abduction scenario, but the sad fact remains that we live in a world where law enforcement officials are made to consider such as this every time they report to work. Saddest of all, I'm afraid, are when these abductions run to children. I pray for all hostages and kidnap victims, but it's for the children that I pray most of all. The good news here is that, despite intensive media coverage of particular incidents, the kidnapping of a child by a stranger is relatively rare, occurring only about two hundred to three hundred times per year, according to a 1990 federally funded study that is still considered authoritative. You'll sometimes see child abduction statistics running much higher, but these alarming "missing children" numbers come from unreliable sources or from lumping together what researchers term "extremely dissimilar social problems," such as runaways and abductions by noncustodial family members.

I don't mean to get off on a rant here, as the comedian Dennis Miller used to say, and I certainly don't mean to minimize the dangers facing our children today—because, frankly, even one child abduction is one too many—but the reality remains that our world is at least a little bit safer than we give it credit for, at least in terms of children. With every compelling, heartbreaking story of a missing child that makes national headlines—from Etan Patz to Adam Walsh, JonBenet Ramsey to Elizabeth Smart to Natalee Holloway—we move further and further from a true understanding of what actually constitutes a "missing" child or a child abduction and what we need to worry about as parents, neighbors and caregivers in order to protect our children. Clearly we need to know what we're talking about when we talk about crimes against our children. After all, it's one thing to teach our kids to be cautious, and it's another to scare the living daylights out of them. We need to spend as much time teaching them to be wary of people in their community they already know—neighbors, teachers, coaches, relatives—as we do teaching them to watch out for strangers. And we need to be ever-vigilant ourselves, keeping a constant and watchful eye on adults and teenagers who come into regular and legitimate contact with our children—not because we don't trust them to do right by our kids, but because we can't always trust our kids to do right by themselves.

Some key points to consider when a child goes missing:

1. **The actions of parents, caregivers and law enforcement are critical in the first few hours—and if the child is not immediately recovered, in the first few days.** Understandably, our emotions will be at a heightened state during this early period, and our decision-making abilities severely taxed, but early and accurate information is essential.

2. **Should your child be missing, you need to make an immediate search of your entire house to ensure your child is not hiding, sleeping, or simply playing beyond earshot.** Dianne and I once feared our youngest son Jon had gone missing. We called and called his name, to no avail. We conducted a room-by-room and area-by-area search of our entire house. As I was about to call the police, we found him sleeping in the back of a closet with a blanket pulled over him: it was a favorite hiding spot, and he had grown tired playing hide-and-seek with his brother and sister the hour before; his siblings had given up trying to find him, and Jon had simply fallen asleep.

3. **If your child doesn't turn up after a thorough search, call the authorities immediately.** The local police, sheriff's

office, and the FBI need to become involved in the search as quickly as possible. In a worst-case scenario, know that we only have a few short hours to find the kidnapper and rescue the child. If your child has simply wandered away, the challenge of traffic, weather, and terrain will require the same rapid response.

4. **Should you believe that your child disappeared due to foul play, you need to preserve the crime scene—your home, or your car, or any other location—so that law officials can conduct an appropriate investigation.** I know of a number of very high-profile kidnappings and murders where apparently well-intentioned family members and friends cleaned the house and otherwise contaminated the crime scene before law enforcement had arrived.

5. **Get to know the law enforcement officer in charge of the search for your child.** Ask any questions you can think of and provide any information asked of you. Realize that family members may appear as logical suspects during the early phase of an investigation. Do not take offense at this. Studies show that in fourteen out of fifteen cases, someone in the immediate family, extended family, or a friend or neighbor will hold some significant information regarding the child's disappearance.

6. **As in the kidnapping of young Elizabeth Smart in Utah, tracker dogs can assist in the search for a missing child, no matter if the child simply wandered away or was carried away against his or her will.** Ask law enforcement officials how quickly they can get such dogs on the scene to search for your child.

7. **In addition to law enforcement and fire and rescue personnel, community groups should be sought to partici-**

pate in the search. The mobilization of church and civic groups can bring together large numbers of searchers with an already existing system of identification and accountability. This search effort should be coordinated with law enforcement officials, who will want to record background information and perhaps conduct police record checks on the search volunteers.

8. **Although law enforcement will want to monitor, trap, trace and record all incoming calls to your residence, office, and perhaps even your cellular telephone, the law enforcement command post and search staging area should ideally be located away from your primary residence.** You will need the privacy of your home to sort out your thoughts, gather your strength and allow you to grab the few moments of rest that will be available to you during such a traumatic event.

9. **Know that you can participate in as little or as much of the search and investigative efforts to find your child as you are capable of—depending, of course, on the law enforcement needs of the investigation.** Some parents and family members quite reasonably prefer to remain home to receive any possible telephone calls from the victim, checking in with the police and the search staging area on a daily basis, while others look to roll up their sleeves and take a more active role.

10. **Keep the matter of your missing child before the media on a daily basis.** Consider the gradual release of photos, background information, and family movies and mementos, which will help to keep your child's face before the local— and, possibly, national—community.

11. **Maintain a log of contacts, thoughts, names, addresses,**

and telephone numbers, along with information provided by outsiders and information supplied by you to the authorities.

12. Some families consider hiring a private investigator to assist in the search, and others might seek the assistance of a psychic in their desperate attempt to find their missing child. Both impulses are common, but you do not want a private investigation to run in conflict with an official investigation. Personally, I don't believe in psychics and always found their involvement counterproductive to any legitimate search, but families are certainly free to go that route at their own risk.

13. Obtain a copy of the U.S. Department of Justice booklet entitled *When Your Child Is Missing: A Family Survival Guideline.* (Order one now and set it aside.) The booklet was written by parents and family members who have gone through the experience of a missing, kidnapped, or murdered child, and contains many ideas from law enforcement and other professionals that can save you time and grief and assist you in focusing your efforts to get your missing child back and deal with the aftermath of such a horrific situation. There is strength in becoming aware of these invaluable lessons, although I pray you will never need to put them into practice.

HOW TO ESCAPE A PREDATOR/KIDNAPPER— WHAT EVERY PARENT AND CHILD SHOULD KNOW

Since sharing the story of my childhood abduction on national television with Oprah Winfrey, many people (including Oprah!) have asked if the reason that I became an FBI agent was because I had been victimized as a child. It would make for an interesting story, to be sure, but I can't say that it's true in my case. Perhaps this was one of the reasons why I did not think to include such a revelation in the hardcover edition of this book. It would have been dramatic and compelling, but it would have been off-point.

Like most victims, I learned to repress the incident while at the same time remembering it vividly. I've often wondered if my childhood victimization was the reason I so quickly sympathized with victims of sexual assault and victims of child predators throughout my career. I don't think so. It might have been a part of it, but it certainly wasn't the whole story. I think I identified with such victims because, like each of us, they were simply human, and no human being should have to undergo such an experience. And yet our numbers are probably in the tens of thousands, maybe hundreds of thousands—victims like myself who have subscribed to the *Omertà*-like code of silence that has been adopted by victims worldwide. This is, perhaps, one of the reasons why I discuss sexual predators in almost every lecture that I give, why I offer tips for parents, children, teens, and others concerning sexual predators, and why I paid to develop and produce a DVD on the subject, *Protecting Children from Predators,* in which I detail some of the common lures used by predators and provide information to help identify these predators before they strike. My private security company has given away thousands of copies at no charge through our website, www.LiveSecure.org, my way of giving thanks that I survived my situation.

My experience is but one of the many reasons that I am an advocate of a "one strike" law concerning sexual predators. No second, third, one-hundredth, or twenty-five-thousandth chance to offend again—that's my take. If one individual sexually assaults another, especially a child, that individual should be put away for life, with no chance for parole and no chance to once again prowl the streets and re-offend. Such laws would, of course, need definition, as many of our states and our federal government considers such legislation. I'm not suggesting that an eighteen-year-old boy who has consensual sex with his sixteen-year-old girlfriend needs to be punished. I am, however, advocating that anyone who abuses his position as an adult or as a person of authority; anyone who makes a child or another person, by means of force, intimidation or abduction, engage in any form of sexual act; anyone who kidnaps or otherwise carries away a person to force them to have sex; anyone who kills such a person during an attempted kidnapping or a forced sexual assault . . . . that this person needs to go to jail for the rest of his or her life. I'll leave it up to the lawyers to add further definition, but if we as parents and caregivers and lawmakers cannot protect our children from such predators, what good are we? Our children are our most precious gift; they expect us to keep them safe. If we don't protect them from such predators, well . . . we simply don't deserve the title of adult. Period.

If you believe as I do that there should be defined "one strike" laws concerning sexual predators in every state and at the national level, then please write your state and federal representatives and tell them that you support such legislation. We cannot afford to continue to lose our precious, innocent children to the actions of sexual predators. We can save them, but we must have a common voice and a common vote.

Most parents I speak to want to know what they can do to keep their children safe. Well, I'm afraid we can never entirely eliminate the risks facing children in today's society, but there are a number of approaches and strategies you can take with your children to minimize the danger. Simply telling our children to be aware of strangers is not enough. In some cases, it doesn't even address the problem, because many children fall victim to a family member, family friend, or other trusted adult in their life. Others are grabbed by strangers within a few feet from their homes or some other public place where we thought they would be safe. Molesters stalk Internet chat rooms looking to develop a relationship with a child they can then lure into a one-on-one meeting. NBC's *To Catch a Predator* has shown the large number of predators who are lurking just on the other side of the firewall of our home computers, waiting for the chance to victimize a child. We need to keep an open line of communication with our children and discuss the common lures that predators may use to gain access to them. Information concerning common predator lures and other information related to personal, family, home, and travel security, as well as our free DVD, *Protecting Children from Predators,* are all available at www.LiveSecure.org.

As a parent or caregiver, you need to consider when you should discuss personal safety and security matters with your child. Think of the following personal security issues as you would bicycle safety. Your child needs to know and understand the rules of the road to avoid an accident, just as he or she needs to understand that some people do bad things. The following checklist covers some of the ways our children could respond to unwanted advances from a sexual predator, and positive initiatives we can take to prevent those advances in the first place.

1. A child should never be afraid to tell his or her parents or other trusted adults if they feel threatened, even if someone has told them not to talk. If they are victimized, it is never their fault and never something they should be ashamed of or something to hide from their parents of other caregivers. Tell your child that you love him and that if he disappears, no matter what his kidnapper says, you will never stop loving him and you will never stop looking for him.

2. Tell your child to never go with anyone they don't want to, and to never let anyone take them away from where the potential kidnapper first approaches them. This is one of the most important things they can do to prevent being taken by a kidnapper.

3. Yell, scream, fight, and run from any potential abductor. No matter what their assailant says, your child should make as much noise and attract as much attention as possible.

4. If someone tries to lure him or her into a vehicle, instruct your child to run the opposite way the vehicle is facing, forcing the kidnapper to turn around to chase the child.

5. Teach your child to run home, to a neighbor's home, into a store or other public place, yelling that someone is trying to kidnap him or her.

6. If your child is on a bicycle, tell him or her to grip the frame. The kidnapper can't get both them and their bike into a car. If they're on the street and unable to run away, tell them to grab a streetlight, traffic sign, trash can, mailbox, or other fixed object while yelling for help.

7. If the kidnapper points a gun at them, tell your child to run away. Most kidnappers don't want to attract attention by shooting a gun and they probably couldn't hit the child even if they fired. It's better to be wounded and left to await help from others than to go off with a kidnapper to some secret hideaway, where in a worst-case scenario the bad guy can violate the child and then kill the only witness against him.

8. If grabbed, children should twist their body and scream, "This is not my Dad!" (Or, "This is not my Mom!")

9. If the assailant grabs your child by his coat or backpack, he or she should twist out of his grip, leaving the assailant with the coat or backpack as your child runs and screams toward another nearby adult. Attract the attention of this adult by grabbing and holding on to him or her, forcing them to respond to your child's plight.

10. If forced into the front seat of a four-door car or van, immediately jump into the back seat; open the rear door and run. (This is a good time to violate another cardinal parent–child rule and avoid wearing a seat belt, which can only slow your child's escape.)

11. Grab the keys from the kidnapper's car and throw them out the window.

12. If in traffic, press on the accelerator (by pushing down on the kidnapper's foot, if needed) and make the car crash into the car in front of it or run off the road. Here again, it's better to risk minor or even serious injury than to entrust your fate to the sick mind of a predator in a kidnap situation.

13. Once again, if your child is in a car, encourage him or her to try to honk the horn, and in this way try to distract the kidnapper and at the same time call attention to the vehicle.

14. If placed in the trunk of a car, look for the emergency trunk release handle (it usually glows in the dark) and pull it hard, push the trunk lid up, and escape. If you can't find the emergency release handle, pull out the wires to the tail lights on both sides of the trunk, thereby attracting attention to the vehicle when the tail and brake lights don't work. Tell police that your child knows how to do this, which will put them on the lookout for cars with malfunctioning tail and brake lights.

15. Remind your child that he or she should not eat or drink anything their kidnapper gives them (it may be drugged).

16. If the kidnapper takes your child into a store, tell him or her to knock things off the shelves, to kick over displays, to break bottles, and to yell and scream they they have been kidnapped. Once again, calling attention to yourself is key.

17. If you're being held in a house, flash the front porch lights off and on. If you're in an upper apartment, flood the bathroom to cause water to pour down into the apartment below.

18. Never stop trying to escape—and always take the opportunity to use a phone to call 911 and ask for help.

19. Discuss and practice these things with your children. While doing everything we can to prevent our children from becoming the victim of a kidnapper, we need to also arm them with the above information to help them escape in the unfortunate event that they are taken by an assailant. Information is all-important and can save the life of your child.

20. And finally, as Winston Churchill once said, remind your child to "Never, never, never, never, never give up."

ABOUT THE AUTHORS

Clint Van Zandt retired from the FBI in 1995 after twenty-five years of service, ending his career as chief hostage negotiator and a supervisor in the Bureau's Behavioral Science Unit, later immortalized in *The Silence of the Lambs*. Upon retirement he started Van Zandt Associates, Inc., an international threat and risk assessment group. In addition to his numerous monthly appearances on a wide variety of news programs, Van Zandt is a regular contributor to *The Abrams Report* and has a weekly column on MSNBC.com. For information about the author and about his personal, family, and home security, please visit www.LiveSecure.org.

Daniel Paisner is the author or coauthor of more than twenty bestselling books, including the *New York Times* bestsellers *Last Man Down*, with New York City Fire Department battalion leader Richard Picciotto; *Book*, with Whoopi Goldberg; and *Mountain, Get out of My Way*, with Montel Williams.